ACCOUNTING ESSENTIALS FOR CAREER SECRETARIES

FIFTH EDITION

Arthur E. Carlson, PhD
Professor of Accounting
School of Business Administration
Washington University, St. Louis

James A. Heintz, DBA, CPA
Associate Professor of Accounting
Indiana University
Bloomington, Indiana

Mary E. Burnet, MBA, CPA
Professor Emeritus of Accounting
Rochester Institute of Technology
Rochester, New York

Published by
SOUTH-WESTERN PUBLISHING CO.

CINCINNATI   WEST CHICAGO, ILL.   DALLAS   PELHAM MANOR, N.Y.   PALO ALTO, CALIF.

Copyright © 1983
by South-Western Publishing Co.
Cincinnati, Ohio

All Rights Reserved

The text of this publication, or any part thereof, may not be reproduced or transmitted in any form or by any means electronic or mechanical, including photocopying, recording, storage in an information retrieval system, or otherwise, without the prior written permission of the publisher.

ISBN: 0-538-01070-3

Library of Congress Catalog Card Number: 82-60122

1 2 3 4 5 K 7 6 5 4 3

Printed in the United States of America

PREFACE

As the world of business and the professions continually grows larger and more complicated, a knowledge of accounting becomes more and more essential. More opportunities are thus created for those persons who are proficient in secretarial skills and who also have an understanding of the accounting process. *Accounting Essentials for Career Secretaries* presents a system of accounting which can be used in any business office. In addition, special attention is paid to accounting problems and situations encountered by attorneys and physicians and dentists.

The accounting cycle and the income statement and balance sheet are presented early in the course. The remaining chapters in the book are an elaboration of the basic material presented earlier. The student is thus continually building upon and reinforcing his or her knowledge of the underlying structure of accounting. Chapter 3 is devoted to accounting for cash and includes a discussion of banking procedure. Chapter 4 covers payroll accounting. The latter chapters of the book which follow those on accounting for attorneys and physicians and dentists take up the end-of-the-period activities.

New features in this fifth edition include "Chapter Objectives" at the beginning of each chapter, "Building Your Accounting Knowledge" review questions at the end of each chapter section (there are one or more sections per chapter), and "Expanding Your Business Vocabulary" terms at the end of each chapter. The vocabulary terms are referenced to the textbook pages on which they appear.

Because of the increasing number of professional corporations in the last few years, an appendix which discusses and illustrates the accounting for professional corporations has been added to Chapter 5, "Accounting for Personal Service (Attorneys)". New material has also been added to Chapter 6 "Accounting for Personal Service (Physicians and Dentists)" which discusses the handling of claims which will be paid by private insurance organizations such as Blue Cross and Blue Shield and government programs such as Medicare and Medicaid.

In order to provide supplementary learning aids, a workbook containing study assignments is available. Accounting problems which may be used for additional work are included in the text following Chapters 4 and 8. Challenge problems, one for each chapter, have been added to the supplementary practical accounting problems which follow Chapters 4 and 8. Each of these problems is based on the material in the chapters or on the appendix to Chapter 5, but the problems involve points not included in the study assignments or in the other supplementary practical accounting problems.

Two practice sets are available for use with the text. One of the sets covers one month's transactions in the office of an attorney (Jerome W. Stearns, Attorney at Law). This set can be effectively started upon the completion of Chapter 5. A second set (Higgins and Salinas, Physicians and Surgeons) provides practice in recording a month's transactions in a physician's office. This set is designed to be started upon the completion of Chapter 6. For those instructors who wish to emphasize the record keeping of a general business, a third set (John H. Roberts, a management consultant), designed to correlate with *College Accounting* is available for use after Chapter 5 or 6. All three sets are designed to give the student a review of the complete accounting cycle.

Tests are available for use following the completion of Chapters 2, 4, 6, and 8.

The authors acknowledge with gratitude the assistance received from the members of the business and professional community whose suggestions contributed to the preparation of this textbook. Special thanks are due to the following persons who provided helpful information: Garry L. Edmondson, Esquire, Attorney and Counselor at Law; Mr. John M. Lindsey, Professor of Law and Law Librarian, Temple University, Philadelphia, Pennsylvania; and Mr. Donald W. Duncan, Professional Management Service, Cincinnati, Ohio.

A. E. Carlson
J. A. Heintz
M. E. Burnet

CONTENTS

Chapter 1	**THE NATURE OF BUSINESS ACCOUNTING**	**1**
	The Accounting Process	3
	The Double-Entry Framework	12
Chapter 2	**ACCOUNTING PROCEDURE**	**25**
	Journalizing Transactions	26
	Posting to the Ledger; The Trial Balance	38
	The Financial Statements	46
Chapter 3	**ACCOUNTING FOR CASH**	**53**
	Cash Receipts and Cash Disbursements	54
	Banking Procedures	63
Chapter 4	**PAYROLL ACCOUNTING**	**82**
	Employee Earnings and Deductions	83
	Payroll Taxes Imposed on the Employer	102
	Chapters 1–4 Supplementary Practical Accounting Problems	**113**
Chapter 5	**ACCOUNTING FOR PERSONAL SERVICE (ATTORNEYS)**	**125**
	The Cash Basis of Accounting for a Personal Service Enterprise	126
	Appendix: The Professional Corporation	152

Chapter 6	**ACCOUNTING FOR PERSONAL SERVICE (PHYSICIANS AND DENTISTS)**	**163**
	The Cash Basis of Accounting for Physicians and Dentists	164
Chapter 7	**THE PERIODIC SUMMARY**	**192**
	End-Of-Period Work Sheet	193
	The Financial Statements	199
Chapter 8	**ADJUSTING AND CLOSING ACCOUNTS AT END OF ACCOUNTING PERIOD**	**208**
	Adjusting Entries	209
	Closing Procedure	212
	Chapters 5–8 Supplementary Practical Accounting Problems	223
Index		247

1

THE NATURE OF BUSINESS ACCOUNTING

CHAPTER OBJECTIVES

> The objectives of this chapter are to enable you:
> ▶ To describe business accounting as it applies to profit-seeking enterprises.
> ▶ To define certain business accounting terms.
> ▶ To explain how selected business transactions affect the business entity, using the accounting equation.
> ▶ To explain the nature of the income statement and the balance sheet, and how they relate to one another.
> ▶ To explain the double-entry framework.
> ▶ To explain the function of the trial balance.

The purpose of business accounting is to provide information about the current financial operations and condition of an enterprise to individuals, agencies, and organizations who have the need and the right to be so informed. These interested parties normally include:

(1) The **owners** of the business — both present and prospective.
(2) The **managers** of the business — managers may or may not own the business. (Often, but not always, the owners and the managers are the same persons.)

(3) The **creditors,** or **suppliers,** of the business — both present and prospective. Creditors or suppliers are those who supply goods and services on credit — meaning that payment need not be made on the date of purchase. The creditor category also includes banks and individuals who lend money to the business.

(4) **Government agencies** — local, state, and national. For purposes of either regulation or taxation — sometimes both — various governmental agencies must be given certain financial information.

In connection with many businesses, some or all of the following also make use of accounting information: customers or clients, labor unions, competitors, trade associations, stock exchanges, commodity exchanges, financial analysts, and financial writers.

Although the information needed by all types of users is not identical, most want data regarding (1) the results of operations — net income or loss — for the current period and (2) the financial status of the business as of a recent date. The demand for the greatest quantity and variety of information usually comes from the managers of the business. They constantly need up-to-the-minute information about the financial activities of every department in their organization. Because accounting relates to so many phases of business, it is not surprising that there are several fields of accounting specialization such as tax work, cost accounting, information systems design and installation, management services, and budget preparation.

Many accountants have but one employer whereas others become qualified as public accountants and offer their services as independent contractors or consultants. Public accountants perform various functions. One of their major activities is **auditing**. This involves the application of standard testing and checking procedures to the records of an enterprise to be certain that acceptable accounting policies and practices have been consistently followed. The purpose of the audit is to provide an independent opinion that the financial information about a business is fairly presented. Public accountants frequently extend their activities into the area of "management services" — a term that covers a variety of specialized consulting assignments. Some states license individuals as **Public Accountants** or **Registered Accountants**, although this practice is declining. All states grant the designation of **Certified Public Accountant** (CPA) to those who meet various prescribed requirements, including the passing of a uniform examination prepared by the American Institute of Certified Public Accountants. A uniform examination is also offered in numerous cities throughout the country by the Institute of Management Accounting of the National Association of Accountants, leading to the designation of **Certified Management Accountant** (CMA). This certificate is designed to give professional status to one-employer accountants.

All of the foregoing comments have related to accounting and accountants in connection with profit-seeking organizations. There are thousands of not-for-profit organizations such as governments, educational institutions, churches, and hospitals that also need to accumulate and dispense information. These organizations also engage a large number of accountants. While the "rules of the game" are somewhat different for not-for-profit organizations, much of the record keeping is identical with that found in profit-seeking organizations.

The accountant has the task of accumulating and dispensing the financial information needed by users. Since such activities touch upon nearly every aspect of the business operation and since financial information is communicated in accounting terms, accounting is said to be the "language of business." Anyone intending to engage in any type of business activity is well advised to learn this language.

THE ACCOUNTING PROCESS

Business accounting may be defined as the art of analyzing and recording financial transactions and certain business-related economic events in a manner that **(1)** classifies and summarizes the information and **(2)** reports and interprets the results. The accounting process itself provides the basis for this definition.

Analyzing is the first step in the accounting process. The accountant must look at a transaction or event that has occurred and determine its fundamental significance to the business so that the information may be properly processed.

Recording traditionally meant writing something by hand. Much of the record keeping in accounting still is done manually, however, technological advances have introduced a variety of bookkeeping machines which typically combine the major attributes of typewriters, calculators, and electronic printing. Today the initial processing sometimes takes the form of holes punched in certain places on a card or a paper tape, of invisible magnetized spots on a special type of tape, or of special characters that can be magnetically or electronically "read" from source documents and thus used to feed information into an electronic computer. Because of the multiple ways information may be processed, the term "data entry" may be substituted for the term "recording" in the accounting process.

Classifying relates to the process of sorting or grouping like things together rather than merely keeping a simple, diary-like narrative record of numerous and varied transactions and events.

Summarizing is the process of bringing together various items of information to determine or explain a result.

Final processing, or **reporting**, refers to the process of communicating the results. In accounting, it is common to use tabular arrangements rather than narrative-type reports. Sometimes, a combination of the two is used.

Interpreting refers to the steps taken to direct attention to the significance of various matters and relationships. Percentage analyses and ratios often are used to help explain the meaning of certain related bits of information. Footnotes to financial reports and special captions may also be valuable in the interpreting phase of accounting.

Accounting and Bookkeeping

A person involved with or responsible for such functions as forms and records design, accounting policy making, data analysis, report preparation, and report interpretation may be referred to as an **accountant**. A person who records or enters information in accounting records may be referred to as a **bookkeeper**. Bookkeeping is the recording phase of the accounting process. That term goes back to the time when formal accounting records were in the form of books — pages bound together. While this still is sometimes the case, modern practice favors the use of loose-leaf or computer-generated records and cards. When the language catches up with practice, the designation "record keeper" or **information processor** may replace "bookkeeper."

Accounting Elements

A **business entity** is a particular individual, association, or other organization for which formal records are kept and periodic reports are made. Properties of value that are owned by a business entity are called **assets**.

Assets. Properties such as money, accounts receivable, merchandise, furniture, fixtures, machinery, buildings, and land are common examples of business assets. An **account receivable** is an unwritten promise by a customer to pay at a later date for goods sold or for service rendered.

It is possible to conduct a business or a professional practice with very few assets. A doctor of medicine, for example, may have relatively few assets, such as money, accounts receivable, instruments, laboratory equipment, and office equipment. In many cases, a variety of assets are necessary. A merchant must have a large selection of merchandise to sell and store equipment with which to display the merchandise. A manufacturer must have an inventory of parts and materials, tools and various sorts of machinery with which to make or assemble the product.

Liabilities. A legal obligation of a business to pay a debt is a business **liability**. Debts can be paid with money, goods, or services, but usually are paid in cash. Liabilities represent one type of ownership interest in a business — an outside interest.

The most common liabilities are accounts payable and notes payable. An **account payable** is an unwritten promise to pay a supplier for property purchased on credit or for a service rendered. Formal written promises to pay suppliers or lenders specified sums of money at definite future times are known as **notes payable**. A business also may have one or more types of taxes payable classified as liabilities.

Owner's Equity. The amount by which the business assets exceed the business liabilities is termed the **owner's equity** in the business. The word "equity" used in this sense represents a second type of ownership interest in a business — an inside interest. The terms **proprietorship**, **net worth**, or **capital** are sometimes used as synonyms for owner's equity. If there are no business liabilities, the owner's equity in the business is equal to the total amount of the assets of the business.

A business that is owned by one person traditionally is called a **proprietorship**. The person owning the interest in a business is known as the proprietor. A distinction must be made between the business assets and liabilities and nonbusiness assets and liabilities that a proprietor may have. For example, the proprietor probably owns a home, clothing, and a car, and perhaps owes the dentist for dental service. These are personal, nonbusiness assets and liabilities. The formal accounting records for the enterprise will relate to the business entity only; any nonbusiness assets and liabilities of the proprietor should be excluded. While the term "owner's equity" can be used in a very broad sense, its use in accounting is nearly always limited to the meaning: business assets minus business liabilities.

Frequent reference will be made to the owner's acts of investing money or other property in the business and to the withdrawal of money or other property from the business. In either case, property is changed from the category of a nonbusiness asset to a business asset or vice versa. These distinctions are important if the owner is going to make decisions based on the financial condition and results of the business apart from nonbusiness affairs.

The Accounting Equation

The relationship between the three basic accounting elements can be expressed in the form of a simple equation known as the **accounting equation**.

ASSETS = LIABILITIES + OWNER'S EQUITY

This equation reflects the fact that outsiders and insiders have an interest in all of the assets of a business. When the amounts of any two of these elements are known, the third can always be calculated.

LIABILITIES = ASSETS − OWNER'S EQUITY

OWNER'S EQUITY = ASSETS − LIABILITIES

For example, Nancy Deppen has business assets on December 31 in the sum of $30,200. The business liabilities on that date consist of $1,200 owed for supplies purchased on account and $1,500 owed to a bank on a note. The owner's equity element of the business may be calculated by subtracting the total liabilities from the total assets, $30,200 − $2,700 = $27,500. These facts about the business can also be expressed in equation form as follows:

ASSETS = LIABILITIES + OWNER'S EQUITY
$30,200 $2,700 $27,500

A closer examination of the owner's equity will show how the equation maintains equality. One way to increase the owner's equity in the business is to increase the assets. To increase the assets and owner's equity, Deppen may **(1)** invest more money or other property in the business or **(2)** operate the business profitably.

For example, if one year later the assets are $45,700 and the liabilities are $2,600, the status of the business would be as follows:

ASSETS	=	LIABILITIES	+	OWNER'S EQUITY
$45,700		$2,600		$43,100

The fact that Deppen's equity in the business had increased by $15,600 (from $27,500 to $43,100) does not prove that she had made a profit (often called net income) equal to the increase. Increases and decreases in owner's equity must be analyzed. If the records indicated that she invested additional money during the year in the amount of $7,000 and did not withdraw any funds for personal use, the remainder of the increase in her equity ($8,600) would have been due to profit (net income).

If the records indicated she invested no additional funds, withdrew assets in an amount of $9,400 cash for personal use, and increased her equity by $25,000 as a result of a profitable operation, the net effect would also account for the $15,600 ($25,000 − $9,400) increase. It is essential that the business records show the changes in owner's equity due to events that are part of regular business operations and the changes in owner's equity due to investments and withdrawals of assets by the owner.

Transactions

Any activity of an enterprise which involves the exchange of values is referred to as a **transaction**. These values frequently are expressed in terms of money. Buying and selling property and performing services are common transactions. The following typical transactions are analyzed to show that each represents an exchange of values.

Typical Transactions	Analysis of Transactions
(1) Purchased equipment for cash, $1,250.	Money was exchanged for equipment.
(2) Received cash in payment of professional fees, $300.	Professional service was rendered in exchange for money.
(3) Paid office rent, $250.	Money was exchanged for the right to use property.
(4) Paid an amount owed to a supplier, $700.	Money was given in settlement of a debt that may have resulted from the purchase of property on account or from services rendered by a supplier.
(5) Paid wages in cash, $150.	Money was exchanged for services rendered.
(6) Borrowed $3,000 at a bank giving a 9 percent interest-bearing note due in 30 days.	A liability known as a note payable was incurred in exchange for money.
(7) Purchased office equipment on account, $500.	A liability known as an account payable was incurred in exchange for office equipment.

Effect of Transactions on the Accounting Equation

Each transaction affects one or more of the three basic accounting elements. For example, in transaction (1) the purchase of equipment for cash represents both an increase and a decrease in assets. The assets increased because equipment was acquired; the assets decreased because cash was disbursed. The office equipment in transaction (7) had been purchased on account, thereby creating a liability. The transaction results in an increase in assets (equipment) with a corresponding increase in liabilities (accounts payable). Neither of these transactions has any effect upon the owner's equity element of the equation.

The effect of any transaction on the basic elements of the accounting equation may be indicated by increasing or decreasing a specific asset, liability or owner's equity account. To illustrate: assume that Edward Foote, an attorney, decided to go into practice for himself. During the first month of this venture (June, 1983), the following transactions relating to the practice took place:

Transaction (a)

An Increase in an Asset Offset by an Increase in Owner's Equity

Foote opened a bank account with a deposit of $8,000. This transaction caused the new business to receive the asset cash; and since Foote contributed the assets, the owner's equity element was increased by the same amount. As a result of this transaction, the equation for the business would appear as follows:

ASSETS	=	LIABILITIES	+ OWNER'S EQUITY
Cash			Edward Foote, Capital
(a) $8,000			$8,000

Transaction (b)

An Increase in an Asset Offset by an Increase in a Liability

Foote purchased office equipment (desk, chairs, file cabinet, etc.) for $4,100 on 30 days credit. This transaction caused the asset office equipment to increase by $4,100 and resulted in an equal increase in the liability accounts payable. Updating the foregoing equation by this (b) transaction gives the following result:

ASSETS		=	LIABILITIES	+ OWNER'S EQUITY
Cash +	Office Equipment		Accounts Payable	Edward Foote, Capital
Bal. $8,000				$8,000
(b)	$4,100		$4,100	
Bal. $8,000	$4,100		$4,100	$8,000

Transaction (c)

An Increase in One Asset Offset by a Decrease in Another Asset

Foote purchased office supplies (stationery, legal pads, pencils, etc.) for cash, $640. This transaction caused a $640 increase in the asset office supplies that exactly offset the $640 decrease in the asset cash. The effect on the equation is as follows:

	ASSETS			=	LIABILITIES	+	OWNER'S EQUITY
	Cash	Office Equipment	Office Supplies		Accounts Payable		Edward Foote, Capital
Bal.	$8,000	$4,100			$4,100		$8,000
(c)	− 640		$640				
Bal.	$7,360	$4,100	$640		$4,100		$8,000

Transaction (d)

A Decrease in an Asset Offset by a Decrease in a Liability

Foote paid $2,500 on account to the company from which the office equipment was purchased. (See Transaction (b).) This payment caused the asset cash and the liability accounts payable both to decrease $2,500. The effect on the equation is as follows:

	ASSETS			=	LIABILITIES	+	OWNER'S EQUITY
	Cash	Office Equipment	Office Supplies		Accounts Payable		Edward Foote, Capital
Bal.	$7,360	$4,100	$640		$4,100		$8,000
(d)	− 2,500				− 2,500		
Bal.	$4,860	$4,100	$640		$1,600		$8,000

Transaction (e)

An Increase in an Asset Offset by an Increase in Owner's Equity Resulting from Revenue

Foote received $1,800 cash from a client for professional services. This transaction caused the asset cash to increase $1,800, and since the cash was received for services performed by the business, the owner's equity increased by the same amount. The effect on the equation is as follows:

	ASSETS			=	LIABILITIES	+	OWNER'S EQUITY
	Cash	Office Equipment	Office Supplies		Accounts Payable		Edward Foote, Capital
Bal.	$4,860	$4,100	$640		$1,600		$8,000
(e)	1,800						1,800
Bal.	$6,660	$4,100	$640		$1,600		$9,800

Transaction (f)

A Decrease in an Asset Offset by a Decrease in Owner's Equity Resulting from Expense

(1) Foote paid $350 for office rent for June. This transaction caused the asset cash to be reduced by $350 with an equal reduction in owner's equity. The effect on the equation is as follows:

	ASSETS				LIABILITIES	+	OWNER'S EQUITY
	Cash +	Office Equipment +	Office Supplies		Accounts Payable		Edward Foote, Capital
Bal.	$6,660	$4,100	$640	=	$1,600		$9,800
(f1) −	350						− 350
Bal.	$6,310	$4,100	$640		$1,600		$9,450

(2) Foote paid a bill for telephone service, $42. This transaction, like the previous one, caused a decrease in the asset cash with an equal decrease in the owner's equity. The effect on the equation is as follows:

	ASSETS				LIABILITIES	+	OWNER'S EQUITY
	Cash +	Office Equipment +	Office Supplies		Accounts Payable		Edward Foote, Capital
Bal.	$6,310	$4,100	$640	=	$1,600		$9,450
(f2) −	42						− 42
Bal.	$6,268	$4,100	$640		$1,600		$9,408

The Financial Statements

A set of records that make up an accounting information system is maintained to fill a variety of needs. Foremost is to provide source data for use in preparing various reports, including those referred to as financial statements. The two most important of these are the income statement and the balance sheet.

The Income Statement. The income statement, sometimes called the profit and loss statement or operating statement, shows the net income (net profit) or net loss for a specified period of time and how it was calculated. A very simple income statement has been prepared relating to the business of Edward Foote for the first month's operation, June, 1983. This statement contains information that was obtained by analysis of the changes in the owner's equity element of the business for the month. This element went from zero to $9,408. Part of this increase, $8,000, was due to the initial investment made by Foote. Since an investment is not classified as income or expense to the business, it is not considered in the income statement. The remainder of the increase, $1,408, was due to Foote's earning income and incurring expense. Transaction (e) involved revenue of $1,800; transactions (f1) and (f2) involved expenses of $350 and $42, respectively. Taken together, these transactions explain the net income of $1,408, as it appears in the statement below:

```
              EDWARD FOOTE, ATTORNEY
                   Income Statement
                For the Month of June, 1983
Professional fees.................................................... $1,800
Expenses:
   Rent expense.................................................... $350
   Telephone expense.............................................. 42      392
Net income for month................................................ $1,408
```

The Balance Sheet. The **balance sheet**, sometimes called a **statement of financial condition** or **statement of financial position**, shows the assets, liabilities, and owner's equity of a business at a specified date. A balance sheet for Foote's business as of June 30, 1983, is shown below.

```
              EDWARD FOOTE, ATTORNEY
                     Balance Sheet
                     June 30, 1983
       Assets                            Liabilities
Cash..................... $ 6,268   Accounts payable........ $ 1,600
Office supplies..........     640
Office equipment.........   4,100        Owner's Equity
                                    Edward Foote, capital..... 9,408
                                    Total liabilities and
Total assets............. $11,008      owner's equity........ $11,008
```

BUILDING YOUR ACCOUNTING KNOWLEDGE

1. Identify the four types of information users found in connection with virtually every business enterprise.
2. Which group of information users demands the greatest quantity and variety of information? Why?
3. Why is accounting called the "language of business?"
4. What is the major difference between a management accountant and a public accountant?
5. Identify the six major phases of the accounting process, and indicate what is done in each phase.

6. Why is it necessary to distinguish between the business assets and liabilities and the nonbusiness assets and liabilities of the single proprietor?
7. In what other way than by making a profit can the owner's equity be increased?
8. In what other way than by suffering a loss can the owner's equity be decreased?

Report No. 1-1

> *A workbook of study assignments is provided for use with this textbook. Each study assignment is referred to as a report. The work involved in completing Report No. 1-1 requires a knowledge of the principles developed in the preceding textbook discussion. Before proceeding with the following discussion, complete Report No. 1-1 in accordance with the instructions given in the study assignments.*

THE DOUBLE-ENTRY FRAMEWORK

The meanings of the terms asset, liability, and owner's equity were explained in the preceding pages. Examples were given to show how each business transaction causes a change in one or more of the three basic accounting elements. Transaction (a) shown on page 8 involved an increase in an asset with a corresponding increase in owner's equity. Transaction (b) involved an increase in an asset which caused an equal increase in a liability. Transaction (c) involved an increase in one asset which was offset by a decrease in another. Each of the transactions illustrated a dual effect. This is always true. A change, increase or decrease, in any asset, any liability, or in owner's equity is always accompanied by an offsetting change within the basic accounting elements.

The fact that each transaction has two aspects — a dual effect upon the accounting elements — provides the basis for what is called **double-entry bookkeeping**. This term describes a processing system that involves recording the two aspects that are involved in every transaction. Double entry does not mean that a transaction is recorded twice; instead, it means that both of the two aspects of each transaction are recorded.

Double entry is known to have been practiced for at least 500 years. The method has endured largely because it has several virtues; it is orderly, fairly simple, and very flexible. There is no transaction that cannot be recorded in a double-entry manner. Double entry promotes accuracy. Its use makes it impossible for certain types of error to remain undetected for very long. For example, if one aspect of a transaction is properly recorded but the other aspect is overlooked, it will soon be found that the records as a whole are "out of balance." The accountant then knows that something is wrong, checks the transaction to discover the trouble and then makes the needed correction.

The Account

It has been explained previously that the assets of a business may consist of a number of items, such as cash, accounts receivable, merchandise, equipment, buildings, and land. The liabilities may consist of one or more items, such as accounts payable and notes payable. A separate record should be kept of each asset and of each liability. Later it will be shown that a separate record should also be kept of the increases and decreases in owner's equity.

A form or record used to keep track of the increases and decreases in each item that result from business transactions is known as an **account**. There are many types of account forms in general use. They may be ruled on sheets of paper and bound in a book form or kept in a loose-leaf binder; they may be ruled on cards and kept in a file of some sort; or they may be developed as computer print-outs. An illustration of a standard account form is shown below:

Standard Form of Account

The three major parts of the standard account form are **(1)** the title and the account number, **(2)** the debit side, and **(3)** the credit side. This account form is designed to facilitate the recording of the essential information regarding each transaction that affects the account. Each account should be given an appropriate title that will indicate whether it is an asset, a liability, or an owner's equity account. Before any entries are recorded in an account, the title and number of the account should be entered on the horizontal line at the top of the form. The standard account form is divided into two equal parts or sections which are ruled identically to facilitate recording increases and decreases. The left side is called the debit side, while the right side is called the credit side. The Date columns are used for recording the dates of transactions. The Item columns may be used for entering a brief description of a transaction when deemed necessary. The Posting Reference columns will be discussed later. The amount column on the left is headed "Debit" while that on the right is headed "Credit." The Debit and Credit columns are used for recording the amounts of transactions.

To determine the balance of an account at any time, it is necessary only to total the amounts in the Debit and Credit columns, and calculate the difference between the two totals. To save time, a **T account** is commonly used for instructional purposes. It consists of a two-line drawing resembling the capital letter T and is sometimes referred to as a skeleton form of account.

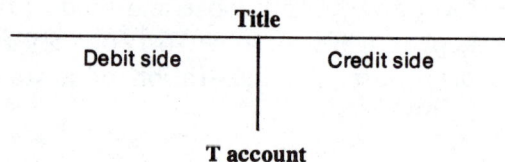

T account

Debits and Credits

To **debit** an account means to enter an amount on the left or debit side of the account. To **credit** an account means to enter an amount on the right or credit side of the account. The abbreviation for debit is Dr. and for credit Cr. (based on the Latin terms "debere" and "credere"). Sometimes the word **charge** is used as a substitute for debit. Increases in assets are recorded on the left side of the accounts; increases in liabilities and in owner's equity are recorded on the right side of the accounts. Decreases in assets are recorded on the right side of the accounts; decreases in liabilities and in owner's equity are recorded on the left side of the accounts. Recording increases and decreases in the accounts in this manner will reflect the basic equality of assets to liabilities plus owner's equity (Assets = Liabilities + Owner's Equity); at the same time it will maintain equality between the total amounts debited to all accounts and the total amounts credited to all accounts (Debits = Credits). These basic relationships may be illustrated in the following manner:

ASSETS	=	LIABILITIES + OWNER'S EQUITY

All Asset Accounts

Debit to enter increases (+)	Credit to enter decreases (−)

All Liability Accounts

Debit to enter decreases (−)	Credit to enter increases (+)

All Owner's Equity Accounts

Debit to enter decreases (−)	Credit to enter increases (+)

TOTAL DEBITS	=	TOTAL CREDITS

Use of Asset, Liability, and Owner's Equity Accounts

To illustrate the application of the double-entry process, the transactions discussed on pages 8–10 will be analyzed and their effect on the accounting elements will be indicated by showing the proper entries in T accounts. As before, the transactions are identified by letters; dates are omitted intentionally.

Transaction (a)

An Increase in an Asset Offset by an Increase in Owner's Equity

Edward Foote, an attorney, started a business by investing $8,000 in cash.

Cash		Edward Foote, Capital
(a) 8,000		(a) 8,000

Analysis: As a result of this transaction the business acquired an asset, cash. The amount of money invested represents Foote's equity in the business; thus the amount of the asset cash is equal to the owner's equity in the business. Separate accounts are kept for the asset cash and for the owner's equity. To record the transaction as an increase in an asset and an increase in owner's equity, the cash account was debited and Foote's capital account was credited for $8,000.

Transaction (b)

An Increase in an Asset Offset by an Increase in a Liability

Purchased office equipment (desk, chairs, file cabinet, etc.) for $4,100 on 30 days' credit.

Office Equipment		Accounts Payable	
(b) 4,100			(b) 4,100

Analysis: As a result of this transaction the business acquired a new asset, office equipment. The debt incurred as a result of purchasing the equipment on 30 days' credit is a liability, accounts payable. Thus, the outside interest in the business has increased by $4,100. Separate accounts are kept for office equipment and for accounts payable. The purchase of office equipment caused an increase in the assets of the business. Therefore, the asset account, Office Equipment, was debited for $4,100. The purchase also caused an increase in a liability. Therefore the liability account, Accounts Payable was credited for $4,100.

Transaction (c)

An Increase in One Asset Offset by a Decrease in Another Asset

Purchased office supplies (stationery, legal pads, pencils, etc.) for cash, $640.

Cash		Office Supplies	
(a) 8,000	(c) 640	(c) 640	

Analysis: As a result of this transaction the business acquired a new asset, office supplies. The addition of this asset was offset by a decrease in the asset cash. Notice there is no change in total assets. To enter the transaction properly, Office Supplies was debited and Cash was credited for $640. This is the second entry in the cash account; the account was previously debited for $8,000 when Transaction (a) was recorded.

It is proper to enter office supplies as an asset at the time of purchase even though they will become an expense when used. The procedure in accounting for supplies used will be discussed later.

Transaction (d)

A Decrease in an Asset Offset by a Decrease in a Liability

Paid $2,500 on account to the company from which the office equipment was purchased. (See Transaction (b).)

	Cash				Accounts Payable		
(a)	8,000	(c)	640	(d)	2,500	(b)	4,100
		(d)	2,500				

Analysis: This transaction resulted in a decrease in the liability accounts payable with a corresponding decrease in the asset cash; hence, it was recorded by debiting Accounts Payable and by crediting Cash for $2,500. Note that this is the second entry in the accounts payable account and the third entry in the cash account. At this point in time, the outside interest in the business has decreased by $2,500.

Revenue and Expense

The owner's equity element of a business entity or professional enterprise may be increased in two ways as follows:

(1) The owner may invest additional money or other property in the enterprise. Such investments result in an increase both in the assets of the enterprise and in the owner's equity, but they do not further enrich the owner. More property merely is invested in the enterprise and less property outside of the enterprise.
(2) Revenue may be derived from sales of goods or services, or from other sources.

As used in accounting, the term **revenue** in nearly all cases refers to an increase in the owner's equity in a business resulting from transactions involving asset inflows except the investment of assets in the business by its owner. In most cases, an increase in owner's equity due to revenue results from an addition to the assets without any change in the liabilities. Often it is cash that is increased. However, an increase in cash and other assets can occur in connection with several types of transactions that do not involve revenue. For this reason, revenue is often defined in terms of a change in owner's equity rather than a change in assets. Any transaction that causes owner's equity to increase, except for investments in the business by its owner, involves revenue.

The owner's equity element of a business entity or professional enterprise may be decreased in two ways as follows:

(1) The owner may withdraw assets (cash or other property) from the business enterprise.
(2) Expenses may be incurred in operating the enterprise.

As used in accounting, the term **expense** in nearly all cases means a decrease in the owner's equity in a business caused by transactions involving asset outflows other than a withdrawal by the owner. When an expense is incurred, either the assets are reduced or the liabilities are increased. In either event, owner's equity is reduced. If a transaction causing a reduction is not a withdrawal of assets by the owner, an expense is incurred. Common examples of expense are rent of office or store, salaries of employees, telephone service, supplies consumed, and many types of taxes.

If during a specified period of time, the total increases in owner's equity resulting from revenue exceed the total decreases resulting from expenses, it may be said that the excess represents the **net income** or net profit for the period.

> **Revenue > Expenses = Net Profit**

On the other hand, if the expenses of the period exceed the revenue, such excess represents a **net loss** for the period.

> **Expenses > Revenue = Net Loss**

The time interval used in the measurement of net income or net loss can be determined by the owner. It may be a month, a quarter (three months), a year, or some other period of time. Any accounting period of twelve months' duration is usually referred to as a **fiscal year**. The fiscal year frequently coincides with the calendar year.

Transactions involving revenue and expense always cause a change in the owner's equity element of an enterprise. Such changes could be recorded by debiting an account called Owner's Equity for expense and crediting it for revenue. If this practice were followed, however, the credit side of the owner's equity account would contain a mixture of increases due to revenue and to the investment of assets in the business by the owner, while the debit side would contain a mixture of decreases due to expenses and to the withdrawal of assets from the business by the owner. In order to determine the net income or the net loss for each accounting period, a careful analysis of the owner's equity account would be required. It is, therefore, better practice to record revenue and expenses in separate accounts.

When a transaction produces revenue, the amount of the revenue should be credited to an appropriate revenue account. When a transaction involves expense, the amount of the expense should be debited to an appropriate expense account. The relationship of these accounts to the owner's equity account and the application of the debit and credit theory to the accounts are indicated in the following diagram:

All Owner's Equity Accounts	
Debit to enter decreases (−)	Credit to enter increases (+)

All Expense Accounts		All Revenue Accounts	
Debit to enter increases (+)	Credit to enter decreases (−)	Debit to enter decreases (−)	Credit to enter increases (+)

The revenue and expense accounts are called **temporary owner's equity accounts** because it is customary to close them (set their balances back to zero) at the end of each accounting period. It is important to recognize that the credit side of each revenue account is serving temporarily as a part of the credit side of the owner's equity account. Increases in owner's equity are entered as credits. Thus increases in owner's equity resulting from revenue should be credited to revenue accounts. The debit side of each expense account is serving temporarily as a part of the debit side of the owner's equity account. Decreases in owner's equity are entered as debits. Thus decreases in owner's equity resulting from expense should be debited to expense accounts.

Use of Revenue and Expense Accounts

To illustrate the application of the double-entry process in recording transactions that affect revenue and expense accounts, the transactions that follow will be analyzed and their effect on the accounting elements will be indicated by showing the proper entries in T accounts. These transactions represent a continuation of the transactions completed by Edward Foote, an attorney, in the conduct of his practice. (See pages 15–17 for Transactions (a) to (d).)

Transaction (e)

An Increase in an Asset Offset by an Increase in Owner's Equity Resulting from Revenue

Received $1,800 in cash from a client for professional services rendered.

Cash				Professional Fees	
(a) 8,000	(c) 640			(e)	1,800
(e) 1,800	(d) 2,500				

Analysis: This transaction results in an increase in the asset cash with a corresponding increase in owner's equity because of revenue from professional fees. To record the transaction properly, Cash was debited and an appropriate account for the revenue was credited for $1,800. Accounts should always be given a descriptive title that will aid in classifying them in relation to the accounting elements. In this case the revenue account was given the title, Professional Fees. Note that this is the fourth entry in the cash account and the first entry in the account, Professional Fees.

Transaction (f)

A Decrease in an Asset Offset by a Decrease in Owner's Equity Resulting from Expense

(1) Paid $350 for office rent for one month.

Cash				Rent Expense	
(a) 8,000	(c) 640		(f1)	350	
(e) 1,800	(d) 2,500				
	(f1) 350				

Analysis: This transaction resulted in a decrease in the asset cash with a corresponding decrease in owner's equity because of expense. To record the transaction properly, Rent Expense was debited and Cash was credited for $350. This is the first entry in the rent expense account and the fifth entry in the cash account.

(2) Paid bill for telephone service, $42.

Cash				Telephone Expense	
(a) 8,000	(c) 640		(f2)	42	
(e) 1,800	(d) 2,500				
	(f1) 350				
	(f2) 42				

Analysis: This transaction is identical with the previous one except that telephone expense rather than rent expense was the reason for the decrease in owner's equity. To record the transaction properly, Telephone Expense was debited and Cash was credited for $42. This is the first entry in the telephone expense account and the sixth entry in the cash account.

The Trial Balance

It is a fundamental principle of double-entry bookkeeping that the sum of the assets is always equal to the sum of the liabilities and owner's equity. In order to maintain this equality in recording transactions, the sum of the debit entries must always be equal to the sum of the credit entries. To determine whether this equality has been maintained, it is customary to take a trial balance periodically. A **trial balance** is a list of all of the accounts showing the title and balance of each account. The **balance** of any account is the amount of difference between the total debits and the total credits to that account. To determine the balance of each account, the debit and credit amount columns should be totaled. This procedure is called **footing** the amount columns as illustrated below:

```
                    Cash
(a)          8,000  | (c)      640
(e)          1,800  | (d)    2,500
      6,268  9,800  | (f1)     350
                    | (f2)      42
                    |        3,532
```

If there is only one item entered in a column, no footing is necessary. To find the balance of an account, it is necessary only to determine the difference between the footings by subtraction.

Since asset and expense accounts are debited for increases, these accounts normally have **debit balances**. Since liability, owner's equity, and revenue accounts are credited to record increases, these accounts normally have **credit balances**. The balance of an account should be entered on the side of the account that has the larger total. The footings and balances of accounts should be entered in small figures just below the last entry. A pencil is generally used for this purpose. If the two footings of an account are equal in amount, the account is said to be **in balance**.

The accounts of Edward Foote are reproduced on page 22. To show their relationship to the fundamental accounting equation, the accounts are arranged in three columns under the headings of Assets, Liabilities, and Owner's Equity. The footings and the balance are printed in italics. Note the position of the footings directly under the debit and credit amount columns of the cash account, and the position of the balance on the left side of the cash account. (The balance of the accounts payable account is shown on the credit side in italics.) It is not necessary to enter the balances of the other accounts because there are entries on only one side of those accounts.

| ASSETS | = | LIABILITIES | + | OWNER'S EQUITY |

Cash
(a)	8,000	(c)	640
(e)	1,800	(d)	2,500
6,268	9,800	(f1)	350
		(f2)	42
			3,532

Accounts Payable
(d)	2,500	(b)	4,100
			1,600

Edward Foote, Capital
(a)	8,000

Office Supplies
(c)	640

Professional Fees
(e)	1,800

Office Equipment
(b)	4,100

Rent Expense
(f1)	350

Telephone Expense
(f2)	42

A trial balance of Edward Foote's accounts is shown below. The trial balance was taken on June 30, 1983; therefore, this date is

Edward Foote, Attorney
Trial Balance
June 30, 1983

Account	Dr. Balance	Cr. Balance
Cash	6268 00	
Office Supplies	640 00	
Office Equipment	4100 00	
Accounts Payable		1600 00
Edward Foote, Capital		8000 00
Professional Fees		1800 00
Rent Expense	350 00	
Telephone Expense	42 00	
	11400 00	11400 00

Edward Foote's Trial Balance

shown on the third line of the heading. The trial balance shows that the debit and credit totals are equal in amount. This is proof that in recording Transactions (a) to (f) inclusive the total of the debits was equal to the total of the credits.

A trial balance is not a formal statement or report. Normally, it is never seen by anyone except the accountant or bookkeeper. It is used as an aid in preparing the income statement and the balance sheet. If the trial balance is studied in conjunction with the income statement and the balance sheet shown on page 11, it will be seen that those statements could have been prepared quite easily from the information that this trial balance provides.

BUILDING YOUR ACCOUNTING KNOWLEDGE

1. Identify at least three ways in which account record forms may be developed and kept.
2. What is the standard form of account designed to facilitate?
3. What are the three major parts of the standard account form?
4. Explain the basis of the abbreviations "Dr." for debit and "Cr." for credit.
5. What word is sometimes used as a substitute for debit?
6. In most cases an increase in owner's equity due to revenue results from what event?
7. When an expense is incurred, what may be the effect on the assets? What may be the effect on the liabilities?
8. What is the purpose of the trial balance?

Report No. 1-2

Refer to the study assignments and complete Report No. 1-2 in accordance with the instructions given therein. The work involved in completing the assignment requires a knowledge of the principles developed in the preceding discussion. Any difficulty experienced in completing the report will indicate a lack of understanding of these principles. In such event further study, using the vocabulary words on page 24, should be helpful. After completing the report, you may continue with the textbook discussion in Chapter 2 until the next report is required.

EXPANDING YOUR BUSINESS VOCABULARY

What is the meaning of each of the following terms?

account (p. 13)
accountant (p. 4)
accounting equation (p. 6)
account payable (p. 5)
account receivable (p. 4)
assets (p. 4)
auditing (p. 2)
balance (p. 21)
balance sheet (p. 11)
bookkeeper (p. 4)
business accounting (p. 3)
business entity (p. 4)
capital (p. 5)
charge (p. 14)
credit (p. 14)
credit balances (p. 21)
debit (p. 14)
debit balances (p. 21)
double-entry bookkeeping (p. 12)
expense (p. 18)
fiscal year (p. 18)
footing (p. 21)

in balance (p. 21)
income statement (p. 10)
information processor (p. 4)
liability (p. 5)
net income (p. 18)
net loss (p. 18)
net worth (p. 5)
notes payable (p. 5)
operating statement (p. 10)
owner's equity (p. 5)
profit and loss statement (p. 10)
proprietorship (p. 5)
revenue (p. 17)
statement of financial condition (p. 11)
statement of financial position (p. 11)
temporary owner's equity accounts (p. 19)
transaction (p. 7)
trial balance (p. 21)
T account (p. 14)

2

ACCOUNTING PROCEDURE

CHAPTER OBJECTIVES

> The objectives of this chapter are to enable you:
> ▶ To recognize the flow of the financial data in an accounting information system — the basic accounting cycle.
> ▶ To explain the purpose of a book of original entry.
> ▶ To describe the chart of accounts as a means of classifying financial information, using an account numbering system.
> ▶ To perform the journalizing and posting process.
> ▶ To prepare the income statement and the balance sheet.

The principles of double-entry bookkeeping were explained and illustrated in the preceding chapter. To avoid complicating these principles, the mechanics of collecting and classifying information about business transactions were ignored. In actual practice, the first record of a transaction, sometimes called the source document, is in the form of a business paper, such as a check stub, receipt, cash register tape, sales ticket, or purchase invoice. The information supplied by source documents is an aid in analyzing transactions to determine their effect upon the accounts.

JOURNALIZING TRANSACTIONS

The record or book in which the first formal double-entry record of a transaction is made is called a **journal**. The act of recording transactions in a journal is called **journalizing**. It is necessary to analyze each transaction before it can be journalized properly. The purpose of a series of journal entries is to provide a chronological record of all transactions completed by the business showing the date of each transaction, titles of the accounts to be debited and credited, and the amounts of the debits and credits. The journal then provides all the information needed to transfer the debits and credits to the proper accounts. When the accounts are grouped together, they collectively comprise a ledger. The flow of data concerning transactions can be illustrated in the following manner:

Business transactions are evidenced by various **SOURCE DOCUMENTS** ⟶ The source documents provide the information needed to enter the transactions in a **JOURNAL** ⟶ The journal provides the information needed to transfer the debits and credits to the accounts which collectively comprise a **LEDGER**

Source Documents

The term source document covers a wide variety of forms and papers. Almost any document that provides information about a business transaction can be called a **source document**.

SOURCE DOCUMENTS

Examples:	Provide information about:
(1) Check stubs or carbon copies of checks	Cash disbursements
(2) Receipt stubs, carbon copies of receipts, cash register tapes, or memos of cash register totals	Cash receipts
(3) Copies of sales tickets or sales invoices issued to customers or clients	Sales of goods or services
(4) Purchase invoices received from suppliers	Purchases of goods or services

The Journal

A journal is commonly referred to as a **book of original entry** because the first formal accounting record of a transaction is made in a journal from source document information. The format of the pages of a journal varies with the type and size of an enterprise and the nature of its operations. Although a wide variety of journals are used in business, the simplest form of journal is a two-column journal. A standard form of such a journal is illustrated below. A **two-column journal** has only two amount columns, one for debit amounts and one for credit amounts. In the illustration, the columns have been numbered to facilitate the following discussion.

Standard Two-Column Journal

Column 1 is the Date column. The year is written in small figures at the top of the column immediately below the column heading and need be repeated only at the top of each new page unless an entry for a new year is made farther down on the page. The **Date column** is a double column, the perpendicular single rule being used to separate the month from the day. Thus in writing the date, the name of the month should be written or abbreviated to the left of the single line. The number designating the day of the month should be written to the right of this line. The name of the month need be shown only for the first entry on a page unless an entry for a new month is made farther down on the page.

Column 2 is generally referred to as the Description or explanation column. The **Description column** is used to record the titles of the accounts affected by each transaction, together with a description of the transaction. Two or more accounts are affected by each transaction, and the titles of all accounts must be recorded. The titles of the accounts debited are written first, followed by the titles of the accounts credited. A separate line should be used for each account title. The titles of the accounts to be debited are written at the extreme left of the column, while the titles of the accounts to be credited are usually indented one-half inch (about 1.3 centimeters). The description should be written immediately following the credit entry and indented an additional one-half inch.

Column 3 is the **Posting Reference column** sometimes referred to as a folio column. No entries are made in this column at the time of journalizing the transactions; such entries are made only at the time of posting which is the process of entering the debit and credit elements in the proper accounts in the ledger. This procedure will be explained in detail later in this chapter.

Column 4, the **Debit amount column**, is a column in which the amount that is to be debited to an account should be written on the same line on which the title of that account appears in the description column.

Column 5, the **Credit amount column**, is a column in which the amount that is to be credited to an account should be written on the same line on which the title of that account appears in the description column.

Journalizing

Journalizing involves recording the significant information concerning each transaction either **(1)** at the time the transaction occurs or **(2)** subsequently, but in the chronological order in which it and the other transactions occurred. For every transaction, the entry should record the date, the title of each account affected, the amounts, and a brief description. Before a transaction can be entered properly, it must be analyzed in order to determine:

(1) Which accounts are affected by the transaction.
(2) What effect the transaction has upon each of the accounts involved, that is, whether the balance of each affected account is increased or decreased.

To illustrate the journalizing process, assume that a business purchased a calculator on June 20 for $95 in cash. The asset accounts affected are Office Equipment and Cash. Office Equipment was increased and Cash was decreased upon purchase of the calculator. The following information would be recorded in a two-column journal:

DATE	DESCRIPTION	POST. REF.	DEBIT	CREDIT
June 20	Office Equipment		9500	
	Cash			9500
	Purchased a calculator.			

The Chart of Accounts

In analyzing a transaction prior to journalizing it, the accountant or bookkeeper must know which accounts are being kept. When an accounting system is established for a new business, the first step is to decide which accounts are required. The accounts used will depend upon the information needed or desired. Ordinarily, it is desirable to keep a separate account for each type of asset and each type of liability, since it is certain that information will be desired in regard to what is owned and what is owed. A permanent **owner's equity** or **capital account** should be kept in order that information may be available as to the owner's interest in the business. Furthermore, it is advisable to keep separate accounts for each type of revenue and each kind of expense. The revenue and expense accounts are temporary accounts that are used in recording increases and decreases in owner's equity from day-to-day business transactions apart from changes caused by the owner's investments and withdrawals. The specific accounts to be kept for recording increases and decreases in owner's equity depend upon the nature and sources of the revenue and the nature of the expenses incurred in earning the revenue.

A professional person or an individual engaged in operating a small enterprise may need to keep relatively few accounts. On the other hand, a large business may need to keep a great many accounts because of the complexity of the operation. Regardless of the number, accounts can be segregated into the three major classes, assets, liabilities, and owner's equity, and should be grouped according to these classes in the ledger. Asset accounts are placed first, liability accounts second, and owner's equity accounts, including revenue and expense accounts, last. A list of all the accounts used by a business is called a **chart of accounts**. It has become a general practice to give each account a number and to keep the accounts in numerical order. The numbering usually follows a consistent pattern and becomes a code. For example, asset accounts may be assigned numbers that always start with "1" or "2," liability accounts with "3" or "4," owner's equity accounts with "5," revenue accounts with "6," and expense accounts with "7" or "8."

To illustrate, assume that on December 1, 1983, Robert Half enters the employment agency business under the name of The Robert Half Personnel Agency. Since the accounts are to be kept on the calendar-year basis, the first accounting period will be for one month only, that is, for the month of December. A two-column journal and a ledger will be used. Half realizes that there will not be a need for many accounts at present because the business is new but that additional accounts may be added as the need arises. A chart of the accounts for the agency is shown below:

THE ROBERT HALF PERSONNEL AGENCY
CHART OF ACCOUNTS

Assets*
- 111 Cash
- 181 Office Supplies
- 211 Office Equipment

Liabilities
- 318 Accounts Payable

Owner's Equity
- 511 Robert Half, Capital
- 521 Robert Half, Drawing

Revenue
- 611 Placement Fees

Expenses
- 821 Rent Expense
- 822 Salary Expense
- 823 Travel and Entertainment Expense
- 824 Telephone Expense
- 825 Office Supplies Expense
- 839 Miscellaneous Expense

*Words in heavy type represent headings and not account titles.

CORRECTION NOTICE

The references to the Robert Half Personnel Agency in this chapter are not intended to reflect in any way on the real Robert Half or his franchisee corporations and Robert Half International, Inc., the franchisor of the Robert Half organization, believed to be the world's largest employment service specializing in the placement of accountants and bookkeepers on a permanent and temporary basis. Unlike the example presented in this chapter, Robert Half never charges a fee to any job applicant. And the Robert Half organization and its franchisees have substantially more equity than shown in this textbook. References to Robert Half have been changed to Donald Mays in printings after the first printing, and some students in the same class may have a first printing and some a later printing.

SOUTH-WESTERN PUBLISHING CO.

Journalizing Procedure Illustrated

To illustrate journalizing procedures, the transactions completed by The Robert Half Personnel Agency through December 31, 1983, will be journalized. A narrative of the transactions follows which provides all of the information needed in journalizing the transactions. Some of the transactions are analyzed to explain their effect upon the accounts. The analysis will immediately follow the journal entry.

THE ROBERT HALF PERSONNEL AGENCY
NARRATIVE OF TRANSACTIONS
Thursday, December 1, 1983

Half invested $3,500 cash in a business enterprise to be known as The Robert Half Personnel Agency.

DATE	DESCRIPTION	POST. REF.	DEBIT	CREDIT
1983 Dec. 1	Cash		3500 00	
	Robert Half, Capital			3500 00
	Original investment			
	in personnel agency.			

Analysis: As a result of this transaction, the business acquired the asset cash in the amount of $3,500. Since Half contributed this asset, the transaction caused an increase of $3,500 in owner's equity. Accordingly, the entry to record the transaction is a debit to Cash and a credit to Robert Half, Capital, for $3,500.

Note that the following steps are involved:

(1) Since this was the first entry on the journal page, the year is written at the top of the Date column.
(2) The month (abbreviated) and day are written on the first line in the Date column.
(3) The title of the account to be debited, Cash, is written on the first line at the extreme left of the Description column. The amount of the debit, $3,500, is written on the same line in the Debit column.
(4) The title of the account to be credited, Robert Half, Capital, is written on the second line indented one-half inch from the left side of the Description column. The amount of the credit, $3,500, is written on the same line in the Credit column.
(5) The explanation of the entry is started on the next line indented an additional one-half inch. The second line of the explanation is also indented the same distance as the first.

Friday, December 2

Paid office rent for December, $400.

DATE	DESCRIPTION	POST. REF.	DEBIT	CREDIT
1983 Dec. 2	Rent Expense		400 00	
	Cash			400 00
	Paid December rent.			

Analysis: This transaction resulted in an increase in an expense, with a corresponding decrease in the asset cash. The increase in the expense represents a decrease in owner's equity. The transaction is recorded by debiting Rent Expense and by crediting Cash for $400.

Half ordered several pieces of office equipment. Since the dealer did not have in stock what Half wanted, the articles were ordered from the factory. Delivery is not expected until the latter part of the month. Pending arrival of the equipment, the dealer loaned Half some used office equipment. No entry is required until the new equipment is received.

Tuesday, December 6

Purchased office supplies from the Clark Peeper Co. on account, $327.

6	Office Supplies	327 00	
	Accounts Payable		327 00
	Clark Peeper Co.		

Analysis: In this transaction, the business acquired a new asset which represented an increase in the total assets. A liability was also incurred because of the purchase on account. The transaction is recorded by debiting Office Supplies and crediting Accounts Payable for $327. As these supplies are consumed, the amount will become an expense of the business.

Wednesday, December 7

Paid the Continental Telephone Co. $35 covering the cost of installing a telephone in the office, together with the first month's service charges payable in advance.

7	Telephone Expense	35 00	
	Cash		35 00
	Paid telephone bill.		

Analysis: This transaction caused an increase in an expense and a corresponding decrease in the asset cash. The transaction is recorded by debiting Telephone Expense and by crediting Cash for $35.

Thursday, December 8

Paid $9 for a subscription to a trade journal.

	8 Miscellaneous Expense		9 00	
	Cash			9 00
	Trade journal sub.			

Analysis: This transaction resulted in an increase in an expense and a corresponding decrease in the asset cash. The transaction is recorded by debiting Miscellaneous Expense and by crediting Cash for $9.

Friday, December 9

Received $750 from Bradley Swalwell for placement services rendered.

	9 Cash		750 00	
	Placement Fees			750 00
	Bradley Swalwell.			

Analysis: This transaction resulted in an increase in the asset cash with a corresponding increase in revenue from placement fees. The transaction is recorded by debiting Cash and by crediting Placement Fees for $750. In keeping the accounts, Half follows the practice of not recording revenue until it is received in cash. This practice is common to professional and personal service enterprises.

Monday, December 12

Paid the Aldine Travel Service $165 for an airplane ticket to be used the next week for an employment agency convention trip.

	12 Travel and Entertainment Expense		165 00	
	Cash			165 00
	Airplane fare—convention.			

Analysis: This transaction resulted in an increase in an expense and a corresponding decrease in the asset cash. The transaction is recorded by debiting Travel and Entertainment Expense and by crediting Cash for $165.

Thursday, December 15

Paid Mary Wurtz $500 covering her salary for the first half of the month. Wurtz is employed by Half as a secretary and bookkeeper at a salary of $1,000 a month.

15	Salary Expense	500 00	
	Cash		500 00
	Paid secretary's salary.		

Analysis: This transaction resulted in an increase in salary expense with a corresponding decrease in the asset cash. The transaction is recorded by debiting Salary Expense and by crediting Cash for $500. (The matter of payroll taxes is purposely ignored at this point. These taxes will be discussed in detail in Chapter 4.)

Note that the Posting Reference column has been left blank in the eight preceding journal entry illustrations. This is because the column is not used until the amounts are posted to the accounts in the ledger, a process to be described starting on page 38. Account numbers are shown in the Posting Reference column of the journal illustrated on pages 36 and 37, since the illustration shows how the journal appears after the posting has been completed.

The journal entries for the following transactions (as well as for those to this point) are illustrated on pages 36 and 37.

Tuesday, December 20

Received $600 from Robert Lewis for placement services rendered.

Thursday, December 22

Half withdrew $800 for personal use.

Analysis: Amounts of cash withdrawn for personal use by the owner of a business enterprise represent a decrease in owner's equity. Although the amounts withdrawn might be recorded as debits to the owner's capital account, it is better practice to record withdrawals in a separate account, Robert Half, Drawing, since this makes it easier to summarize the owner's withdrawals. This transaction is recorded in the journal by debiting Robert Half, Drawing, and by crediting Cash for $800.

Friday, December 23

Received $700 from Leesa Gornish for services rendered.

Wednesday, December 28

Paid $60 membership dues in the National Placement Officers' Association.

Thursday, December 29

Received the office equipment ordered December 2. These items were purchased on account from the Shaw-Walker Office Equipment Co. for $3,050. The dealer removed the used equipment that had been loaned to Half.

Friday, December 30

Paid the Clark-Peeper Co. $327 for the office supplies purchased on December 6.

Analysis: This transaction caused a decrease in the liability accounts payable with a corresponding decrease in the asset cash. The transaction is recorded by debiting Accounts Payable and by crediting Cash for $327.

Received from Ellen Lim $550 for placement services rendered.

Paid Wurtz $500 covering her salary for the second half of the month.

Office supplies used during the month, $55.

Analysis: By referring to the transaction of December 6, it will be noted that office supplies amounting to $327 were purchased and were recorded as an asset. By taking an inventory, counting the supplies in stock at the end of the month, Half was able to determine that the expense of supplies used during the month amounted to $55. The total expenses for the month of December would not be reflected properly if the supplies used during the month were not taken into consideration. Therefore, the expense of supplies used is recorded by debiting the expense account, Office Supplies Expense, and by crediting the asset account, Office Supplies, for $55.

Proving the Journal

Because a double entry is made for each transaction, the equality of debit and credit entries on each page of the journal may be

JOURNAL

PAGE 1

DATE	DESCRIPTION	POST. REF.	DEBIT	CREDIT
1983 Dec. 1	Cash	111	3500.00	
	Robert Half, Capital	511		3500.00
	Original investment in personnel agency.			
2	Rent Expense	821	400.00	
	Cash	111		400.00
	Paid December rent.			
6	Office Supplies	181	327.00	
	Accounts Payable	318		327.00
	Clark-Peeper Co.			
7	Telephone Expense	824	35.00	
	Cash	111		35.00
	Paid telephone bill.			
8	Miscellaneous Expense	839	9.00	
	Cash	111		9.00
	Trade journal sub.			
9	Cash	111	750.00	
	Placement Fees	611		750.00
	Bradley Swalwell.			
12	Travel and Entertainment Expense	823	165.00	
	Cash	111		165.00
	Airplane fare, convention.			
15	Salary Expense	822	500.00	
	Cash	111		500.00
	Paid secretary's salary.			
20	Cash	111	600.00	
	Placement Fees	611		600.00
	Robert Lewis.			
22	Robert Half, Drawing	521	800.00	
	Cash	111		800.00
	Withdrawn for personal use.			
23	Cash	111	700.00	
	Placement Fees	611		700.00
	Leesa Gornish.			
28	Miscellaneous Expense	839	60.00	
	Cash	111		60.00
	N.P.O.A. dues.			
29	Office Equipment	211	3050.00	
	Accounts Payable	318		3050.00
	Shaw-Walker Office Equip. Co.		10896.00	10896.00

The Robert Half Personnel Agency Journal
(continued on next page)

	JOURNAL			PAGE 2
DATE	DESCRIPTION	POST. REF.	DEBIT	CREDIT
1983 Dec. 30	Accounts Payable	318	327 00	
	Cash	111		327 00
	Clark-Peeper Co.			
30	Cash	111	550 00	
	Placement Fees	611		550 00
	Ellen Lim.			
30	Salary Expense	822	500 00	
	Cash	111		500 00
	Paid secretary's salary.			
30	Office Supplies Expense	825	55 00	
	Office Supplies	181		55 00
	Cost of supplies used during December.			
			1432 00	1432 00

The Robert Half Personnel Agency Journal
(concluded)

proved merely by totaling the amount columns. The total of each column is entered as a footing immediately under the last entry. When a page of the journal is filled, the footings may be entered just under the last single horizontal ruled line at the bottom of the page as shown in the illustration on page 36. When it is desirable to prove the equality of debits and credits on a page that is not filled, the footings should be entered immediately under the last entry as shown in the above illustration.

BUILDING YOUR ACCOUNTING KNOWLEDGE

1. Where is the first formal accounting record of a transaction usually made?
2. Name a source document that provides information about each of the following types of business transactions:
   (a) cash disbursement

(b) cash receipt
(c) sale of goods or services
(d) purchase of goods or services
3. What information usually is written in each of the following columns of the journal?
(a) Date column
(b) Description column
(c) Debit amount column
(d) Credit amount column
4. What is the first step in establishing an accounting system for a new business?
5. Name the five types of financial statement items for which it is ordinarily found desirable to keep separate accounts.
6. Which two types of accounts are temporarily used to record increases and decreases in owner's equity from most day-to-day business transactions?
7. In what order are the accounts customarily placed in the ledger?

Report No. 2-1

> *Refer to the study assignments and complete Report No. 2-1. To complete this assignment correctly, the principles developed in the preceding discussion must be understood. Review the text assignment if necessary. After completing the report, continue with the following textbook discussion until the next report is required.*

POSTING TO THE LEDGER; THE TRIAL BALANCE

The purpose of a journal is to provide a chronological record of financial transactions expressed as debits and credits to accounts. Accounts are kept to supply management with desired information in summary form. Collectively, the accounts are known as the **general ledger**, or often simply as "the ledger." The account forms may be on sheets of paper or on cards. When on sheets of paper, the sheets may be bound in book form or kept in a loose-leaf binder. Usually a separate page or card is used for each account. The accounts should be classified properly in the ledger; that is, the asset accounts should be grouped together, the liability accounts together, and the owner's equity accounts together. Proper grouping of the accounts in the ledger is an aid in preparing the various reports desired by the owner. Half decided to keep all of the accounts for the personnel agency in a loose-leaf ledger. The numbers shown in the agency's chart of accounts on page 30 were used as a guide in arranging the accounts in the ledger. The ledger is reproduced on pages 41–43. Note that the accounts are in numerical order.

Since Half makes few purchases on account, a separate account is not kept for each supplier. When invoices are received for items purchased on account, the invoices are checked and entered in the journal by debiting the proper accounts and by crediting Accounts Payable. The credit balance of Accounts Payable indicates the total amount owed to suppliers. After each invoice is recorded, it is filed in an unpaid invoice file, where it remains until it is paid in full. When an invoice is paid in full, it is removed from the unpaid invoice file and then filed under the name of the supplier for future reference. The balance of the accounts payable account may be proved at any time by determining the total of the unpaid amounts of the invoices.

Posting

The process of transferring information from the journal to the ledger is known as **posting**. All amounts entered in the journal should be posted to the accounts kept in the ledger in order to summarize the results. Such posting may be done daily or at frequent intervals. The ledger is not a reliable source of information until all of the transactions recorded in the journal have been posted. Since the accounts provide the information needed in preparing financial statements, an accurate posting procedure must be maintained.

Posting from the journal to the ledger involves entering the following information in the accounts:

(1) The date of each transaction.
(2) The amount of each transaction.
(3) The page of the journal from which each transaction is posted.

The posting procedure also requires that after the page of the journal has been posted to the ledger account, the number of that account should be entered in the Posting Reference column in the journal so as to provide a cross-reference between the journal and the ledger.

The first entry of the agency to be posted from the journal occurred on December 1, 1983, and required a debit to cash of $3,500.

The posting is, as illustrated below, accomplished by **(1)** entering the year, "1983," the month, abbreviated "Dec.," and the day, "1," in the Date column of the cash account, **(2)** entering the amount, $3,500, in the Debit column, **(3)** entering the number "1" in the Posting Reference column since the posting came from Page 1 of the journal, and **(4)** entering the cash account number 111 in the Posting Reference column of the journal on the same line as the debit to Cash for $3,500. The same pattern is followed in posting the credit part of the entry, $3,500, to Robert Half, Capital, Account No. 511.

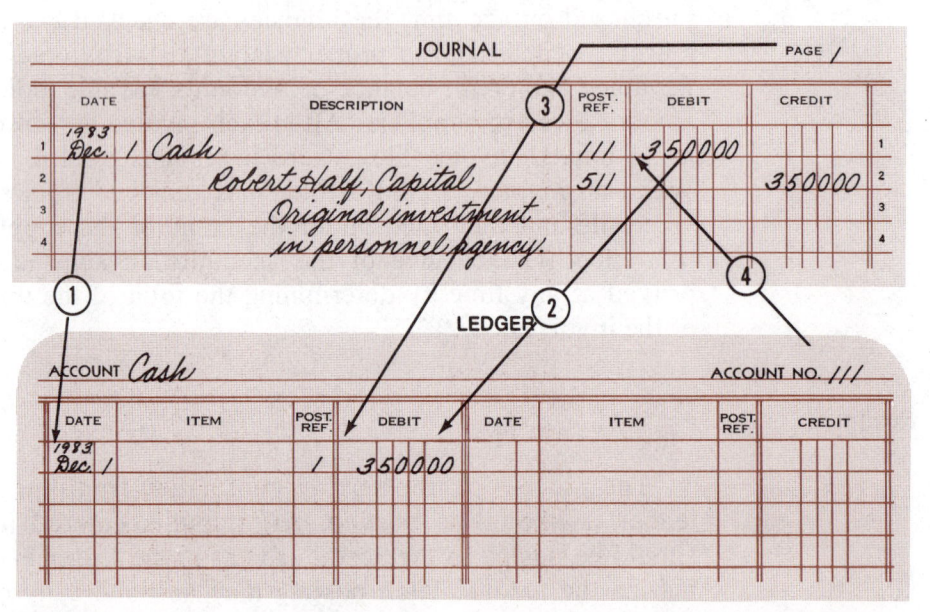

JOURNAL — PAGE 1

DATE	DESCRIPTION	POST. REF.	DEBIT	CREDIT
1983 Dec. 1	Cash	111	3500 00	
	Robert Half, Capital	511		3500 00
	Original investment in personnel agency.			

LEDGER

ACCOUNT Cash — ACCOUNT NO. 111

DATE	ITEM	POST. REF.	DEBIT	DATE	ITEM	POST. REF.	CREDIT
1983 Dec. 1		1	3500 00				

ACCOUNT Robert Half, Capital — ACCOUNT NO. 511

DATE	ITEM	POST. REF.	DEBIT	DATE	ITEM	POST. REF.	CREDIT
				1983 Dec. 1		1	3500 00

Reference to the journal of The Robert Half Personnel Agency (reproduced on pages 36 and 37) and its ledger (reproduced on pages 41–43) will indicate that a similar procedure is followed in posting every amount from the journal. Note also that in the ledger, the year "1983" is entered only at the top of each Date column, and that the month "Dec." is entered only with the first posting to an account.

Chapter 2 Accounting Procedure

ACCOUNT Cash — ACCOUNT NO. 111

DATE	ITEM	POST. REF.	DEBIT	DATE	ITEM	POST. REF.	CREDIT
1983 Dec. 1		1	3500 00	1983 Dec. 2		1	400 00
9		1	750 00	7		1	35 00
20		1	600 00	8		1	9 00
23		1	700 00	12		1	165 00
30	3,504.00	2	550 00	15		1	500 00
			6100 00	22		1	800 00
				28		1	60 00
				30		2	327 00
				30		2	500 00
							2796 00

ACCOUNT Office Supplies — ACCOUNT NO. 181

DATE	ITEM	POST. REF.	DEBIT	DATE	ITEM	POST. REF.	CREDIT
1983 Dec. 6	272.00	1	327 00	1983 Dec. 30		2	55 00

ACCOUNT Office Equipment — ACCOUNT NO. 211

DATE	ITEM	POST. REF.	DEBIT	DATE	ITEM	POST. REF.	CREDIT
1983 Dec. 29		1	3050 00				

ACCOUNT Accounts Payable — ACCOUNT NO. 318

DATE	ITEM	POST. REF.	DEBIT	DATE	ITEM	POST. REF.	CREDIT
1983 Dec. 30		2	327 00	1983 Dec. 6		1	327 00
				29	3,050.00	1	3050 00
							3377 00

ACCOUNT Robert Half, Capital — ACCOUNT NO. 511

DATE	ITEM	POST. REF.	DEBIT	DATE	ITEM	POST. REF.	CREDIT
				1983 Dec. 1		1	3500 00

The Robert Half Personnel Agency Ledger
(continued on next page)

Account: Robert Half, Drawing — Account No. 521

DATE	ITEM	POST. REF.	DEBIT	DATE	ITEM	POST. REF.	CREDIT
1983 Dec. 22		1	800 00				

Account: Placement Fees — Account No. 611

DATE	ITEM	POST. REF.	DEBIT	DATE	ITEM	POST. REF.	CREDIT
				1983 Dec. 9		1	750 00
				20		1	600 00
				23		1	700 00
				30		2	550 00
							2600 00

Account: Rent Expense — Account No. 821

DATE	ITEM	POST. REF.	DEBIT	DATE	ITEM	POST. REF.	CREDIT
1983 Dec. 2		1	400 00				

Account: Salary Expense — Account No. 822

DATE	ITEM	POST. REF.	DEBIT	DATE	ITEM	POST. REF.	CREDIT
1983 Dec. 15		1	500 00				
30		2	500 00				
			1000 00				

Account: Travel and Entertainment Expense — Account No. 823

DATE	ITEM	POST. REF.	DEBIT	DATE	ITEM	POST. REF.	CREDIT
1983 Dec. 12		1	165 00				

The Robert Half Personnel Agency Ledger
(continued)

Chapter 2   Accounting Procedure

ACCOUNT Telephone Expense							ACCOUNT NO. 824
DATE	ITEM	POST. REF.	DEBIT	DATE	ITEM	POST. REF.	CREDIT
1983 Dec. 7		1	35 00				

ACCOUNT Office Supplies Expense							ACCOUNT NO. 825
DATE	ITEM	POST. REF.	DEBIT	DATE	ITEM	POST. REF.	CREDIT
1983 Dec. 30		2	55 00				

ACCOUNT Miscellaneous Expense							ACCOUNT NO. 839
DATE	ITEM	POST. REF.	DEBIT	DATE	ITEM	POST. REF.	CREDIT
1983 Dec. 8		1	9 00				
28		1	60 00				
			69 00				

The Robert Half Personnel Agency Ledger
(concluded)

As seen from the preceding discussion, when the posting is completed, the same information is provided in both the journal and the ledger as to the date, the amount, and the effect of each transaction. A cross-reference from each book to the other book is provided by the Posting Reference column. Each entry in the journal may be traced to the ledger by referring to the account numbers indicated in the Posting Reference column of the journal. The cross reference also makes it possible to trace the entry in the ledger to the journal by referring to the page indicated in the Posting Reference column. By referring to pages 36 and 37, it will be seen that the account numbers were inserted in the Posting Reference column. This was done as each part of the posting was completed.

The Trial Balance

As indicated in Chapter 1, the purpose of a trial balance is to prove that the totals of the debit and credit balances in the ledger are equal. In a double-entry framework, equality of debit and credit balances in the ledger must be maintained. A trial balance may be taken daily, weekly, monthly, or whenever desired. Before taking a trial balance, all transactions should be journalized and the posting should be completed in order that the effect of all transactions to date will be reflected in the ledger accounts.

Footing Accounts. Prior to taking a trial balance it is necessary to **(1) foot** — add the amounts recorded on the debit and credit side of each account and **(2)** determine the balance of the account. The footing process is illustrated below. The footings are recorded immediately below the last item in both the debit and credit amount columns of the account. The footings should be written in small figures close to the preceding line so that they will not interfere with the recording of an item on the next ruled line. At the same time, the **balance** (the difference between the footings) is computed and recorded in small figures in the Item column of the account on the side with the larger footing. In other words, if an account has a debit balance, the balance should be written in the Item column on the debit or left side of the account just below the line on which the last regular entry appears and in line with the footing. If the account has a credit balance, the balance should be written in the Item column on the credit or right side of the account just below the line in which the last regular entry appears.

ACCOUNT Cash · ACCOUNT NO. 111

DATE	ITEM	POST. REF.	DEBIT	DATE	ITEM	POST. REF.	CREDIT
1983 Dec. 1		1	3500.00	1983 Dec. 2		1	400.00
9		1	750.00	7		1	35.00
20		1	600.00	8		1	9.00
23		1	700.00	12		1	165.00
30	3,304.00	2	550.00	15		1	500.00
			6100.00	22		1	800.00
				28		1	60.00
				30		2	327.00
				30		2	500.00
							2796.00

Reference to the accounts kept in the ledger shown on pages 41–43 reveals that the accounts have been footed and shows how the footings and the balances are recorded. When only one item has been posted to an account, regardless of whether it is a debit or a credit amount, no footing is necessary.

Care should be used in computing the balances of the accounts. If an error is made in adding the amount columns or in determining the difference between the footings, the error will be carried to the trial balance and considerable time may be required to locate the mistake. Most accounting errors result from carelessness. For example, a bookkeeper may write an account balance on the wrong side of an account by mistake or may enter figures so illegibly that they may be misread later. Neatness in writing the amounts is just as important as accuracy in determining the footings and the balances.

Preparing the Trial Balance. It is important that the following procedure be followed in preparing a trial balance:

(1) Head the trial balance showing (a) the name of the individual, firm, or organization, (b) the title of the report, "Trial Balance," and (c) the date. The date shown is the last day of the month even though the last business day occurs a day or two earlier. A December 31 trial balance might be prepared by the bookkeeper on January 3, however, the accounts should reflect only transactions through December 31.

(2) List the account titles in order, showing each account number.

(3) Record the account balances, entering debit balances in the left amount column and credit balances in the right amount column.

(4) Add the columns and record the totals, ruling a single line across the amount columns above the totals and a double line below the totals in the manner shown in the illustration below.

Robert Half Personnel Agency
Trial Balance
December 31, 1983

Account	Acct. No.	Dr. Balance	Cr. Balance
Cash	111	3304 00	
Office Supplies	181	272 00	
Office Equipment	211	3050 00	
Accounts Payable	318		3050 00
Robert Half, Capital	511		3500 00
Robert Half, Drawing	521	800 00	
Placement Fees	611		2600 00
Rent Expense	821	400 00	
Salary Expense	822	1000 00	
Travel and Entertainment Expense	823	165 00	
Telephone Expense	824	35 00	
Office Supplies Expense	825	55 00	
Miscellaneous Expense	839	69 00	
		9150 00	9150 00

Model Trial Balance

A trial balance is usually prepared on ruled paper though it can be written on plain paper if desired. The illustration on page 45 shows the trial balance as of December 31, 1983, of the ledger of The Robert Half Personnel Agency.

Even though the trial balance indicates that the ledger is in balance, there still may be errors in the ledger. For example, if a journal entry has been made in which the wrong accounts were debited or credited, or if an item has been posted to the wrong account, the ledger will still be in balance. It is important, therefore, that extreme care be used in preparing the journal entries and in posting them to the ledger accounts.

BUILDING YOUR ACCOUNTING KNOWLEDGE

1. What useful purpose is served by proper grouping of the accounts in the ledger?
2. When does the ledger become a reliable source of information?
3. Name the three elements of information normally entered in each ledger account involved in the posting process.
4. What information is entered in the Posting Reference column of the journal as each amount is posted to the proper account in the ledger?
5. Where should the footings of an account be recorded?
6. Where should the balance of an account be recorded?
7. Explain why there still may be errors in the ledger even though the trial balance indicates that the ledger is in balance. Give examples of two such types of errors.

Report No. 2-2

> *Refer to the study assignments and complete Report No. 2-2. To complete this assignment correctly, the principles developed in the preceding discussion must be understood. Review the text assignment if necessary. After completing the report, continue with the following textbook discussion until the next report is required.*

THE FINANCIAL STATEMENTS

The transactions completed by The Robert Half Personnel Agency during the month of December were recorded in a two-column journal (see pages 36 and 37). The debits and credits were subsequently posted to the proper accounts in a ledger (see pages 41–43). At the end of the month, a trial balance was taken as a means of proving that the equality of debits and credits had been maintained throughout the journalizing and posting process (see page 45).

Although the trial balance of The Robert Half Personnel Agency taken as of December 31 contains a list of all of the accounts, shows the amounts of their debit and credit balances, and proves the equality of these debit and credit balances, it does not clearly present all of the information that Half may need regarding either the results of operations during the month or the status of the business at the end of the month. To meet these needs, it is usual practice to prepare two financial statements — the income statement and the balance sheet.

The Income Statement

An **income statement** is an itemized statement that provides information regarding the results of operations during a specified period of time. It is a statement of the changes in owner's equity resulting from the revenue and expenses of a specific period (month, quarter, or year). Such changes are entered originally in temporary owner's equity accounts known as revenue and expense accounts. Changes in owner's equity resulting from investments or withdrawals of assets by the owner are not included in the income statement because they involve neither revenue nor expense.

The **heading** of an income statement consists of the following:

(1) The name of the business.
(2) The title of the statement.
(3) The period of time covered by the statement.

The **body** of an income statement consists of (1) an itemized list of the sources and amounts of revenue received during the period, and (2) an itemized list of the various expenses incurred during the period. The income statement reflects the **matching concept** (matching the revenues and expenses of a business on a periodic basis). It is said that this matching process is the "heart" of income measurement.

An income statement prepared from The Robert Half Personnel Agency trial balance showing the results of operations for the month ended December 31, 1983, is reproduced at the top of page 48.

The financial statements usually are prepared first on ruled paper. Such handwritten copies may then be typed so that a number

Robert Half Personnel Agency
Income Statement
For the Month Ended December 31, 1983

Revenue:		
Placement fees		$2,600.00
Expenses:		
Rent expense	$400.00	
Salary expense	1,000.00	
Travel and entertainment expense	165.00	
Telephone expense	35.00	
Office supplies expense	55.00	
Miscellaneous expense	69.00	
Total expenses		1,724.00
Net income		$876.00

Income Statement

of copies will be available for those who are interested in examining the statements. Since the typewritten copies are not on ruled paper, dollar signs are included in the handwritten copy so that the typist will understand just when they are to be inserted. Note that a dollar sign is placed beside the first amount in each column and the first amount below a ruling in each column. The income statement illustrated above is shown on two-column ruled paper; however, the columns do not have any debit-credit significance. The only source of revenue was placement fees that amounted to $2,600. The total expenses for the month amounted to $1,724. The revenue exceeded the expenses by $876. This represents the amount of the net income for the month. If the total expenses had exceeded the total revenue, the excess would have represented a **net loss** for the month. The information provided by the income statement of The Robert Half Personnel Agency may be summarized in equation form as follows:

REVENUE − EXPENSES = NET INCOME
$2,600 $1,724 $876

It is apparent that the income statement is more informative than the trial balance as to the results of operations for December. The trial balance contains the necessary data for preparing the income statement, but the income statement presents the data in a more meaningful way.

Chapter 2   Accounting Procedure   49

The Balance Sheet

The **balance sheet** is an itemized statement of the assets, liabilities, and owner's equity of a business enterprise as of a specified date. Its purpose is to provide information regarding the status of these basic accounting elements as of the close of business on the date indicated in the heading.

The **heading** of a balance sheet contains the following:

(1) The name of the business.
(2) The title of the statement.
(3) The date of the statement as of the close of business on that day.

The **body** of a balance sheet consists of an itemized list of the assets, the liabilities, and the owner's equity, the latter being the difference between the total amount of the assets and the total amount of the liabilities. A balance sheet for The Robert Half Personnel Agency showing the status of the business when it closed on December 31, 1983, is reproduced on pages 50 and 51. The balance sheet illustrated is arranged like a standard account with the assets listed on the left side and the liabilities and owner's equity listed on the right side. The information provided by the balance sheet of The Robert Half Personnel Agency may be summarized in equation form as follows:

ASSETS	=	LIABILITIES	+	OWNER'S EQUITY
$6,626		$3,050		$3,576

The trial balance was the source of the information needed in listing the assets and liabilities in the balance sheet. The amount of the owner's equity may be calculated by subtracting the total liabilities from the total assets. Thus, Half's equity as of December 31, 1983, is as follows:

Total assets...	$6,626
Less total liabilities	3,050
Owner's equity	$3,576

The owner's equity may also be determined by taking into consideration the following factors:

(1) The **amount invested** in the enterprise by Half on December 1, as shown by the capital account.
(2) The amount of the **net income** of The Robert Half Personnel Agency for December, as shown by the income statement.
(3) The total **amount withdrawn** for personal use during December, as shown by Half's drawing account.

	Robert Half
	Balance
	December
Assets	
Cash	$3304 00
Office supplies	272 00
Office equipment	3050 00
Total assets	$6626 00

Balance Sheet — Account Form *(Left Page)*

The trial balance on page 45 shows that Half's equity in The Robert Half Personnel Agency on December 1 amounted to $3,500. This is indicated by the credit balance of the capital account. The income statement on page 48 shows that the net income of the agency for December amounted to $876. The trial balance also shows that the amount withdrawn by Half for personal use during the month amounted to $800. This is indicated by the debit balance of the drawing account. On the basis of this information, Half's equity in The Robert Half Personnel Agency as of December 31, 1983, is as follows:

Amount of capital, December 1		$3,500
Net income for December	$876	
Less amount withdrawn for personal use during the month	800	76
Capital as of close of business, December 31		$3,576

BUILDING YOUR ACCOUNTING KNOWLEDGE

1. What is the purpose of an income statement?
2. Why are changes in owner's equity resulting from investments or withdrawals of assets by the owner not included in the income statement?
3. What are the three parts of the heading of an income statement?

Chapter 2   Accounting Procedure   51

Personnel Agency
Sheet
31, 1983

	Liabilities		
Accounts payable		$3050.00	
Total liabilities			$3050.00
	Owner's Equity		
Robert Half, capital			
Capital, Dec. 1, 1983		$3500.00	
Net income	$876.00		
Less withdrawals	800.00		
Net increase		76.00	
Capital, Dec. 31, 1983			3576.00
Total liabilities and owner's equity			$6626.00

Balance Sheet — Account Form *(Right Page)*

4. What is the purpose of a balance sheet?
5. What are the three parts of the heading of a balance sheet?
6. What is the source of information for preparing both the income statement and the balance sheet?
7. Owner's equity can be calculated by subtracting total liabilities shown by the balance sheet from total assets shown by the balance sheet. What three factors may be used to prove the amount of owner's equity calculated in this manner?

Report No. 2-3

> Refer to the study assignments and complete Report 2-3. This assignment provides a test of your ability to apply the principles developed in Chapters 1 and 2 of this textbook. The textbook and the study assignments go hand in hand, each serving a definite purpose in the learning process. Inability to solve correctly any problem included in the report indicates that you have failed to master the principles developed in the textbook. Further study, with the aid of the vocabulary list on page 52, should be helpful in this regard. After completing the report, you may proceed with Chapter 3 until the next report is required.

EXPANDING YOUR BUSINESS VOCABULARY

What is the meaning of each of the following terms:

balance (p. 44)
balance sheet (p. 49)
book of original entry (p. 27)
capital account (p. 29)
chart of accounts (p. 29)
Credit amount column (p. 28)
Date column (p. 27)
Debit amount column (p. 28)
Description column (p. 27)
foot (p. 44)
general ledger (p. 38)

income statement (p. 47)
journal (p. 26)
journalizing (p. 26)
matching concept (p. 47)
owner's equity (p. 29)
posting (p. 39)
Posting Reference column (p. 28)
source document (p. 26)
two-column journal (p. 27)

3

ACCOUNTING FOR CASH

CHAPTER OBJECTIVES

The objectives of this chapter are to enable you:

▶ To explain the meanings of the term "cash" as it is used in accounting.

▶ To describe **internal control** as it relates to the handling of cash.

▶ To explain the operation of a petty cash fund and to prepare a special multicolumn record of cash disbursements.

▶ To describe banking procedures relating to the use of commercial bank checking accounts, and to prepare a bank statement reconciliation.

In the preceding chapters, the purpose and nature of business accounting, transaction analysis, and the framework of double entry bookkeeping were introduced. Explanations and illustrations were given of **(1) journalizing** (recording transactions in a general journal — a book of original entry), **(2) posting** (transferring the entries to the accounts that, taken together, comprise the general ledger), **(3)** taking a trial balance, and **(4)** using the latter to prepare an income statement and a balance sheet (two basic and important financial statements).

This chapter is devoted to a discussion of the handling of and accounting for cash receipts and cash disbursements, including various considerations that are involved when cash is kept in a commercial bank.

CASH RECEIPTS AND CASH DISBURSEMENTS

The term "cash" has several different, though not totally dissimilar, meanings. In a very narrow sense, **cash** means currency and coins. In a broader sense, cash includes checks, drafts, and money orders. All of these, including currency and coins, are sometimes called cash items. Usually, any reference to the **cash receipts** of a business relates to the receipt of checks, drafts, and money orders payable to the business, as well as to the receipt of currency and coins. The cash account balance, as well as the amount shown for cash in a balance sheet, normally includes cash and cash items on hand plus the amount on deposit in a bank checking account. In some cases, the balance sheet figure for cash includes amounts on deposit in more than one bank. On the balance sheet, it is rather rare to make a distinction between "cash on hand" and "cash in bank," but sometimes this is done.

A good policy for a business enterprise to adopt is one which requires that all cash and cash items which it receives be deposited in a bank. When this is done, its total cash receipts will equal its total deposits in the bank. It is also a good policy to make arrangements with the bank so that all checks and other cash items received by the business from customers or others in the usual course of business will be accepted by the bank for deposit only. This will cause the records of cash receipts and disbursements of the business to agree item by item with the bank's record of deposits and withdrawals.

The Cash Account

The cash account is debited when cash is increased and credited when cash is decreased. This account normally has a debit balance.

Cash Receipts. Cash and cash items received by a business are known as cash receipts. It is vital that an accurate and timely record be kept of cash receipts. When the volume of the receipts is large both in number and in amount, procedures designed to reduce the danger of mistake and **embezzlement** (the unauthorized taking of business cash by an employee) should be followed. When numerous receipts of currency and coins from customers are given in person for goods or services just received, it is customary to use a **cash register**. Such a machine provides a listing of amounts recorded as the money is received. A cash register may have the capability of accumulating subtotals that permit classification of amounts — sales by departments or products, for example.

When money comes in by mail (nearly always checks), a pre-supplied form showing the remitter's name, address, and the amount on the enclosed check or money order is usually enclosed. A good example of this is the top part of a monthly statement that the customer has received as shown below.

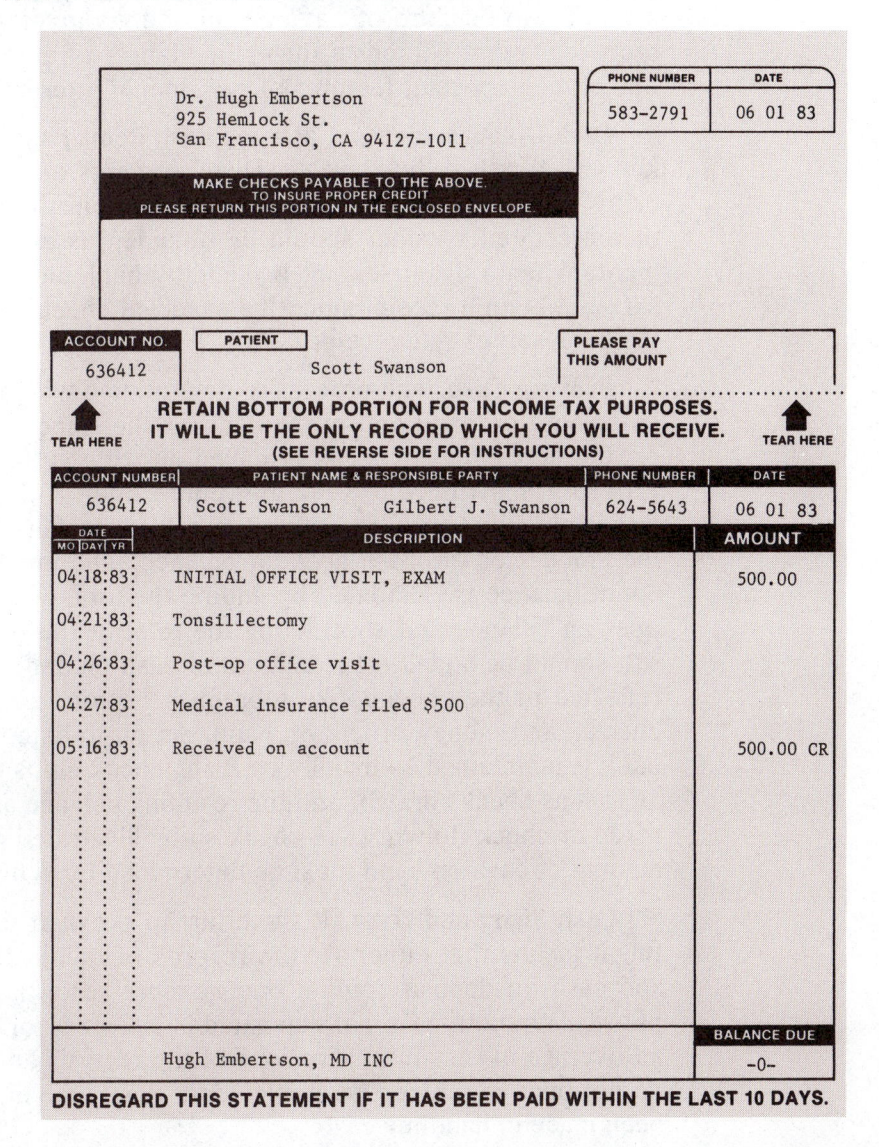

PHONE NUMBER	DATE
583-2791	06 01 83

Dr. Hugh Embertson
925 Hemlock St.
San Francisco, CA 94127-1011

MAKE CHECKS PAYABLE TO THE ABOVE.
TO INSURE PROPER CREDIT
PLEASE RETURN THIS PORTION IN THE ENCLOSED ENVELOPE.

ACCOUNT NO.	PATIENT	PLEASE PAY THIS AMOUNT
636412	Scott Swanson	

**RETAIN BOTTOM PORTION FOR INCOME TAX PURPOSES.
IT WILL BE THE ONLY RECORD WHICH YOU WILL RECEIVE.
(SEE REVERSE SIDE FOR INSTRUCTIONS)**

TEAR HERE ⬆   ⬆ TEAR HERE

ACCOUNT NUMBER	PATIENT NAME & RESPONSIBLE PARTY	PHONE NUMBER	DATE
636412	Scott Swanson Gilbert J. Swanson	624-5643	06 01 83

DATE MO/DAY/YR	DESCRIPTION	AMOUNT
04 18 83	INITIAL OFFICE VISIT, EXAM	500.00
04 21 83	Tonsillectomy	
04 26 83	Post-op office visit	
04 27 83	Medical insurance filed $500	
05 16 83	Received on account	500.00 CR

Hugh Embertson, MD INC

BALANCE DUE
-0-

DISREGARD THIS STATEMENT IF IT HAS BEEN PAID WITHIN THE LAST 10 DAYS.

Sometimes a written receipt must be prepared by the business. A carbon copy of the receipt or the returned portion of the monthly statement provides the source document for the cash received. In any case, the initial record of each amount received should be prepared by someone other than the bookkeeper to provide good internal control. The money received, including checks and money orders, is placed in the custody of whoever is authorized to handle bank deposits and cash on hand. The bookkeeper uses the initial records in preparing proper journal entries for cash receipts. Under such a plan, the bookkeeper does not actually handle any cash; instead cash receipts are entered from records prepared by other persons. The procedure of having transactions involving cash handled by two or more persons reduces the danger of embezzlement and is one of the important features of a system of internal control.

Cash Disbursements. Cash and cash items paid by a business are known as **cash disbursements**. Disbursements may be made in cash or by bank check. When a disbursement is made in cash, a receipt or a receipted voucher should be obtained as evidence of the payment. When a disbursement is made by bank check, it is not necessary to obtain a receipt since the canceled check that is returned by the bank serves as a receipt.

Proving Cash. The process of determining whether the amount of cash, both on hand and in the bank, is the same amount that exists on the accounting records is called **proving cash**. Cash should be proved at least once a week and, more often if the volume of cash transactions is large. The first step is to determine from the records the amount of the cash account balance. The most recent cash account balance is calculated by adding the total of the receipts to the opening balance and subtracting the total of the payments. The result should be equal to the amount of cash on deposit in the bank as reflected in the checkbook stubs plus the total of currency, coins, checks, and money orders on hand. An up-to-date record of cash in bank is maintained — usually by using check stubs to show deposits as well as checks drawn, and the resulting balance after each deposit made or check drawn. (See check stubs illustrated on page 71.) The amount of cash on hand must be determined by actual count.

Cash Short and Over. If the effort to prove cash is not successful, it means that either **(1)** the records of receipts, disbursements, and cash on deposit contain one or more recording errors, **(2)** the physical count of cash not deposited is incorrect, or **(3)** a shortage or an overage exists. If verifications of the records and the cash count do not uncover any error, it is evident that some mistake must have been made in handling cash.

Finding that cash is slightly short or over is not unusual. If there are numerous cash transactions, it is difficult to avoid occasional errors in making change. There is always the danger of shortages due to dishonesty, but most discrepancies are the result of mistakes. Many businesses have a special ledger account entitled **Cash Short and Over** which is used to keep track of day-to-day shortages and overages of cash. If, in the effort to prove cash, it is found that a shortage exists, the amount is treated as a cash disbursement transaction involving a debit to Cash Short and Over. Any overage discovered is regarded as a cash receipt transaction involving a credit to Cash Short and Over. By the end of the fiscal year, it is likely that the cash short and over account will have both debits and credits. If the total of the debits exceeds the total of the credits, the balance represents an expense or loss; if the reverse is the case, the balance represents revenue.

The Petty Cash Fund

When all cash receipts are deposited in a bank, an office fund known as a **petty cash fund** may be established for paying small items. ("Petty" means small or little.) Such a fund eliminates the necessity of writing checks for small amounts.

Operating a Petty Cash Fund. To establish a petty cash fund, a check is written for the amount that is to be set aside in the fund. The amount may be $50, $100, $125, or any amount considered necessary. The check is made payable to the person who will have custody of the fund. That person's name, followed by a comma and the words, "Petty Cashier" appears on the check as the payee. When the check is cashed by the bank, the money is placed in a cash drawer, a cash register, or a safe at the depositor's place of business; and a designated individual in the office is authorized to make payments from the fund. The person responsible for the fund should be able to account for the full amount of the fund at any time.

Disbursements from the fund should not be made without obtaining some sort of receipt. A special form of receipt, showing the name of the payee, the purpose of the payment, and the account to be charged for each petty cash disbursement, is known as a **petty cash voucher**. A form of petty cash voucher is shown on page 58. Such a voucher should be used for each expenditure.

The check written to establish the petty cash fund may be entered in the journal by debiting Petty Cash Fund and by crediting Cash. When it is necessary to replenish the fund, the petty cashier usually prepares a statement of the expenditures, properly classi-

Petty Cash Voucher

No. 4　　　　　　　　　　Date December 14, 1983
Paid to Barbara K. Moran　　　　Amount
For American Red Cross　　　　　15 | 00
Charge to Charitable Contributions Expense
Payment received:
Barbara K. Moran　　Approved by Al Boes

Petty Cash Voucher

fied. A check is then written for the exact amount of the total expenditures. This check is entered in the journal by debiting the proper accounts indicated in the statement and by crediting Cash.

To illustrate, assume that on July 1, Marcia's Boutique established a petty cash fund for $75, and that on July 30 the fund was replenished for $62.50 after classifying and totaling the petty cash vouchers. The journal entries to record these transactions are:

July	1	Petty Cash Fund	75.00	
		Cash		75.00
		To establish petty cash fund.		
	30	Automobile Expense	14.00	
		Supplies Expense	26.00	
		Postage Expense	19.00	
		Miscellaneous Expense	3.50	
		Cash		62.50
		Replenishment of petty cash fund.		

The petty cash fund is thus a revolving fund. The petty cash account balance does not change in amount unless the fund is increased or decreased. The actual amount of cash in the fund plus the total of the petty cash vouchers should be equal to the amount originally deposited to the petty cash fund. This commonly used method for handling petty cash is referred to as the **imprest method**.

Petty Cash Disbursements Record. When a petty cash fund is maintained, it is good practice to keep a formal record of all disbursements from the fund. The **petty cash disbursements record** is a special multicolumn record that supplements the regular accounting records. No posting is done from this special record. Various types of records have been designed for recording petty cash transactions. One of the standard forms is illustrated on pages 60 and 61. The headings of the Distribution columns may vary with each enterprise, depending upon the desired classification of the expenditures. The headings represent accounts that eventually are to be charged for the expenditures. The desired headings may either be printed on the form or they may be written in. Often account numbers instead of account titles are used in the headings to indicate the accounts to be charged.

The petty cashier should have a document for each disbursement made from the petty cash fund. Whether or not a receipt or receipted invoice is obtained, the petty cashier should prepare a voucher. The vouchers should be numbered consecutively.

A typical petty cash disbursements record is reproduced on pages 60 and 61. It is a part of the records of Al Boes, a business consultant. Since Boes is out of the office much of the time, a petty cash fund is provided from which the secretary is authorized to make petty cash disbursements not to exceed $25 each. A narrative of the petty cash transactions completed by Pauline Curtis, Boes' secretary, during the month of December follows:

AL BOES

NARRATIVE OF PETTY CASH TRANSACTIONS

Dec. 1 Issued check for $125 payable to Pauline Curtis, Petty Cash Fund Cashier. The check is cashed and the proceeds placed in a petty cash fund.

> This transaction is recorded in the journal by debiting Petty Cash Fund and by crediting Cash. A memorandum entry is also made in the Description column of the petty cash disbursements record reproduced on pages 60 and 61.

DATE	DESCRIPTION	POST. REF.	DEBIT	CREDIT
19-- Dec. 1	Petty Cash Fund		125 00	
	Cash			125 00
	To establish petty cash fund.			

During the month of December, the following disbursements were made from the petty cash fund:

PETTY CASH DISBURSEMENTS

DAY	DESCRIPTION	VOU. NO.	TOTAL AMOUNT	Tel. Exp.	Auto Exp.
	AMOUNTS FORWARDED				
1	Received in fund 125.00				
6	Automobile repairs	1	16 40		16 40
7	Client luncheon	2	11 50		
13	Al Boes, personal use	3	25 00		
14	American Red Cross	4	15 00		
15	Typewriter repairs	5	8 75		
17	Traveling expense	6	9 25		
20	Washing automobile	7	4 50		4 50
22	Postage expense	8	1 50		
23	Salvation Army	9	8 00		
27	Postage stamps	10	15 00		
28	Long distance call	11	3 60	3 60	
			118 50	3 60	20 90
			118 50	3 60	20 90
31	Balance		6.50		
31	Received in fund		118.50		
	Total		125.00		

Al Boes' Petty Cash Disbursements Record (Left Page)

Dec. 6 Paid $16.40 to Jim Smith of Smith's Auto for having the company automobile serviced. Petty Cash Voucher No. 1.

7 Reimbursed Boes $11.50 for the amount spent in entertaining a client at lunch. Petty Cash Voucher No. 2.

13 Gave Boes $25 for personal use. Petty Cash Voucher No. 3.

> This item is entered in the Amount column provided at the extreme right of the petty cash disbursements record since no special distribution column has been provided for recording amounts withdrawn by the owner for personal use.

14 Gave the American Red Cross a $15 donation. Petty Cash Voucher No. 4.

15 Paid $8.75 for typewriter repairs. Petty Cash Voucher No. 5.

16 Reimbursed Boes $9.25 for traveling expenses. Petty Cash Voucher No. 6.

Chapter 3 Accounting for Cash 61

Post. Exp.	Char. Cont. Exp.	Travel & Ent. Exp.	Misc. Exp.	ACCOUNT	AMOUNT
		11 50			
				Al Boes, Drawing	25 00
	15 00				
			8 75		
		9 25			
1 50					
	8 00				
15 00					
16 50	23 00	20 75	8 75		25 00
16 50	23 00	20 75	8 75		25 00

FOR MONTH OF December 1983. PAGE 1

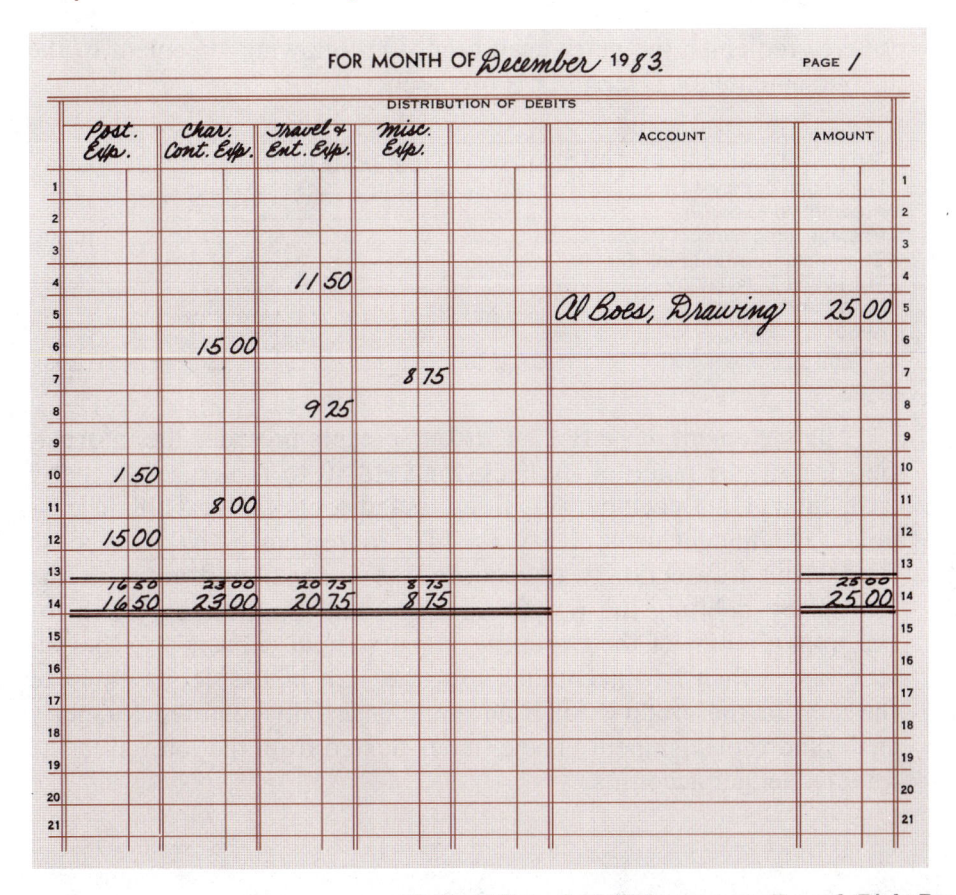

Al Boes' Petty Cash Disbursements Record (Right Page)

Dec. 20 Paid $4.50 to Mike Butler of Glow Car Care for having the company automobile washed. Petty Cash Voucher No. 7.
 22 Paid $1.50 for mailing a package. Petty Cash Voucher No. 8.
 23 Donated $8 to the Salvation Army. Petty Cash Voucher No. 9.
 27 Paid $15 for postage stamps. Petty Cash Voucher No. 10.
 28 Reimbursed Boes $3.60 for a long distance telephone call made from a booth. Petty Cash Voucher No. 11.

Proving the Petty Cash Disbursements Record. To prove the petty cash disbursements record, it is first necessary to foot all of the amount columns. The sum of the footings of the Distribution columns should equal the footing of the Total Amount column. After proving the footings, the totals are recorded and the record is ruled as shown in the illustration. The illustration shows that a total of $118.50 was paid out during December. Since this is an appropriate time to replenish the petty cash fund, the following statement of the disbursements for December is prepared:

STATEMENT OF PETTY CASH DISBURSEMENTS FOR DECEMBER
Telephone Expense	$ 3.60
Automobile Expense	20.90
Postage Expense	16.50
Charitable Contributions Expense	23.00
Travel and Entertainment Expense	20.75
Miscellaneous Expense	8.75
Al Boes, Drawing	25.00
Total disbursements	$118.50

The statement of petty cash disbursements provides the information for the issuance of a check for $118.50 to replenish the petty cash fund. On December 30, Boes issued a check for $118.50 payable to Pauline Curtis, Petty Cashier to replenish the petty cash fund. This transaction was recorded as a compound entry in the journal by debiting the proper accounts and by crediting Cash for the total amount of the expenses. A **compound entry** is one that affects more than two accounts, with the sum of the debits equal to the sum of the credits. Such an entry is usually required for petty cash fund replenishment. The entry is posted from the journal to the affected ledger accounts.

JOURNAL PAGE 15

DATE	DESCRIPTION	POST. REF.	DEBIT	CREDIT
1983 Dec. 30	Telephone Expense		3 60	
	Automobile Expense		20 90	
	Postage Expense		16 50	
	Charitable Contributions Expense		23 00	
	Travel and Entertainment Expense		20 75	
	Miscellaneous Expense		8 75	
	Al Boes, Drawing		25 00	
	Cash			118 50
	Replenishment of petty cash fund.			

After footing and ruling the petty cash disbursements record, the balance in the fund and the amount received to replenish the fund may be recorded in the Description column below the ruling as shown in the illustration. It is customary to carry the total forward to the top of a new page as a memorandum entry before recording any of the transactions for the following month.

BUILDING YOUR ACCOUNTING KNOWLEDGE

1. What is the usual source documentation of cash receipts in currency and coin when they are numerous and given in person? What form of source documentation usually accompanies money that comes in by mail?
2. Why should transactions involving cash be handled by two or more persons?
3. Why is it not unusual to find that the cash balance at the end of the day is slightly short or over?
4. What does a debit balance in the cash short and over account represent? What does a credit balance in this account represent?
5. What is the purpose of a petty cash fund?
6. What should be obtained from the receiving party each time a petty cash disbursement is made?
7. From what source is the information for issuing a check to replenish the petty cash fund obtained?

Report No. 3-1

> *Refer to the study assignments and Complete Report No. 3-1. After completing the report, proceed with the textbook discussion until the next report is required.*

BANKING PROCEDURES

A bank is a financial institution that receives deposits, lends money, makes collections, and renders other services, such as providing vaults for the safekeeping of valuables and handling trust funds for its customers. Most banks offer facilities for both checking accounts and savings accounts.

Checking Account

The majority of all money payments in the United States are made by checks. Commercial paper drawn on funds in a bank account and payable on demand is called a **check**. It involves three original parties: **(1)** the depositor who orders the bank to pay a certain amount of money is known as the **drawer**; **(2)** the bank in which the drawer has money on deposit is known as the **drawee**; and **(3)** the person directed to receive the money is known as the **payee**. The drawer and payee may be the same person, though the payee named in such a case usually is "Cash," or the name of the drawee bank.

A check is **negotiable** (meaning that the right to receive the money can be transferred to someone else) if it complies with the following requirements: **(1)** it is in writing; **(2)** it is signed by the drawer; **(3)** it contains an unconditional order to pay a specified amount of money; **(4)** it is payable on demand; and **(5)** it is payable to the order of another party or to the bearer. The payee transfers the right to receive the money by **indorsing** the check. This procedure requires writing his or her name and sometimes other pertinent information on the back of the check. If the payee simply signs on the back of the check, customarily near the left end, the signature is called a **blank indorsement**. This makes the check payable to any bearer. If there are added words such as "For deposit," "Pay to any bank or banker," or "Pay to Mel Blank only," it is called a **restrictive indorsement**. A widely used business practice when indorsing checks for deposit is to use a rubber stamp similar to that illustrated below.

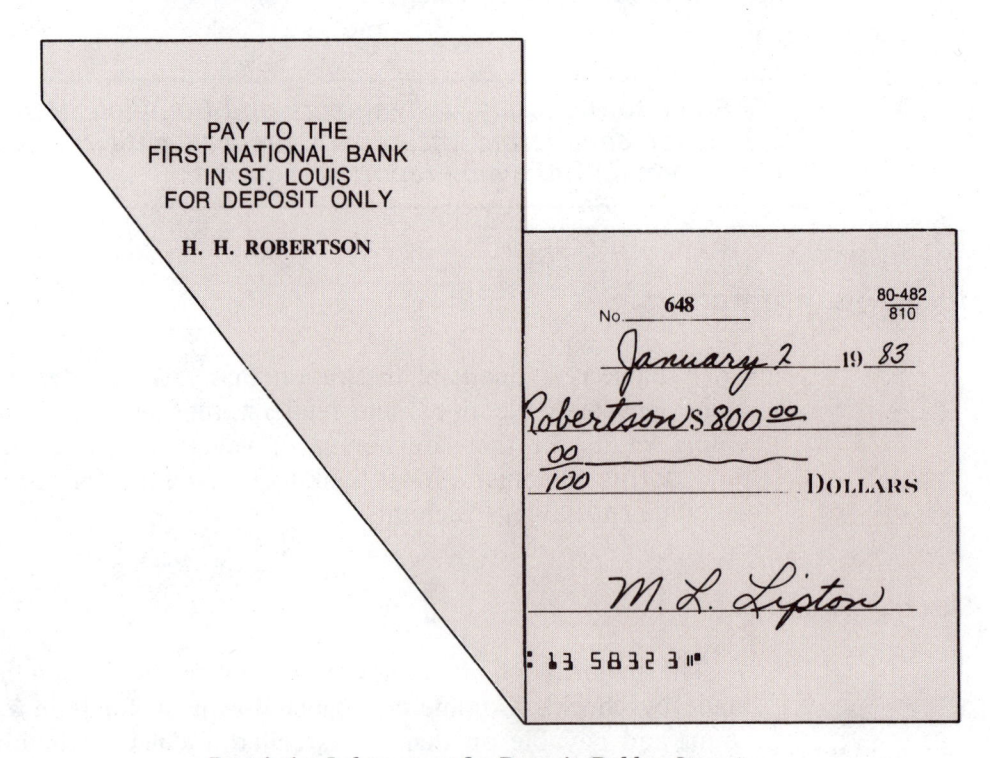

Restrictive Indorsement for Deposit (Rubber Stamp)

Important factors in connection with a checking account are: **(1)** opening the account, **(2)** making deposits, **(3)** making withdrawals, **(4)** recording bank transactions, and **(5)** reconciling the bank statement.

Opening a Checking Account. To open a checking account with a bank, it is necessary to obtain the approval of an official of the bank and to make an initial deposit. Money, checks, bank drafts, money orders, and other cash items usually are accepted for deposit, subject to their verification as to amount and validity.

Banks usually require new depositors to sign their names on a card or form as an aid in verifying the depositor's signature on checks that may be issued, on cash items that may be indorsed for deposit, and on other business papers that may be presented to the bank. The form a depositor signs to give the bank a sample signature is called a **signature card**. If desired, depositors may authorize others to sign checks and other business forms on their behalf. A person who is so authorized is required to sign the depositor's name along with his or her own signature on a signature card and on all documents subsequently executed on behalf of the depositor. To aid in identification, the depositor's social security number is also shown. A signature card is one of the safeguards that a bank uses to protect its own interests as well as the interests of its depositors.

Making Deposits. To make a deposit with a bank, it is necessary to use certain forms prescribed by that bank and to observe the rules of the bank with regard to acceptable and unacceptable deposit items. In preparing the deposit, paper money should be arranged in the order of the denominations, the smaller denominations being placed on top. The bills should be all stacked face up and top up. Coins (pennies, nickels, dimes, quarters, half dollars and dollars) that are to be deposited in considerable quantities should be wrapped in coin wrappers, which the bank provides, unless the bank has a coin-sorting machine. The name and account number of the depositor should be written on the outside of each coin wrapper as a means of identification in the event that a mistake has been made in counting the coins. All checks being deposited must be indorsed. The indorsement on the check illustrated on page 64 was made by means of a rubber stamp.

Deposit Ticket. A printed form with a detailed listing of items being deposited is called a **deposit ticket**. Banks provide these forms for depositors. A filled-in deposit ticket, typical of the type that most banks provide, is reproduced on page 66. Note that the number of the depositor's account is preprinted at the bottom in

Accounting for Cash — Chapter 3

Deposit ticket			4-5/810
		Amount	
First National Bank in St. Louis	Currency	$ 822	00
St. Louis, Missouri	Coin	38	27
	Checks 4-5	290	40
Date October 13, 1983	List 80-459	620	00
	checks 4-97	560	00
	singly		
H. H. ROBERTSON	Be sure all items are endorsed		
For credit of 2650 S. Hanley Rd.			
St. Louis, MO 63144-9892			
	Total	2,330	67

⑆081000058⑆ 13 6725 4⑈

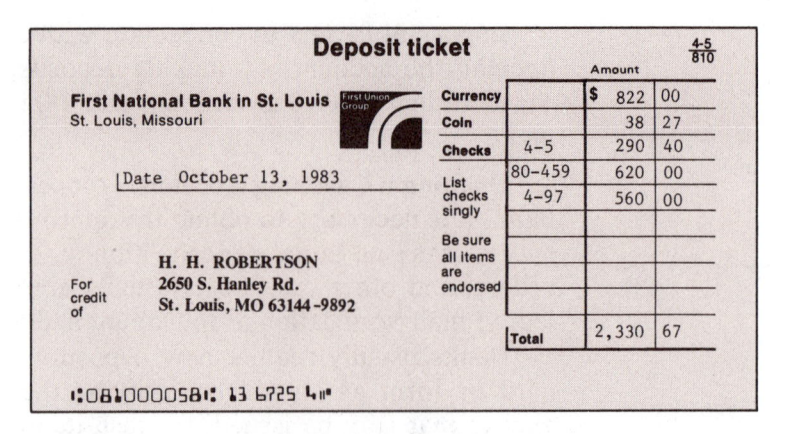

Deposit Ticket

numbers that can be "read" by electronic equipment used by banks. These numbers are called **MICR numbers**, which stands for magnetic ink character recognition. This series of digits, which is also preprinted at the bottom of all of the depositor's checks, is actually a code used in sorting and routing deposit slips and checks. In the first set of digits, 081000058, the first "8" indicates that the bank is in the Eighth Federal Reserve District. The third digit "1" is the reserve bank or branch serving the district. The fourth digit "0" indicates that the item is for immediate credit. A "1" in the fourth position would indicate that the credit to the bank is delayed by one day. The depositor in either case receives immediate credit to his/her account. The number "5" is a number assigned to the First National Bank in St. Louis. The last number "8" is known as a check digit and is used to verify the accuracy of the eight preceding digits in computer processing. Because this numbering method was established by the American Bankers Association, code numbers used in sorting and routing deposit tickets are also known as **ABA numbers**. The second set of digits, 13-6725-4, is the number assigned by the First National Bank in St. Louis to H. H. Robertson's account.

It is common practice to prepare deposit tickets in duplicate so that one copy, when receipted by the bank teller, may be retained by the depositor. In preparing a deposit ticket, the date should be written in the space provided. The amounts of cash represented by currency and by coins should be entered in the amount column of the deposit ticket on the lines provided for these items.

Each check to be deposited should be listed on a separate line of the deposit ticket as shown in the illustration. In listing checks on the deposit ticket, the instructions of the bank should be observed in describing the checks for identification purposes. Banks usually prefer that depositors identify checks being deposited by showing the ABA number of the bank on which the check is drawn. The ABA number for the first check listed on the deposit ticket is $\frac{4-5}{810}$. The number "4" is the number assigned to the city in which the bank is located and the number "5" is assigned to the specific bank. The denominator "810" is the check routing number, but only the numerator is used in identifying the deposit.

The total of the cash and other items deposited should be entered on the deposit tickets. The deposit tickets, prepared in duplicate, together with the cash and the other items deposited, should be delivered to the receiving teller of the bank. The teller processes the deposit tickets and returns the duplicate to the depositor.

A depositor may personally obtain cash at the time of making a deposit by indicating on the deposit slip the portion of the total of items listed to be returned to him or her, with the remainder to constitute the deposit. Alternatively, a check may be drawn payable to the depositor, or usually, just to "Cash."

If a duplicate deposit ticket is not used, the bank may provide the depositor with a machine-printed receipt for each deposit. Some banks use **automatic teller machines** in preparing the receipts. The use of such machines saves the time required to make the manual entries and eliminates the need for making duplicate copies of deposit tickets. Such machines are not only timesaving, but they also promote accuracy in the handling of deposits. A deposit that consists exclusively of checks often is mailed to the bank with a single deposit ticket. Later, a machine-printed deposit receipt and a new deposit envelope are mailed back to the depositor.

The deposits handled by each teller during the day may be accumulated in the automatic teller machine so that at the end of the day the total amount of the deposits received by the teller is automatically recorded by the machine. This amount may be proved by counting the cash and cash items accepted by a teller for deposit during the day.

Dishonored Checks. A check that a bank refuses to pay is described as a **dishonored check**. A depositor guarantees all items deposited and is liable to the bank for the amount involved if any item is not honored when presented for payment. When a check or other cash item is deposited with a bank and is not honored upon presentation to the bank upon which it is drawn, the depositor's bank may charge the amount of the dishonored item to the depositor's account or may present it to the depositor for reimbursement. It is not uncommon for checks that have been deposited to be returned to the depositor for various reasons accompanied with a **debit advice**. As indicated on the debit advice shown below, the most common reason for checks being returned unpaid is that they are **NSF checks** ("not sufficient funds" remain in the drawer's account to cover them).

Debit Advice

Issuance of a check on a bank without sufficient funds on deposit with that bank to cover the check when it is presented for payment is called an **overdraft**. Under the laws of most states, issuance of such a check is illegal. When a dishonored check is charged to the depositor's account, the amount should be deducted from the balance shown on the depositor's checkbook stub.

Most overdraft checks are not the result of any dishonest intent on the part of the drawer of such checks. Either the depositor thought that there was money in the account when the check was written, due to an error in keeping the checkbook, or expected to get a deposit to the bank in time to "cover" the check before it reached the bank for payment. It is commonly considered to be something of a disgrace to the drawer of a check if the bank will not honor (pay) it. In recent years, many banks have made available plans that guarantee that all checks, within prescribed limits as to amount, will be honored even if the depositor's balance is too low. This amounts to a prearrangement with the bank to make a loan to the depositor. These plans have been given names such as "Ready Reserve Account," "Instant Cash," and others. Arrangements of this sort are parts of larger plans that involve such things as picture checks, no minimum balance requirement, bank statements that list checks paid in numerical order, check guarantee cards, travelers checks without fee, safe-deposit boxes, and even bank credit cards. The bank may charge a monthly fee for any or all of these services.

Such comprehensive plans are not widely subscribed to by businesses (in contrast to individuals).

Postdated Checks. Checks dated after the date that the check was written and issued are known as **postdated checks**. For example, a check written and issued on March 1 is dated March 15. The recipient of the postdated check should not deposit it before the date specified on the check (March 15) because it is not legally acceptable as cash until that date. One reason for issuing a postdated check may be that the maker does not have sufficient funds in the bank at the time of issuance which in this case is March 1, but expects to have a sufficient amount on deposit by the time the check is presented for payment on or after the date of the check (March 15). When a postdated check is presented to the bank on which it is drawn and payment is not made, it is handled by the bank in the same manner as any other dishonored check and the payee should treat it as a dishonored check. Generally, it is not considered good practice for a business to issue postdated checks.

Making Deposits by Mail. As indicated earlier, bank deposits may be made either over the counter or by mail. The over-the-counter method of making deposits is frequently used, but it may not always be convenient to make deposits over the counter. If the depositor lives at a great distance from the bank, it may be more convenient to make deposits by mail. When deposits are made by mail, the bank may provide the depositor with a supply of deposit tickets, a self-addressed, prestamped envelope, and a form which is subsequently returned with a machine-printed receipt for the deposit.

Night Deposits. Many banks provide night deposit service. A common practice is for the bank to have a night safe with an opening on the exterior of the bank building. Upon signing a night depository contract, the bank supplies the depositor with a key to the outside door of the safe, together with a bag that has an identifying number and in which valuables may be placed, and two keys to the bag itself. Once the depositor places the bag in the night deposit safe, it cannot be retrieved because it moves to a vault in the bank that is accessible to bank employees only. Since only the depositor is provided with keys to the bag, the depositor or an authorized representative must go to the bank to unlock the bag. The depositor may or may not deposit the funds that had been placed previously in the night deposit safe.

Night deposit banking service is especially valuable to those individuals and concerns that accumulate cash and other cash items which they cannot take to the bank during regular banking hours and that do not have safe facilities in their own places of business.

Making Withdrawals. The amount deposited in a bank checking account may be withdrawn either by the depositor or by any other person who is properly authorized to make withdrawals from the depositor's account. Such withdrawals are accomplished by the use of checks signed by the depositor or by others having the authority to sign checks drawn on the account.

Checkbook. Checks used by businesses are usually bound in the form of a book with two or three blank checks to a page and perforated so that they may be removed singly. Checks may be provided by the bank (often for a charge) or purchased directly from firms that specialize in the manufacture of check forms.

To the left of each check is a small form called a **check stub** that contains space to record all relevant information about the check. Sometimes the depositor is provided with a checkbook that, instead of containing stubs, is accompanied by a small register book in which the relevant information is noted. The information contained on the stub or on the register includes the check number, date, payee, amount, the purpose of the check and often the account to be charged, along with the bank balance before the check was issued, current deposits if any, and the resulting balance after issuing the check.

The depositor's name and address normally are printed on each check and the MICR numbers are shown along the bottom edge. Often the check number is preprinted in the upper right corner. Sometimes, checks come bound in the form of a pad. There may be a blank page after each check for use in making a carbon copy of the check. The carbon copy is not a check; it is merely a copy of what was typed or written on the original check and provides the essential information for recording an entry in the formal records.

Writing a Check. The first step in writing a check is to complete the check stub or check register. This plan insures that the drawer will retain a record of each check issued. Second, the name of the payee is written on the check. Third, the amount of the check is written on the check in both figures and words. If the amount shown on the check in figures does not agree with the amount shown in words, the bank usually contacts the drawer for the correct amount or returns the check unpaid.

Care must be used in writing the amount on the check in order to avoid any possibility that the payee or a subsequent holder may change the amount. If the instructions given on page 71 are followed

Chapter 3   Accounting for Cash   71

in the preparation of a check, it will be difficult to change the amount.

(1) The amount shown in figures should be written so that there is no space between the dollar sign and the first digit of the amount.

(2) The amount stated in words should be written beginning at the extreme left on the line provided for this information. The cents should be written in the form of a common fraction; if the check is for an even number of dollars, use two ciphers or the word "no" as the numerator of the fraction. If a vacant space remains, a line should be drawn from the amount stated in words to the word "Dollars" on the same line with it, as illustrated below.

Checks and Stubs

A machine frequently used to write or print the amount of a check in figures and in words is known as a **checkwriter**. The use of a checkwriter is desirable because it practically eliminates the possibility of changing the amount of a check.

As the fourth step in writing a check, the purpose for which a check is drawn is often noted in the lower left-hand corner of the check itself. Indicating the purpose on the check provides information for the benefit of the payee and provides a specific receipt for the drawer. In the fifth step, the signature of the drawer is written on the lower right hand corner of the check in the same manner as on the signature card.

Banks usually, but not always, will return checks issued by a depositor after the checks have been paid. If canceled checks are returned to the depositor with the bank statement, the checks constitute receipts that the depositor should retain for future reference. The checks will have been indorsed by the payee and any subsequent holders. The checks may be attached to the stubs from which they were removed originally or they may be filed.

Electronic Processing of Checks. It is now nearly universal practice to use checks that, like deposit tickets, can be processed by MICR (magnetic ink character recognition) equipment. Imprinted in magnetic ink along the lower margin of the check is a series of numbers or digits in the form of a code that indicates (1) the identity of the Federal Reserve district in which the bank is located and a routing number, (2) the identity of the bank, and (3) the account number assigned to the depositor. Sometimes the check number is also shown. In processing checks with electronic equipment, the first bank that handles the check imprints the amount in magnetic ink characters to further aid in the processing of the check. The amount is printed directly below the signature line in the lower right-hand corner of the check.

Checks imprinted with the bank's number, the depositor's number, and the amount — all in MICR characters — can be posted electronically to the customer's account. The two checks reproduced on page 71 illustrate magnetic ink characters along the lower margins, as well as check stubs properly completed.

Recording Banking Transactions. A depositor should keep a record of the transactions completed with the bank. The checkbook stubs, as shown in the illustration on page 71, serve this purpose. The record consists of detailed information concerning each check written and an amount column in which are recorded (1) the balance brought forward, (2) the amount of deposits to be added, and (3) the amount of each check to be subtracted. The purpose is to keep a detailed record of deposits made and checks issued and to indicate the balance in the checking account after each check is drawn.

As the amount of each check is recorded in the journal, a check mark is placed immediately after the account title written on the stub to indicate that the check has been recorded. If the canceled check is subsequently received from the bank, the amount shown on the stub may be checkmarked to indicate that the canceled check has been received.

Records Kept by a Bank. The usual transactions completed by a bank with a depositor are:

(1) Accepting deposits made by the depositor.
(2) Paying checks issued by the depositor.
(3) Lending money to the depositor.
(4) Collecting the amounts of various kinds of commercial paper, such as matured notes or bonds, for the account of the depositor.

The bank keeps an account for each depositor. Each transaction affecting the depositor's account is recorded by either debiting or crediting the depositor's account, depending upon the effect of the transaction.

When a bank accepts a deposit, the account of the depositor is credited (increased) for the amount of the deposit. The deposit increases the bank's liability to the depositor. When the bank pays a check that has been drawn on the bank, it debits (decreases) the account of the depositor for the amount of the check. If the bank makes a collection for the depositor, the net amount of the collection is credited to the account. At the same time, the bank notifies the depositor that the collection has been made using a form similar to the one shown below.

```
                                                    Date April 19, 1983
Credit
Your account has been credited for

    Redemption of Treasury Bill ........ $15,000.00
    Less collection charge .............      15.00

                                 Account number | T.C. | Total amount
                                   13-6725-4    |      | $14,985.00

         H. H. ROBERTSON          First National Bank in St. Louis
                                  St. Louis, Missouri        First Union
                                                             Group

                                  by    R. A. R.
```

Credit Advice

Bank Statement. A statement of account rendered to each depositor once a month by a bank is called a **bank statement**. An illustration of a widely used form of bank statement is shown on page 74. Some banks provide statements that also present information

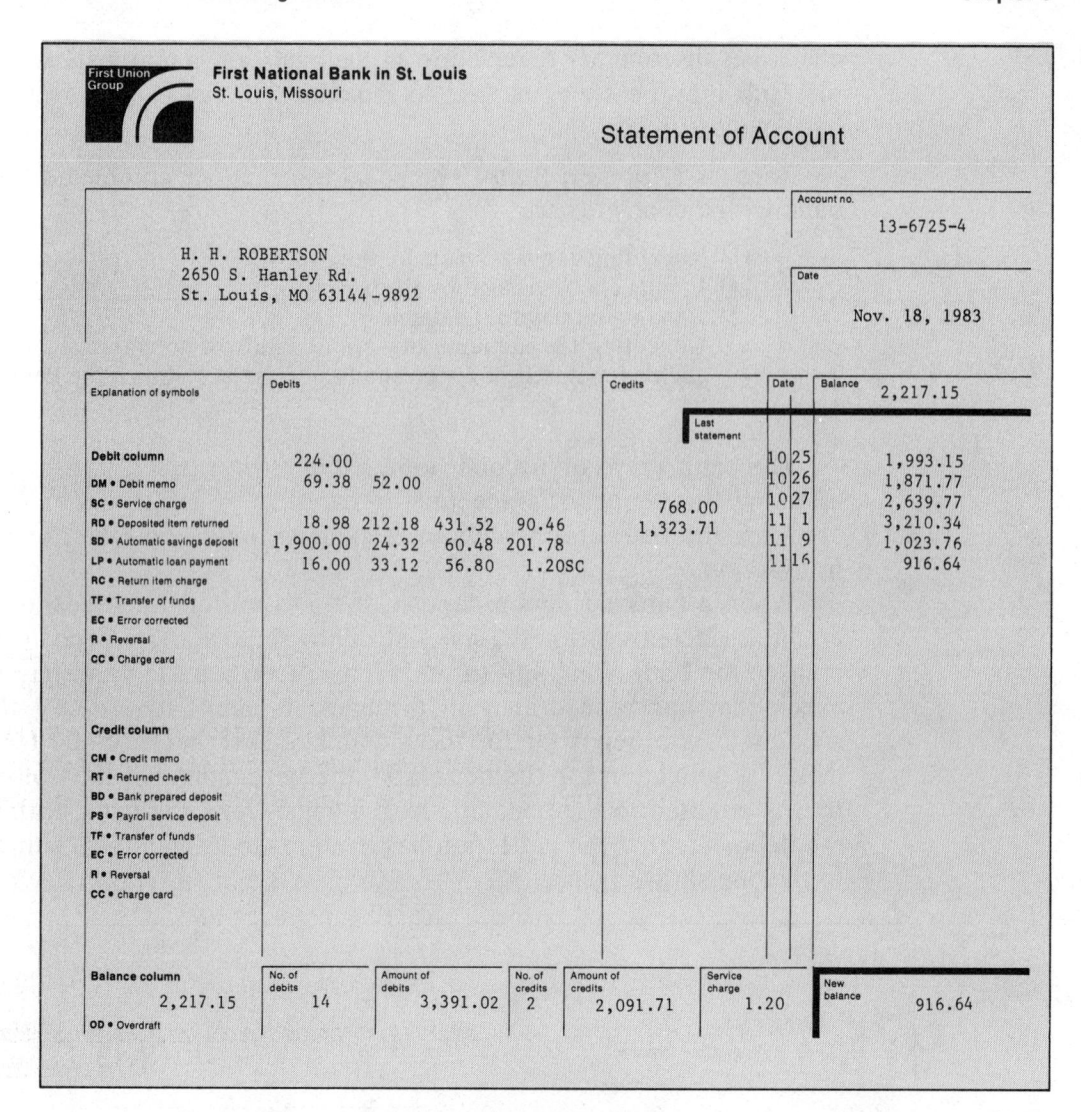

Statement of Account

First National Bank in St. Louis
St. Louis, Missouri

Account no. 13-6725-4

H. H. ROBERTSON
2650 S. Hanley Rd.
St. Louis, MO 63144-9892

Date: Nov. 18, 1983

Explanation of symbols

Debit column
- DM • Debit memo
- SC • Service charge
- RD • Deposited item returned
- SD • Automatic savings deposit
- LP • Automatic loan payment
- RC • Return item charge
- TF • Transfer of funds
- EC • Error corrected
- R • Reversal
- CC • Charge card

Credit column
- CM • Credit memo
- RT • Returned check
- BD • Bank prepared deposit
- PS • Payroll service deposit
- TF • Transfer of funds
- EC • Error corrected
- R • Reversal
- CC • charge card

Debits	Credits	Date	Balance
	Last statement		2,217.15
224.00		10 25	1,993.15
69.38 52.00		10 26	1,871.77
	768.00	10 27	2,639.77
18.98 212.18 431.52 90.46	1,323.71	11 1	3,210.34
1,900.00 24.32 60.48 201.78		11 9	1,023.76
16.00 33.12 56.80 1.20SC		11 16	916.64

Balance column: 2,217.15
No. of debits: 14
Amount of debits: 3,391.02
No. of credits: 2
Amount of credits: 2,091.71
Service charge: 1.20
New balance: 916.64

OD • Overdraft

Bank Statement

regarding savings accounts and loan accounts, for those depositors who have such accounts. Very commonly, however, a separate statement is furnished for each type of account.

The statement illustrated is for a checking account. It is a report showing (1) the balance on deposit at the beginning of the period, (2) the amount of deposits made during the period (credits), (3) the amounts of checks honored during the period (debits), (4) other items charged to the depositor's account during the period, and (5) the balance on deposit at the end of the period. With the bank statement, the depositor usually also receives all checks paid by the bank during the period, together with any other vouchers representing items charged to the account.

Reconciling the Bank Statement. A depositor ordinarily keeps one or more records of bank-related transactions. A bank also keeps records of transactions with each depositor. The depositor's records of transactions with the bank should be brought into agreement with the bank's records of transactions with the depositor at periodic intervals — usually once a month.

As soon as possible after a bank statement is received, the depositor should try to make it agree with the bank balance record kept on the check stubs, a procedure known as **reconciling the bank statement**. The balance shown on the bank statement may not be the same as the amount shown on the check stubs for one or more of the following reasons:

(1) Checks issued during the period may not have been presented to the bank for payment before the statement was prepared. These are known as **outstanding checks**. Some of the checks issued may fall into this category.

(2) Deposits may not have been recorded by the bank on the bank statement. These are known as **deposits in transit**. Such a deposit may have been mailed, or placed in the night depository and not recorded by the bank until the day following the date of the statement.

(3) The bank may have credited the depositor's account for an amount collected, but the depositor may not as yet have noted it on the check stubs since the credit advice has not yet been received.

(4) Service charges or other charges may appear on the bank statement that the depositor has not recorded on the check stubs.

(5) The depositor may have erred in keeping the bank account record.

(6) The bank may have erred in keeping its account with the depositor.

Each bank usually provides a form for completing the bank reconciliation on the back of the bank statement. If a depositor is unable to reconcile the bank statement, a report on the matter should be made to the bank immediately.

A suggested procedure in reconciling the bank statement is enumerated below:

(1) The amount of each deposit recorded on the bank statement is checked with the amount recorded on the check stubs. Any deposit recorded on the check stub but not recorded on the bank statement should be added to the bank statement balance as a deposit in transit.

(2) The amount of each canceled check is compared both with the amount recorded on the bank statement and with the amount recorded on the depositor's check stubs. When making this comparison, it is a good plan to place a check mark by the amount recorded on each check stub to indicate that the canceled check has been returned by the bank and its amount verified.

(3) The outstanding checks are listed, totaled, and deducted from the bank balance. The information needed for this list may be obtained by examining the check stubs and noting the amounts that have not been checkmarked.

(4) The amounts of any items listed on the bank statement that represent credits or charges to a depositor's account which have not been entered on the check stubs are added to or deducted from the balance on the check stubs and are recorded in the journal that is being used to record cash receipts and disbursements.

(5) Any error discovered on the check stubs or bank statement will require an adjustment to the check stub balance or bank balance depending on the nature of the error. A journal entry will also be necessary to correct for any check stub errors.

After completion of the foregoing procedure, the adjusted balance shown on the check stubs should equal the adjusted bank balance. A reconciliation of the bank balance shown in the statement reproduced on page 74 with the most recent check stub balance is presented below.

H. H. ROBERTSON
Reconciliation of Bank Statement
November 18, 1983

(1)	Balance, November 18, per bank statement..............		$ 916.64
(2)	Add deposit, November 18...		729.81
			$1,646.45
(3)	Less checks outstanding, November 18:		
	No. 426..	$136.00	
	No. 429..	27.84	
	No. 431..	272.40	436.24
(4)	Adjusted bank balance...		$1,210.21
(5)	Balance, November 18, per check stub		$1,211.50
(6)	Less: Bank service charge..	$ 1.20	
(7)	Error on stub for Check No. 404	.09	1.29
(8)	Adjusted check stub balance.......................................		$1,210.21

In making the reconciliation of the H. H. Robertson bank statement as of November 18, 1983, the following steps, which correspond with the numbers in the reconciliation, were completed:

(1) The November 18 bank balance, $916.64, was copied from the bank statement.
(2) A deposit of $729.81, placed in the night depository on November 18 and therefore not shown on the bank statement, was added to the November 18 bank balance to agree with the check stub that reflected the deposit on that date.
(3) The outstanding Checks Nos. 426, 429, and 431 were listed, totaled, and $436.24 was subtracted from the bank balance. These checks had not been presented to the bank for payment and thus were not returned with the bank statement.
(4) The adjusted bank balance as of the close of business November 18, was calculated as $1,210.21.
(5) The check stub balance as of November 18 was copied from the last check stub bearing that date, in the amount of $1,211.50.
(6) A bank service charge of $1.20 shown at the bottom of the bank statement was subtracted from the check stub balance.
(7) A checkbook error was discovered. Check No. 404 was written for $18.98 and recorded in the check stub as $18.89. This error required the check stub balance to be decreased by $.09.
(8) The adjusted check stub balance as of the close of business, November 18, was calculated as $1,210.21 and was equal to the adjusted November 18 bank balance.

In step number 6 above, a bank service charge was mentioned. A service charge may be made by a bank for the handling of checks and other items. The basis and the amount of such charges vary with different banks in different localities.

When a bank statement indicates that a service charge has been made, the depositor should record the amount of the service charge by debiting an expense account, such as Miscellaneous Expense, and by crediting Cash.

Miscellaneous Expense	1.20	
Cash		1.20
Bank service charge for November.		

The error noted in step number 7 above was discovered when the canceled checks that were returned with the bank statement were matched against the check stubs. It was found that, although Check No. 404 had been written for $18.98, the amount was shown as $18.89 on its stub. This is called a **transposition error**, because the "9" and the "8" were transposed; i.e., their order was reversed. On Stub No. 404, and the others that followed, the bank balance shown was $.09 overstated. The correct amount, $18.98, should be shown on Stub No. 404, and the bank balance shown on the stub of the last check used should be corrected by reducing the amount by $.09. If Check No. 404 was in payment of a telephone bill, an entry should be made debiting Telephone Expense and crediting Cash.

Telephone Expense	.09	
Cash		.09
Correction of checkbook error.		

If the bank the enterprise is dealing with does not return canceled checks, the comparison outlined in Step 2 at the top of page 76 will be between the amounts recorded on the bank statement and the amounts recorded on the depositor's check stubs. Steps (3), (4), and (5) remain unchanged.

Keeping a Ledger Account for Each Bank

As explained previously, the depositor may keep a checkbook for each bank account. The depositor may also keep a ledger account for each bank. The title of such an account usually is the name of the bank. Sometimes, more than one account is kept with a bank, in which case each account should be correctly labeled. Such terms as "commercial," "executive," and "payroll" are used to identify the accounts.

The bank account is debited for the amount of each deposit and should be credited for the amount of each check written. The account should also be debited or credited for any other items that may have been handled directly by the bank, including collections and service charges.

When both a cash on hand account and a bank account are kept in the ledger, the following procedure should be observed in recording transactions affecting these accounts:

(1) Cash receipts are recorded as debits in the cash on hand account.
(2) Cash payments and bank deposits are recorded as credits to the cash on hand account.
(3) Cash deposits and bank collections are recorded as debits to the bank account.
(4) Checks written and bank charges are recorded as credits to the bank account.

Cash on Hand		First National Bank in St. Louis	
Debit	Credit	Debit	Credit
(1) For all receipts of cash and cash items.	(2) For all payments in cash. For all bank deposits.	(3) For all deposits. For collection of amounts for the depositor.	(4) For all checks written. For all service charges. For all other charges such as for dishonored checks.

Under this method of accounting for cash and banking transactions, the cash on hand account will be in balance when all cash on hand has been deposited in the bank. When the account is in balance, it means that the account has a zero balance since the total of the debits is equal to the total of the credits. To prove the balance of the cash on hand account at any time, it is necessary only to count the cash and cash items on hand and to compare the total with the cash on hand account balance. To prove the bank account balance, it is necessary to reconcile the bank statement in the same manner in which it was reconciled when only a memorandum record of bank transactions was kept on the check stubs.

The cash on hand account can be dispensed with when a bank account is kept in the ledger and all cash receipts are deposited in the bank. All disbursements except small expenditures made from a petty cash fund are made by check. Daily, or at frequent intervals, the receipts are deposited in the bank. If all cash received during the month has been deposited before the books are closed at the end of the month, the total amount of the bank deposits will equal the total cash receipts for the month. If all disbursements made during the month are made by check, the total amount of checks issued will be the total disbursements for the month.

Savings Account

When a savings account is opened in a bank, a signature card must be signed by the depositor. By signing the signature card, the depositor agrees to abide by the rules and regulations of the bank. These rules and regulations vary with different banks and may be altered and amended from time to time. At this time, a **passbook** may be given to the depositor. This is a small book in which the bank teller enters the date and amount of each deposit or withdrawal and initials the entry. The passbook is to be presented at the bank or mailed to the bank along with a deposit or withdrawal slip, each time money is deposited or withdrawn from the account. An alternative practice for depositing or withdrawing money from a savings account is to give the depositor a small register for recording deposits and withdrawals and a pad of deposit-withdrawal forms. This procedure eliminates the use of the passbook. Each time a deposit or withdrawal from savings is made, the appropriate part of one of the forms is filled in, signed, recorded in the register and presented or mailed to the bank with deposit items or other documents. The bank gives a machine-printed receipt to the depositor or returns it by mail. There should be a separate savings account in the ledger to record these activities. Sometimes, the name of the bank is in the title of the account, for example, "First National Bank in St. Louis — Savings Account."

At least once each quarter, the bank mails a credit advice to the depositor, indicating the amount of interest credited to the account. This should be entered in the depositor's register upon receipt. The depositor should also record the amount in the business accounts by a debit to the savings account and by a credit to Interest Earned. The interest is revenue earned whether withdrawn or not and is taxable to the depositor.

First National Bank in St. Louis — Savings Account	xxx	
Interest Earned		xxx
Quarterly interest earned.		

Traditionally, the principal differences between a savings account and a checking account are that interest is paid regularly by the bank on a savings account and withdrawals from a savings account may be made at the bank or by mail by the depositor or an authorized agent. Depositors use checking accounts primarily as a convenient means of making payments, while savings accounts are used primarily as a means of accumulating funds with interest.

An increasingly common practice is for the bank to combine savings and checking accounts and get depositor permission to make automatic transfers of funds from the savings portion to the checking portion whenever the latter falls below a specified minimum balance. This amounts to giving the depositor an interest-earning checking account.

BUILDING YOUR ACCOUNTING KNOWLEDGE

1. Name the five requirements with which a check must comply in order to be negotiable.
2. Why do banks usually require a new depositor to fill out a signature card? Why may more than one name appear on a signature card?
3. What is the reason for preparing a deposit ticket in duplicate?
4. Describe the use of MICR numbers in the electronic processing of checks.
5. Name the five major dollar amounts summarized on a bank statement.
6. If a depositor is unable to reconcile a bank statement, what should be done?
7. What journal entry should a depositor make when a bank statement indicates that there has been a service charge?

Chapter 3   Accounting for Cash   **81**

8. What is the primary purpose of a savings account? Are savings accounts in frequent use by businesses?

Report No. 3-2

> *Refer to the study assignments and complete Report No. 3-2. This assignment provides a test of your ability to apply the principles developed in the first three chapters of the textbook. Further study, with the aid of the vocabulary list below, may be helpful in this regard. After completing the report, you may proceed with the textbook discussion in Chapter 4 until the next report is required.*

EXPANDING YOUR BUSINESS VOCABULARY

What is the meaning of each of the following terms?

ABA numbers (p. 66)
automatic teller machine (p. 67)
bank statement (p. 73)
blank indorsement (p. 64)
cash (p. 54)
cash disbursements (p. 56)
cash receipts (p. 54)
cash register (p. 55)
Cash Short and Over (p. 57)
check (p. 63)
check stub (p. 70)
checkwriter (p. 71)
compound entry (p. 62)
debit advice (p. 67)
deposit ticket (p. 65)
deposits in transit (p. 75)
dishonored check (p. 67)
drawee (p. 64)
drawer (p. 63)
embezzlement (p. 54)

imprest method (p. 58)
indorsing (p. 64)
MICR numbers (p. 66)
NSF checks (p. 68)
negotiable (p. 64)
outstanding checks (p. 75)
overdraft (p. 68)
passbook (p. 79)
payee (p. 64)
petty cash disbursements record (p. 58)
petty cash fund (p. 57)
petty cash voucher (p. 57)
postdated checks (p. 69)
proving cash (p. 56)
reconciling the bank statement (p. 75)
restrictive indorsement (p. 64)
signature card (p. 65)
transposition error (p. 77)

4

PAYROLL ACCOUNTING

CHAPTER OBJECTIVES

The objectives of this chapter are to enable you:

▶ To explain and perform the three major functions of payroll accounting: **(1)** determination of employee earnings and deductions, **(2)** determination of employer payroll taxes, and **(3)** proper recording of the expenses, liabilities, and cash disbursements in connection with (1) and (2).

▶ To explain those government laws and regulations that primarily affect payroll accounting.

▶ To describe and prepare selected forms and records that are required or desirable in payroll accounting.

▶ To explain selected manual and mechanical record-keeping methods used in the payroll area.

Employers need to maintain detailed and accurate payroll accounting records for both financial and legal reasons. The financial reason is simply that payroll expenditures represent a major part of the total expenditures of most companies. Payroll accounting records provide data useful in the analysis, classification, and control of these expenditures. In addition, payroll accounting information is invaluable in contract discussions with labor unions, in the settlement of company-union grievances, and in determining employee pension benefits.

The legal reason for maintaining payroll accounting records is that employers are required by federal, state, and local laws to do so. Companies must accumulate payroll data both for the business as a whole and for each employee. Clearly, accurate payroll accounting is essential to the survival of most businesses.

EMPLOYEE EARNINGS AND DEDUCTIONS

The first step in determining the amount to be paid to an employee is to calculate the employee's total or gross earnings for the pay period. The second step is to determine the amounts of deductions that are required either by law or by specific agreement between the employer and the employee. Depending upon a variety of circumstances, either or both of these steps may be relatively simple or quite complicated. An examination of the factors that must be considered in performing these two steps follows.

Employees and Independent Contractors

Not every individual who performs services for a business is considered to be an employee. A public accountant, lawyer, or management consultant who sells services to a business does not necessarily become its employee. Neither does a plumber nor an electrician who is hired to make specific repairs or installations on business property. These people are told what to do, but not how to do it, and the compensation that they receive for their services is called a **fee**. Any person who agrees to perform a service for a fee and is not subject to the control of those for whom the service is performed is called an **independent contractor**.

In contrast, an **employee** is one who is under the control and direction of an employer with regard to the performance of services. The difference between an independent contractor and an employee is an important legal distinction. The nature and extent of the responsibilities of a contractor and a client to each other and to third parties are quite different from the mutual obligations of an employer and the employee. Of particular importance for payroll accounting purposes is the fact that the various government laws and regulations regarding employee deductions, employer payroll taxes, records, and reports apply only to employees.

Types of Compensation

Compensation for managerial or administrative services usually is called **salary**. A salary normally is expressed in terms of a month or a year. Compensation either for skilled or for unskilled labor usually is referred to as **wages**. Wages ordinarily are expressed in terms of hours, weeks, or pieces of accomplishment. The terms salaries and wages often are used interchangeably in practice.

Supplements to basic salaries or wages of employees include bonuses, commissions, cost-of-living adjustments, pensions, and profit sharing plans. Compensation also may take the form of goods, lodging, meals, or other property, and as such is measured by the fair market value of the property or service given in payment for the employee's efforts. This chapter demonstrates proper accounting for basic salaries and wages of employees paid in cash.

Determination of Total Earnings

An employee's earnings commonly are based on the time worked during the payroll period. Sometimes earnings are based on units of output or of sales during the period. Compensation based on time requires a record of the time worked by each employee. If there are only a few employees, a record of times worked may be kept in a memorandum book. Where there are many employees, time clocks commonly are used to record time spent on the job each day. With time clocks, a time card is provided for each employee and the clock is used to record arrival and departure times on the card. Alternatively, plastic cards or badges with holes punched in them for basic employee data are now being used in computer-based timekeeping systems. Whatever method is used, the total time worked during the payroll period must be computed.

Employees often are entitled to compensation at more than their regular rate of pay for work during certain hours or on certain days. If the employer is engaged in Interstate Commerce, the Federal Fair Labor Standards Act (commonly known as the Wages and Hours Law) provides that all employees covered by the Act must be paid one and one-half times the regular rate for all hours worked over 40 per week. Labor-management agreements often require extra pay for certain hours or days. In such cases, hours worked in excess of eight per day or work on Sundays and specified holidays may be paid for at higher rates.

To illustrate, assume that the company which employs Donald Schramm pays time and a half for all hours worked in excess of 40 per week and double time for work on Sunday. Schramm's regular rate is $8 per hour; and during the week ended April 16, Schramm worked nine hours each day Monday through Friday, six hours on Saturday and four on Sunday. Schramm's total earnings for the week ended April 16, are computed as follows:

40 hours @ $8	$320
11 hours @ $12	132*
4 hours (on Sunday) @ $16	64
Total earnings for the week	$516

*Schramm worked 9 hours each day Monday through Friday and 6 hours on Saturday — a total of 51 hours. Forty hours would be paid for at the regular rate and 11 hours at time and a half.

An employee who is paid a regular monthly or annual salary may also be entitled to premium pay for any overtime. If this is the case, it is necessary to compute the regular hourly rate of pay before computing the overtime rate. To illustrate, assume that Linda Herer receives a regular salary of $1,400 a month and that Herer is entitled to overtime pay at the rate of one and one-half times the regular hourly rate for any time worked in excess of 40 hours per week. Herer's overtime pay is computed as follows:

$1,400 × 12 months............$16,800 annual pay
$16,800 ÷ 52 weeks............$323.08 pay per week
$323.08 ÷ 40 hours.............$8.08 pay per regular hour
$8.08 × 1½.........................$12.12 overtime pay per hour

Deductions from Total Earnings

An employee's take-home or **net pay** typically is significantly less than the total earnings or **gross pay** described above. The difference between an employee's gross and net pay generally can be explained by three factors: **(1)** employee FICA (Federal Insurance Contributions Act) tax withheld by the employer, **(2)** employee federal income taxes (and state and city income taxes where applicable) withheld by the employer, and **(3)** other deductions based on special agreements between the employer and the employee.

Employees' FICA Tax Withheld. The Federal Insurance Contributions Act (FICA) requires most employers to withhold certain amounts from employees' earnings for contributions to the old-age, survivors, and disability insurance (OASDI) and health insurance for the aged (HIP) programs. These withheld amounts are commonly referred to as **FICA taxes**.

Each employee is required to have a social security number for payroll accounting purposes. A completed form SS-5, the official form used in applying for an account number is illustrated below:

Application for Social Security Number (Form SS-5)

The earnings base against which the FICA tax is applied and the tax rate have been changed several times since the law was first enacted and are subject to change by Congress at any time in the future. These base and rate changes, however, do not affect the accounting principles and procedures for payroll. Therefore, for the sake of convenience in this chapter, the rate is assumed to be 5.6 percent of taxable wages paid during the calendar year for OASDI plus 1.4 percent for HIP for a total FICA rate of 7.0%. It is also assumed that the first $30,000 of earnings paid to each employee in any calendar year is taxable. Any amount of compensation paid in excess of $30,000 is assumed to be exempt from the tax.

State and Local Taxes. In addition to the federal requirements described above, a few states require employers to withhold a percentage of the employees' wages for unemployment compensation benefits or for disability benefits. In some states and cities, employers are also required to withhold a percentage of the employees' wages for other types of payroll taxes.

Employees' Income Tax Withheld. Under federal law, employers are required to withhold certain amounts from the total earnings of each employee to be applied toward the payment of the employee's federal income tax. The amount to be withheld each pay period is based on (1) the total earnings of the employee, (2) the marital status of the employee, (3) the number of withholding allowances claimed by the employee, and (4) the length of the employee's pay period.

Each employee is required to furnish the employer with an Employee's Withholding Allowance Certificate, Form W-4, showing marital status and the number of allowances claimed. The marital status of the taxpayer and the number of allowances claimed determine the dollar amount of earnings subject to withholding tax. According to 1979 federal income tax laws, $2,300 for single taxpayers and $3,400 for married taxpayers is excluded from withholding tax. These amounts on which no withholding tax is levied are known as **zero bracket amounts**, that is, they represent income brackets or levels at which the withholding tax is zero. A **withholding allowance** is an allowance of $1,000 on which no federal income tax is withheld from the employee's pay. Each federal income taxpayer is permitted one personal withholding allowance and one for each dependent who qualifies, that is, the taxpayer is entitled to one or more exemptions of $1,000 each from federal income tax based on family status and dependency relationships. The law specifies the relationship that must exist, the extent of support required, and the amount of support that must be provided in order for a person to qualify as a dependent.

In addition to these withholding allowances for personal and dependent exemptions, a taxpayer can qualify for two other types of withholding allowances. First, one **special withholding allowance** can be claimed by each single taxpayer who has only one job, or each married taxpayer whose spouse is not employed. Second, **additional withholding allowances** are permitted to taxpayers who anticipate large itemized deductions. In order to claim one or more additional withholding allowances, an employee's expected total earnings and itemized deductions for the coming year have to be estimated. Based on these expected total earnings and itemized deductions, the schedule and table illustrated on page 89 are used to determine the number of additional withholding allowances to which the employee is entitled.

An allowance certificate completed by John Anthony Indiman is shown on page 88.

To illustrate the use of the schedule and table, John Indiman is married, has a spouse who is not employed, and has one dependent child. Indiman expects earnings of $24,500 and itemized deductions of $4,500 in the coming year. As computed in the schedule, Indiman is therefore entitled to 1 additional withholding allowance. On line 1 of the W-4 form, Indiman claims 5 allowances, calculated as follows:

Withholding Allowance Certificate (Form W-4)

Personal allowances:		
Self...	1	
Wife..	1	2
Special withholding allowance................		1
Allowance for dependent........................		1
Additional withholding allowance............		1
Total withholding allowances.................		5

Most employers use the **wage-bracket method** of determining the amount of tax to be withheld from an employee's pay by tracing the employee's gross pay for a specific time period into the appropriate wage-bracket table provided by the Internal Revenue Service. These tables cover monthly, semimonthly, biweekly, weekly, and daily or miscellaneous periods, and there are separate tables for single and married taxpayers. Copies may be obtained from any local Internal Revenue Service office. A portion of a weekly income tax wage-bracket withholding table for married persons is illustrated on page 89. To use this table, assume that John Indiman (who claims 5 allowances) had gross earnings of $375 for the week ending December 16, 1983. On the line showing the tax on wages of "at least $370, but less than $380," in the column headed "5 withholding allowances," $38.00 is given as the amount to be withheld.

Whether the wage-bracket method or some other method is used in computing the amount of tax to be withheld, the sum of the taxes withheld from an employee's wages only approximates the tax on actual income derived solely from wages. An employee may be liable for a tax larger than the amount withheld. This additional tax will be remitted with the employee's federal income tax return. On the other hand, the amount of the taxes withheld by the employer may be greater than the employee's actual tax liability. In such an event, the employee will be entitled to a refund of the excess taxes withheld, or the excess can be applied to the employee's tax liability for the following year.

Several states and cities have adopted state and city income tax procedures. Some of these states and cities supply employers with withholding allowance certificate forms and income tax withholding tables that are similar in concept and appearance to those used by the federal Internal Revenue Service. Other states determine the amount to be withheld merely by applying a fixed percentage to the federal withholding amount.

Other Deductions. In addition to the compulsory deductions from employee earnings for FICA and income taxes, there are many

WEEKLY Payroll Period – Employee MARRIED – Effective October 1, 1981

| And the wages are- || And the number of withholding allowances claimed is— |||||||||||
At least	But less than	0	1	2	3	4	5	6	7	8	9	10 or more
		The amount of income tax to be withheld shall be—										
$310	$320	$46.20	$41.40	$37.50	$33.70	$29.80	$26.00	$22.50	$19.50	$16.40	$13.40	$10.70
320	330	48.70	43.80	39.50	35.70	31.80	28.00	24.10	21.10	18.00	14.90	12.10
330	340	51.20	46.30	41.50	37.70	33.80	30.00	26.10	22.70	19.60	16.50	13.50
340	350	53.70	48.80	44.00	39.70	35.80	32.00	28.10	24.30	21.20	18.10	15.00
350	360	56.20	51.30	46.50	41.70	37.80	34.00	30.10	26.30	22.80	19.70	16.60
360	370	58.70	53.80	49.00	44.20	39.80	36.00	32.10	28.30	24.40	21.30	18.20
370	380	61.20	56.30	51.50	46.70	41.90	38.00	34.10	30.30	26.40	22.90	19.80
380	390	63.70	58.80	54.00	49.20	44.40	40.00	36.10	32.30	28.40	24.60	21.40
390	400	66.20	61.30	56.50	51.70	46.90	42.10	38.10	34.30	30.40	26.60	23.00
400	410	68.70	63.80	59.00	54.20	49.40	44.60	40.10	36.30	32.40	28.60	24.80
410	420	71.20	66.30	61.50	56.70	51.90	47.10	42.30	38.30	34.40	30.60	26.80
420	430	73.70	68.80	64.00	59.20	54.40	49.60	44.80	40.30	36.40	32.60	28.80
430	440	76.20	71.30	66.50	61.70	56.90	52.10	47.30	42.50	38.40	34.60	30.80
440	450	78.70	73.80	69.00	64.20	59.40	54.60	49.80	45.00	40.40	36.60	32.80
450	460	81.60	76.30	71.50	66.70	61.90	57.10	52.30	47.50	42.70	38.60	34.80
460	470	84.70	78.80	74.00	69.20	64.40	59.60	54.80	50.00	45.20	40.60	36.80
470	480	87.80	81.90	76.50	71.70	66.90	62.10	57.30	52.50	47.70	42.90	38.80
480	490	90.90	85.00	79.00	74.20	69.40	64.60	59.80	55.00	50.20	45.40	40.80
490	500	94.00	88.10	82.10	76.70	71.90	67.10	62.30	57.50	52.70	47.90	43.10
500	510	97.10	91.20	85.20	79.20	74.40	69.60	64.80	60.00	55.20	50.40	45.60
710	720	168.70	161.60	154.50	147.40	140.90	134.30	127.80	121.20	114.70	108.60	102.60
720	730	172.40	165.30	158.20	151.10	144.30	137.70	131.20	124.60	118.10	111.70	105.70
730	740	176.10	169.00	161.90	154.80	147.70	141.10	134.60	128.00	121.50	115.00	108.80
740	750	179.80	172.70	165.60	158.50	151.40	144.50	138.00	131.40	124.90	118.40	111.90
750	760	183.50	176.40	169.30	162.20	155.10	147.90	141.40	134.80	128.30	121.80	115.20
760	770	187.20	180.10	173.00	165.90	158.80	151.60	144.80	138.20	131.70	125.20	118.60
770	780	190.90	183.80	176.70	169.60	162.50	155.30	148.20	141.60	135.10	128.60	122.00
780	790	194.60	187.50	180.40	173.30	166.20	159.00	151.90	145.00	138.50	132.00	125.40
790	800	198.30	191.20	184.10	177.00	169.90	162.70	155.60	148.50	141.90	135.40	128.80
800	810	202.00	194.90	187.80	180.70	173.60	166.40	159.30	152.20	145.30	138.80	132.20

*As of the date of printing, the above Weekly Federal Income Tax Withholding Table is the most current available.

Portion of Weekly Federal Income Tax Wage-Bracket Withholding Table for Married Persons

other possible deductions that generally are voluntary and depend on specific agreements between the employee and employer. Some examples of these deductions are for:

(1) United States savings bond purchases.
(2) Life, accident or health insurance premiums.
(3) Union dues.
(4) Pension plan payments.
(5) Charitable contributions.

Payroll Records

The needs of management and the requirements of various federal and state laws make it necessary for employers to keep records that will provide the following information for each employee:

(1) Name, address, and social security number.
(2) The gross amount of earnings, the date of payment, and the period of employment covered by each payroll.
(3) The gross amount of earnings accumulated since the first of the year.
(4) The amount of any taxes or other items withheld.

Regardless of the number of employees or type of business, three types of payroll records usually need to be prepared by the employer. They are: **(1)** the **payroll register** or payroll journal; **(2)** the payroll check with earnings statement attached; and **(3)** the **earnings record** of the individual employee (on a weekly, monthly, quarterly, or annual basis). These records can be prepared either by manual or by automated methods.

Record-Keeping Methods. A purely **manual system** is one in which all records, journals and ledgers are handwritten. Such systems are rare today. Even very small businesses use cash registers, desk calculators and other machines in performing accounting tasks. In this sense, virtually all accounting systems today are at least partially automated, i.e., they use some kind of machines in the accounting process.

In a manual system, all employee data on the payroll records, such as name, address, social security number, pay rate, hours worked, current earnings, and taxes withheld, are determined, calculated, and recorded manually. In such a system, it often is necessary to record the same data a number of times. For example, identical employee earnings amounts would be recorded on the payroll register, paycheck, and earnings record.

Automated systems can be broken down into two types: mechanical and electronic. A **mechanical system** is one in which various types of accounting machines are used for posting accounts, billing customers, recording payroll, and printing paychecks. An **electronic system** is one in which data are processed by electronic computers. On the following pages, a payroll register, payroll check, and individual employee's earnings record that were prepared using an accounting machine are illustrated.

In a mechanical system, much of the payroll information is recorded simultaneously on the payroll register, paycheck, and earnings record. This is an example of the **write-it-once principle**. It is often desirable to record data on a number of documents and records at the same time, because each time the same information is recopied there is another chance for an error. Many accounting machines are available that perform these functions. Most of these machines also are capable of performing the arithmetic operations necessary in preparing the payroll. Each pay period, accounting personnel still need to provide input to the machines indicating information such as employee name, social security number, gross earnings, taxes withheld, and other deductions.

In a system using electronic computers, not only are the payroll register, paycheck, and earnings record generated simultaneously, but a number of inputs need not be repeated each pay period. Computers have the ability to store internally large amounts of information, such as employee names, social security numbers, withholding allowances, pay rates, FICA and income tax withholding rates, and earnings to date. They also can perform arithmetic and logic functions required in payroll accounting. In a given pay period, based on inputs of employee social security numbers and hours worked, the computer can determine the employee names and other data and calculate gross earnings, all appropriate deductions, and net pay. The computer would then print the paychecks, the payroll register, and updated employees' earnings records.

Both mechanical and electronic processing systems are also available through companies external to an employer's business. These companies, known as **service bureaus** (or automation companies), perform payroll accounting, among other accounting functions, for businesses on a contract basis. A common approach is for the employer to provide a service bureau with whatever inputs the employer would need if the payroll were being prepared on the employer's own mechanical or electronic payroll system. The service bureau then processes these inputs and provides the employer with the completed payroll register, paychecks, and updated employee earnings records.

Computers are also used with payroll accounting systems on a **time sharing** basis. This refers to the use of a single computer by a number of small- to medium-sized businesses who share time on the computer. Thus it is possible for businesses that do not have their own computer to have the use of one by sharing it with other companies. Companies using time sharing have record keeping and processing situations similar to those for companies having their own computers. The main difference is that communication between time sharing users and the computer is normally by means of special telephone lines, remote computer terminals, and other electronic devices at each business location.

In recent years minicomputers have come on the market. They are sufficiently low in price that they may be purchased by even a small business. These computers are easy to operate and can be used for payroll accounting and all other accounting needs of the business.

An important point to note in connection with this discussion of payroll record-keeping methods is that the same inputs and outputs are required in each of the three systems. Even given an electronic computer with substantial data stored in its memory, the inputs required for payroll processing have to be provided to the system at some point in time. The outputs in the form of a payroll register, paychecks, and employee earnings records are basically the same under each of the three systems. This means that the illustrations of payroll records under any of these systems are quite similar. For the sake of convenience and in order to avoid duplication, the illustrations in this chapter are based on a mechanical system only. The forms and procedures illustrated are equally applicable to a manual or an electronic system.

Payroll Register. A payroll register is a multicolumn form used to assemble, compute, and summarize the data required at the end

PAYROLL

NAME	EMPLOYEE NUMBER	NUMBER OF ALLOW.	MARITAL STATUS	EARNINGS REGULAR	EARNINGS OVERTIME	EARNINGS TOTAL	CUMULATIVE TOTAL	TAXABLE EARNINGS UNEMPLOYMENT COMP.	TAXABLE EARNINGS FICA
Becker, Mark P.	1	3	M	280.00		280.00	14,000.00		280.00
Gardner, Debra	2	1	S	320.00	35.00	355.00	17,400.00		355.00
Indiman, John A.	3	5	M	375.00		375.00	19,025.00		375.00
McGrath, Martin D.	4	2	M	590.00	60.00	650.00	30,840.00		
Reiss, Wanda T.	5	2	M	300.00		300.00	15,000.00		300.00
Sorenson, Shawn	6	2	S	400.00	45.00	445.00	21,850.00		445.00
Wight, Albert J.	7	3	M	350.00		350.00	18,220.00		350.00
Zimmer, Joel F.	8	1	S	260.00		260.00	5,200.00	260.00	260.00
				2,875.00	140.00	3,015.00	141,535.00	260.00	2,365.00

Payroll Register — Machine Prepared (Left Page)

of each payroll period. The payroll register used by Central States Diversified, Inc., for the payroll period ended December 16, 1983, is illustrated on page 92 and below. The columnar headings are basically self-explanatory. Detailed information on earnings, taxable earnings, deductions, and net pay is summarized for each employee.

Central States Diversified, Inc., has eight employees. Debra Gardner and Joel Zimmer each claim only one allowance because each has two jobs. Shawn Sorenson claims two allowances because she has only one job. Martin McGrath and Wanda Reiss each claim only two withholding allowances because their spouses also work. Mark Becker and Albert Wight each get the special withholding allowance, but none as yet has any children.

Only the first $30,000 of earnings received in any calendar year is subject to FICA tax. As indicated in the taxable earnings columns, McGrath's earnings for the week ending December 16 are exempt from the FICA tax because earnings totaling $30,000 have already been taxed. In addition to their use in determining the employees' FICA tax, the columns for taxable earnings are needed for determining the employer's payroll taxes. These taxes are discussed on pages 102–104.

Regular deductions are made from the earnings of employees for FICA tax, federal income tax, and city earnings tax. In addition, voluntary deductions are made for the company pension plan (which is a voluntary plan), health insurance, the company credit union, and for the United Way contribution, according to agreement with individual employees. Gardner and McGrath have each authorized Central States Diversified, Inc., to withhold $15 on the payday nearest to the middle of each month for their United Way contributions. After the data for each employee have been entered, the

REGISTER

			DEDUCTIONS							
FICA TAX	FEDERAL INC. TAX	CITY TAX	PENSION PLAN	HEALTH INS.	CREDIT UNION	UNITED WAY	TOTAL	DATE	NET PAY	CK. NO.
19.60	27.70	5.60	8.00		6.25		67.15	Dec. 16, '83	212.85	301
24.85	66.70	7.10			6.25	15.00	119.90	Dec. 16, '83	235.10	302
26.25	38.00	7.50		8.00			79.75	Dec. 16, '83	295.25	303
	133.50	13.00	10.50	9.00	6.25	15.00	187.25	Dec. 16, '83	462.75	304
21.00	35.50	6.00	10.50	9.00	6.25		88.25	Dec. 16, '83	211.75	305
31.15	89.30	8.90	7.00				136.35	Dec. 16, '83	308.65	306
24.50	41.70	7.00		8.00	6.25		87.45	Dec. 16, '83	262.55	307
18.20	41.60	5.20					65.00	Dec. 16, '83	195.00	308
165.55	474.00	60.30	36.00	34.00	31.25	30.00	831.10		2,183.90	

Payroll Register — Machine Prepared (Right Page)

amount columns in the payroll register must be footed and the footings verified as shown below.

Regular earnings		$2,875.00
Overtime earnings		140.00
Gross earnings		$3,015.00
Deductions:		
FICA tax	$165.55	
Federal income tax	474.00	
City earnings tax	60.30	
Pension plan	36.00	
Health insurance premiums	34.00	
Credit union	31.25	
United Way	30.00	831.10
Net amount of payroll		$2,183.90

Whether the payroll system is manual or automated, this footing and verification process must be performed in order to make certain that there is no error in the payroll register. An error could cause the payment of an incorrect amount to an employee or remittance of an incorrect amount to the companies or government agencies for whom funds are deducted from the employees' gross pay.

Payroll Check. Employees may be paid in cash or by check. In some cases today, the employee does not even handle the paycheck. Rather, salary is paid via a **direct deposit** of the check by the employer at the employee's bank. The employee receives the deduction stub from the check and a copy of the deposit slip. Payment by check or direct deposit is strongly preferred because it provides better accounting control. Many businesses prepare a single check for the net amount of the total payroll and deposit it in a special payroll bank account. Individual paychecks are then drawn on that account for the amount due to each employee. Data needed to prepare an individual paycheck for each employee are contained in the payroll register. (In an automated system, the paychecks would normally be prepared at the same time as the payroll register.) The employer furnishes a statement of payroll deductions to each employee along with each wage payment. Paychecks with detachable stubs, like the one for John Indiman illustrated on page 95, are widely used for this purpose. Before such a check is cashed, the stub should be detached and retained by the employee as a permanent record of earnings and payroll deductions.

Employee's Earnings Record. A separate record of each employee's earnings, called an **employee's earnings record**, is kept in order to provide the information needed in preparing the various

Chapter 4   Payroll Accounting   95

Paycheck and Deduction Stub — Machine Prepared

EMPLOYEE'S

NAME	JOHN ANTHONY INDIMAN				
ADDRESS	925 LINCOLN AVENUE				
CITY	ST. LOUIS, MISSOURI 63120-4752				
SEX	Male		NUMBER OF ALLOWANCES		
MARITAL STATUS	Married		5		

EARNINGS				TAXABLE EARNINGS	
REGULAR	OVERTIME	TOTAL	CUMULATIVE TOTAL	UNEMPLOYMENT COMP.	FICA
375.00		375.00	10,125.00		375.00
375.00		375.00	10,500.00		375.00
375.00		375.00	10,875.00		375.00
375.00		375.00	11,250.00		375.00
375.00		375.00	11,625.00		375.00
375.00		375.00	12,000.00		375.00
375.00		375.00	12,375.00		375.00
375.00		375.00	12,750.00		375.00
375.00		375.00	13,125.00		375.00
375.00		375.00	13,500.00		375.00
375.00		375.00	13,875.00		375.00
375.00		375.00	14,250.00		375.00
375.00		375.00	14,625.00		375.00
THIRD QUARTER 4,875.00		4,875.00			4,875.00
375.00		375.00	15,000.00		375.00
375.00		375.00	15,375.00		375.00
375.00		375.00	15,750.00		375.00
375.00		375.00	16,125.00		375.00
375.00	40.00	415.00	16,540.00		415.00
375.00	45.00	420.00	16,960.00		420.00
375.00	40.00	415.00	17,375.00		415.00
375.00	50.00	425.00	17,800.00		425.00
375.00	50.00	425.00	18,225.00		425.00
375.00	50.00	425.00	18,650.00		425.00
375.00		375.00	19,025.00		375.00
FOURTH QUARTER					
YEARLY TOTAL					

Employee's Earnings Record — Machine Prepared (Left Page)

federal, state, and local reports required of employers. A mechanically prepared employee's earnings record used by Central States Diversified, Inc., for John A. Indiman during the last two quarters of the current calendar year is illustrated above and on page 97.

This record may be kept on separate sheets or on cards, which

Chapter 4   Payroll Accounting   97

EARNINGS RECORD

DEPARTMENT	Maintenance	SOCIAL SECURITY NUMBER	307-78-3813
OCCUPATION	Service	DATE OF BIRTH	September 19, 1960
PAY RATE	$375 Weekly	DATE EMPLOYED	January 3, 1979
EMPLOYEE NO.	3	DATE EMPLOYMENT TERMINATED	

			DEDUCTIONS							
FICA TAX	FEDERAL INC. TAX	CITY TAX	PENSION PLAN	HEALTH INS.	CREDIT UNION	UNITED WAY	TOTAL	DATE	NET PAY	CK. NO.
26.25	38.00	7.50		8.00			79.75	July 8, '83	295.25	119
26.25	38.00	7.50		8.00			79.75	July 15, '83	295.25	127
26.25	38.00	7.50		8.00			79.75	July 22, '83	295.25	135
26.25	38.00	7.50		8.00			79.75	July 29, '83	295.25	143
26.25	38.00	7.50		8.00			79.75	Aug. 5, '83	295.25	151
26.25	38.00	7.50		8.00			79.75	Aug. 12, '83	295.25	159
26.25	38.00	7.50		8.00			79.75	Aug. 19, '83	295.25	167
26.25	38.00	7.50		8.00			79.75	Aug. 26, '83	295.25	175
26.25	38.00	7.50		8.00			79.75	Sept. 2, '83	295.25	183
26.25	38.00	7.50		8.00			79.75	Sept. 9, '83	295.25	191
26.25	38.00	7.50		8.00			79.75	Sept. 16, '83	295.25	199
26.25	38.00	7.50		8.00			79.75	Sept. 23, '83	295.25	207
26.25	38.00	7.50		8.00			79.75	Sept. 30, '83	295.25	215
341.25	494.00	97.50		104.00			1,036.75		3,838.25	
26.25	38.00	7.50		8.00			79.75	Oct. 7, '83	295.25	223
26.25	38.00	7.50		8.00			79.75	Oct. 14, '83	295.25	231
26.25	38.00	7.50		8.00			79.75	Oct. 21, '83	295.25	239
26.25	38.00	7.50		8.00			79.75	Oct. 28, '83	295.25	247
29.05	47.10	8.30		8.00			92.45	Nov. 4, '83	322.55	255
29.40	49.60	8.40		8.00			95.40	Nov. 11, '83	324.60	263
29.05	47.10	8.30		8.00			92.45	Nov. 18, '83	322.55	271
29.75	49.60	8.50		8.00			95.85	Nov. 25, '83	329.15	279
29.75	49.60	8.50		8.00			95.85	Dec. 2, '83	329.15	287
29.75	49.60	8.50		8.00			95.85	Dec. 9, '83	329.15	295
26.25	38.00	7.50		8.00			79.75	Dec. 16, '83	295.25	303

Employee's Earnings Record — Machine Prepared (Right Page)

may be filed alphabetically or by employee number for ready reference. The information recorded on this form is obtained from the payroll register in a manual system. In an automated system, the employee's earnings record can be updated simultaneously with the preparation of the payroll register.

Indiman's earnings for the last half of the year up to December 16 are shown on this form. The entry for the pay period ended December 16 is posted from the payroll register illustrated on pages 92 and 93.

The payroll register is a summary of the earnings of all employees for each pay period, while the earnings record is a summary of the annual earnings of each employee. The earnings record illustrated on pages 96 and 97 is designed so that quarterly and yearly totals can be accumulated. Thus the form provides a complete record of the earnings of an employee for the year — information that is needed in preparing an annual report to the employee and the Internal Revenue Service on a form called a Wage and Tax Statement. This report is explained in the following section. The earnings record also provides information on an employee's quarterly earnings, which is needed for filing quarterly reports to government agencies on various forms. These reports will be discussed later in this chapter.

Wage and Tax Statement

Not later than January 31 of each year, the law requires employers to furnish each employee from whom income taxes have been withheld an annual report called a Wage and Tax Statement, Form W-2, showing the total amount of wages paid and the amount of such tax withheld during the preceding calendar year. A completed form W-2 is illustrated on page 99. If the employee's wages are subject to FICA tax as well as federal, state, or local income tax, the employer must report total wages paid and the amounts deducted both for income tax and for FICA tax. Information for this purpose is contained in the employee's earnings record.

The **employer's identification number** appearing on the Wage and Tax Statement is an an identification number assigned to the employer by the Internal Revenue Service. An employer who employs one or more persons must file for an identification number. This number must be shown on all reports required of Central States Diversified, Inc., under the Federal Insurance Contributions Act.

Wage and Tax Statements must be prepared in quadruplicate. Copy A goes to the Social Security Administration. Copies B and C are furnished to the employee; Copy B must be sent in with the employee's federal income tax return, and Copy C is for the employee's files. Copy D is kept by the employer as part of the accounting records. In states or cities which have state or city income tax withholding laws, two more copies are furnished. Copy 1 is sent by the employer to the appropriate state or city tax department, and

Chapter 4   **Payroll Accounting**   99

1 Control number	22222		
2 Employer's name, address, and ZIP code Central States Diversified, Inc. 5221 Natural Bridge St. Louis, MO 63115-8230	3 Employer's identification number 43-0211630	4 Employer's State number 21-686001	
	5 Stat. employee / Deceased / Pension plan / Legal rep.	942 emp. / Sub-total / Correction / Void	
	6 •	7 Advance EIC payment	
8 Employee's social security number 307-78-3813	9 Federal income tax withheld $2,040.60	10 Wages, tips, other compensation $19,775.00	11 FICA tax withheld $1,384.25
12 Employee's name (first, middle, last) John Anthony Indiman		13 FICA wages $19,775.00	14 FICA tips
925 Lincoln Ave. St. Louis, MO 63120-4752		16 Employer's use	
		17 State income tax	18 State wages, tips, etc.	19 Name of State
		20 Local income tax $395.50	21 Local wages, tips, etc. $19,775.00	22 Name of locality St. Louis Co.
15 Employee's address and ZIP code			
Form W-2 Wage and Tax Statement 1983	Copy A For Social Security Administration • See Instructions for Forms W-2 and W-2P	Department of the Treasury Internal Revenue Service	

Wage and Tax Statement (Form W-2)

Copy 2 is sent by the employee with the state or city income tax return.

Accounting for Employee Earnings and Earnings Deductions

In accounting for employee earnings and deductions from earnings, it is desirable to keep separate accounts for **(1)** earnings and **(2)** earnings deductions. Various account titles are used in recording wages, such as Payroll Expense, Salaries Expense, and Salaries and Commissions Expense. The accounts needed in recording earnings deductions depend upon what deductions are involved. It helps in understanding the accounting for these deductions if we recognize that in withholding amounts from employees' earnings, the employer basically is serving as an agent for various groups such as the federal government, insurance companies, and labor unions. Amounts that are withheld and deducted from an employee's gross earnings must be paid by the employer to these groups. Therefore, a separate account should be kept for the liability incurred under each type of deduction, such as employee income tax, FICA tax, and insurance premiums. Examples of several of the major accounts involved in payroll accounting and of a typical journal entry for payroll are presented in the following sections.

Payroll Expense. This is an expense account which is debited for the total amount of the gross earnings of all employees for each pay period. Sometimes separate payroll accounts are kept for the employees of different departments. Thus separate accounts may be kept for Office Salaries Expense, Sales Salaries Expense, and Factory Payroll Expense.

Payroll Expense	
Debit to record gross earnings of employees for each pay period.	

FICA Tax Payable. This is a liability account which is credited for (1) the FICA tax withheld from employees' earnings and (2) the FICA tax imposed on the employer. FICA taxes imposed on the employer are discussed later in the chapter. The account should be debited for amounts paid to the Internal Revenue Service. When all of the FICA taxes have been paid, the account should be in balance.

FICA Tax Payable	
Debit	Credit
to record payment of FICA tax previously withheld or imposed.	to record FICA taxes (1) withheld from employees' earnings and (2) imposed on the employer.

Employees Income Tax Payable. This is a liability account which should be credited for the total income tax withheld from employees' earnings. The account is debited for amounts paid to a bank depository for the Internal Revenue Service. When all of the income taxes withheld have been paid, the account will be in balance. A city or state earnings tax payable account is used in a similar manner.

Employees Income Tax Payable	
Debit	Credit
to record payment of income tax previously withheld.	to record income tax withheld from employees' earnings.

Other Deductions. Pension Plan Deductions Payable is a liability account which is credited with amounts withheld from employees' earnings for any pension plan contributions. The account should be debited for the subsequent payment of these amounts to the pension plan trustee. Accounts for health insurance premiums payable, credit union contributions payable, and United Way contributions payable are similarly used.

Journalizing Payroll Transactions. The information needed to properly record the payment of employee wages and salaries is contained in the payroll register. The totals at the bottom of the columns of the payroll register on pages 92 and 93 provide the basis for the following two-column journal entry to record wages paid on December 16, 1983:

Dec. 16	Payroll Expense	3,015.00	
	FICA Tax Payable		165.55
	Employees Income Tax Payable		474.00
	City Earnings Tax Payable		60.30
	Pension Plan Deductions Payable		36.00
	Health Insurance Premiums Payable		34.00
	Credit Union Contributions Payable		31.25
	United Way Contributions Payable		30.00
	Cash		2,183.90
	Payroll for week ended December 16.		

These amounts are posted to payroll expense and liability accounts such as those illustrated in the preceding paragraphs.

BUILDING YOUR ACCOUNTING KNOWLEDGE

1. Why is it important for payroll accounting purposes to distinguish between an employee and an independent contractor?
2. Name three factors that generally explain the difference between an employee's gross pay and net pay.
3. Identify the four factors that determine the amount of federal income tax that is withheld from an employee's pay each pay period.
4. What factors determine the number of withholding allowances to which a taxpayer is entitled?
5. Identify the three types of payroll records usually needed by an employer.
6. Describe the information contained in the payroll register.
7. Why is it important to foot and verify the footings of the payroll register after the data for all employees have been entered?
8. Distinguish between the payroll register and the employee earnings record.
9. Explain what an employer does with the amounts withheld from an employee's pay.

Report No. 4-1

Complete Report No. 4-1 in the study assignments and submit your working papers to the instructor for approval. After completing the report, continue with the following textbook discussion until the next report is required.

PAYROLL TAXES IMPOSED ON THE EMPLOYER

The various taxes discussed thus far have had one thing in common — they all were levied on the employee. The employer withholds them from the employees' earnings only for the purpose of subsequently paying them to some agency or organization. They do not represent any additional expense of the employer.

In addition to these employee taxes, however, certain taxes are also imposed directly on the employer for various purposes, such as: old-age, survivors, and disability insurance benefits; hospital insurance benefits for the aged; and unemployment, relief, and welfare. Most employers are subject to payroll taxes imposed under the Federal Insurance Contributions Act (FICA) and the Federal Unemployment Tax Act (FUTA). An employer may also be subject to the payroll tax imposed under the unemployment compensation laws of one or more states. This tax is commonly called a **State Unemployment Tax**. All of these employer taxes do represent additional payroll expenses of the employer, as will be demonstrated in subsequent sections.

Employer's FICA Tax

The taxes imposed under the Federal Insurance Contributions Act are levied on employers for exactly the same amounts as employees. As explained on page 86, the rate and the taxable earnings base of the tax may be changed by Congress at any time. It was assumed in this chapter that the combined rate (OASDI and HIP) is 7 percent and the base is $30,000. Thus the employer would be required to pay the employer's share of the FICA tax at a rate of 7% on the first $30,000 of each employee's earnings. Any amount of earnings paid to an employee during a year in excess of $30,000 is exempt from FICA tax. (Note that a total of 14% of each employee's taxable earnings — the employer's share and the employee's share — must be paid periodically to an authorized bank or the Internal Revenue Service.)

Employer's FUTA Tax

Under the Federal Unemployment Tax Act, a payroll tax, called the **FUTA tax**, is levied on employers for the purpose of financing the cost of administering the federal-state unemployment compensation program. This tax is levied only on employers and is not deducted from employees' earnings. Employers who employ one or more persons for at least one day in each of 20 or more calendar weeks in a calendar year, or who pay wages of $1,500 or more in any calendar quarter are subject to this tax. The federal law imposes a specific rate of tax on a specific earnings base but allows a substantial credit against this levy for amounts paid into state unemployment compensation programs. Since all states have such programs, the amounts actually paid to the federal government by most employers are substantially less than the legal maximum. Most of the total amount of tax levied under the FUTA program typically is paid to the state governments.

As in the case of the FICA tax, Congress can and does change both the rate and the taxable base of the FUTA tax from time to time. For the purpose of this discussion, a rate of 3.4 percent with a credit of 2.7 percent for payments to state unemployment programs is assumed. The difference, 0.7 percent (3.4%–2.7%) is the effective federal rate. It is further assumed that the taxable base is the first $6,000 of compensation paid to each employee during the calendar year. Note that both the rate and base are substantially lower than the 7 percent and $30,000 for the FICA tax. It is also important to note that all of the payroll taxes relate to gross wages paid — not to wages earned. Sometimes wages are earned in one quarter or year, but not paid until the following period.

Employer's State Unemployment Tax

All of the states and the District of Columbia have enacted unemployment compensation laws providing for the payment of benefits to qualified unemployed workers. The cost of administering the state unemployment compensation laws is borne by the federal government. Under the federal law an appropriation is made for each year by the Congress from which grants are made to the states to meet the proper administrative costs of their unemployment compensation laws. As a result of this provision, the entire amount paid into the state funds may be used for the payment of benefits to qualified workers. While in general there is considerable uniformity in the provisions of the state laws, there are many variations in coverage, rates of tax imposed, and benefits payable to qualified workers. The date of payment of unemployment taxes also varies from state to state, and a penalty generally is imposed on the employer for late payment. Not all employers covered by the Federal Unemployment Tax Act are covered by the unemployment compensation laws of the states in which they have employees. But most employers of one or more individuals are covered by the federal law.

There are frequent changes in the state laws with respect to coverage, contribution rates required, eligibility to receive benefits, and amounts of benefits payable. In this discussion, it is assumed that the state tax rate is 2.7 percent of the first $6,000 of wages paid each employee each year. However, under the laws of most states there is a **merit-rating system** which provides a tax-saving incentive to employers to stabilize employment. Under this system, an employer's rate may be considerably less than the maximum rate if steady work is provided for the employees, i.e., if none or very few of the employer's workers have applied for unemployment compensation. If an employer qualifies for a lower state rate, the full credit of 2.7 percent would still be allowed in computing the federal unemployment tax due.

To illustrate the merit-rating system and the functioning of the federal-state unemployment tax program as a whole, assume that an employer has a favorable merit rating and is required to pay only 1.0 percent rather than 2.7 percent to the state government. If an employee earns $4,000, this employer would be required to pay a total of $68 in unemployment taxes; $40 to the state government and $28 to the federal government, calculated as follows:

Taxable earnings		$4,000
State unemployment tax rate	×	1.0%
State unemployment tax		$ 40
Taxable earnings		$4,000
Total FUTA rate	3.4%	
Credit for state program	2.7%	
	×	0.7%
Federal unemployment tax		$ 28

Accounting for Employer Payroll Taxes

In accounting for employer payroll taxes, it is acceptable either to use separate accounts for FICA Tax Expense, FUTA Tax Expense, and State Unemployment Tax Expense, or to record all of these taxes in a single account such as Payroll Taxes Expense. Liabilities for FICA, FUTA, and state unemployment taxes normally should be recorded in separate accounts. Examples of the payroll taxes expense and liability accounts and a typical journal entry for payroll taxes are presented in the following sections.

Payroll Taxes Expense. All of the payroll taxes imposed on an employer under the federal and state social security laws are an expense of the employer. For the purpose of this discussion, it is assumed that a single account entitled Payroll Taxes Expense is used in summarizing such taxes. This is an expense account which is debited for all payroll taxes imposed on the employer.

Payroll Taxes Expense	
Debit to record FICA, FUTA, and state unemployment taxes imposed on the employer.	

FICA Tax Payable. This is the same liability account that was illustrated on page 100 and was used to recognize the FICA tax withheld from employees' earnings. As used here, the account is credited to record the FICA tax imposed on the employer. The account is debited when the tax is paid to the Internal Revenue Service. When all of the FICA taxes have been paid, the account should be in balance.

FICA Tax Payable	
Debit to record payment of FICA tax.	Credit to record FICA taxes (1) withheld from employees' earnings and (2) imposed on the employer.

FUTA Tax Payable. In recording the federal unemployment tax, it is customary to keep a separate liability account entitled FUTA Tax Payable. This is a liability account which is credited for the tax imposed on employers under the Federal Unemployment Tax Act. The account is debited for amounts paid to apply on such taxes. When all of the FUTA taxes have been paid, the account should be in balance.

FUTA Tax Payable	
Debit to record payment of FUTA tax.	Credit to record FUTA tax imposed on the employer.

State Unemployment Tax Payable. In recording the tax imposed under state unemployment compensation laws, it is customary to keep a separate liability account entitled State Unemployment Tax Payable. This is a liability account which is credited for the tax imposed on employers under the state unemployment compensation laws. The account is debited for the amount paid to apply on such taxes. When all of the state taxes have been paid, the account should be in balance. Some employers who are subject to taxes imposed under the laws of several states keep a separate liability account for the tax imposed by each state.

State Unemployment Tax Payable

Debit	Credit
to record state unemployment tax paid.	to record state unemployment tax imposed on the employer.

Journalizing Employer's Payroll Taxes. The payroll taxes imposed on employers may be recorded periodically, such as monthly or quarterly. It is more common to record such taxes at the time that wages are paid so that the employer's liability for such taxes and related expenses may be recorded in the same period as the wages on which the taxes are based.

The information needed to properly record employer payroll taxes is contained in the payroll register such as the one illustrated on pages 92 and 93. The totals at the bottom of the two columns for "Taxable Earnings" headed "Unemployment Comp." and "FICA" indicate the total employee earnings on which employer taxes would be levied. The FICA taxable earnings for the pay period involved amounted to $2,365.00. Assuming that the combined rate of the tax imposed on the employer was 7 percent, which is the same as the rate of the tax imposed on each employee, the tax would amount to $165.55. The only earnings in the payroll register that were subject to unemployment compensation taxes were Zimmer's earnings for the year because they had not exceeded the $6,000 taxable base. Zimmer just started working for Central States Diversified, Inc., on August 1, 1983. Federal and state unemployment taxes in this situation can be computed as follows:

State unemployment tax, 2.7% of $260	$7.02
FUTA tax, 0.7% of $260	1.82
Total unemployment taxes	$8.84

The following two-column journal entry would therefore be made to record employer payroll taxes expense on wages paid on December 16. These amounts would be posted to payroll taxes expense and liability accounts such as those illustrated in the preceding paragraphs.

Dec. 16	Payroll Taxes Expense	174.39	
	FICA Tax Payable		165.55
	FUTA Tax Payable		1.82
	State Unemployment Tax Payable		7.02
	Employer payroll taxes for the week ended December 16.		

An alternative approach employed by some businesses is to record employer payroll taxes only when they are paid. Under this approach, the above entry would not be made on December 16. Rather, at the time the employer payroll taxes were paid, an entry would be made debiting Payroll Taxes Expense and crediting Cash (or Bank) for the total amount of the employer payroll taxes.

It is important to note in these illustrations the total cost incurred by an employer in order to employ a person. The employer must of course pay the gross wages of an employee; in part to the employee, and in part to various government agencies and other organizations. In addition to these gross wages, however, the employer must pay payroll taxes on wages paid to an employee up to certain dollar limits. To illustrate this point, assume that an employee earns $20,000 for a year. The total cost of this employee to the employer can be calculated as follows:

Gross wages	$20,000.00
Employer FICA tax, 7% of $20,000	1,400.00
State unemployment tax, 2.7% of $6,000	162.00
FUTA tax, 0.7% of $6,000	42.00
	$21,604.00

Thus, the total cost to an employer of employing a person whose salary is $20,000 is not $20,000, but $21,604.00. Employer payroll taxes clearly are a signficant cost of doing business.

Filing Returns and Making Payroll Tax Payments

Employer responsibilities for filing reports and making payroll tax payments can be broken down into two areas: **(1)** responsibility with respect to FICA and federal income taxes, and **(2)** responsibility with respect to state and federal unemployment taxes. These two areas are discussed in the following sections.

Responsibilities for FICA and Federal Income Taxes. Federal reporting and payment regulations deal jointly with requirements for employee FICA taxes withheld, federal income taxes withheld, and employer FICA taxes. When the cumulative amount withheld from employees for FICA and income tax purposes plus the cumulative amount of employer FICA tax exceeds certain specified dollar amounts as of particular dates, an employer is required to deposit the amount in a District Federal Reserve Bank or some other authorized depository. The dollar amounts and dates have been changed several times in recent years and are subject to change at any time in the future. In general, large employers are required to make deposits about every four days. Medium-size employers generally are required to make deposits by the 15th of each month. In contrast, very small employers may need to make a deposit only at the end of each quarter. For the sake of convenience in this chapter, it is assumed that the cumulative amount of FICA and income taxes at the end of each month must be deposited by the 15th of the following month.

At the time any one of these tax deposits is made, the employer should submit to the depository bank a completed copy of the Federal Tax Deposit — Withheld Income and FICA Taxes, Form 501. An example of this form is shown on page 109.

To illustrate the accounting procedure for recording the payment of employees' FICA and income taxes withheld and employer's FICA tax, assume that on February 15, Central States Diversified, Inc., issued a check in payment of the following taxes imposed with respect to wages paid during the first four payroll weeks of January:

Employees' income tax withheld from wages		$1,875.90
FICA tax:		
Withheld from employees' wages	$789.45	
Imposed on employer	789.45	1,578.90
Amount of check		$3,454.80

The journal entry to properly record this transaction would be as follows:

Feb. 15	FICA Tax Payable		1,578.90	
	Employees Income Tax Payable		1,875.90	
	Cash			3,454.80
	Remitted $3,454.80 in payment of taxes.			

Another major form that the employer must file in connection with employee FICA and income taxes withheld and cumulative employer FICA taxes is Form 941. This is the Employer's Quarterly

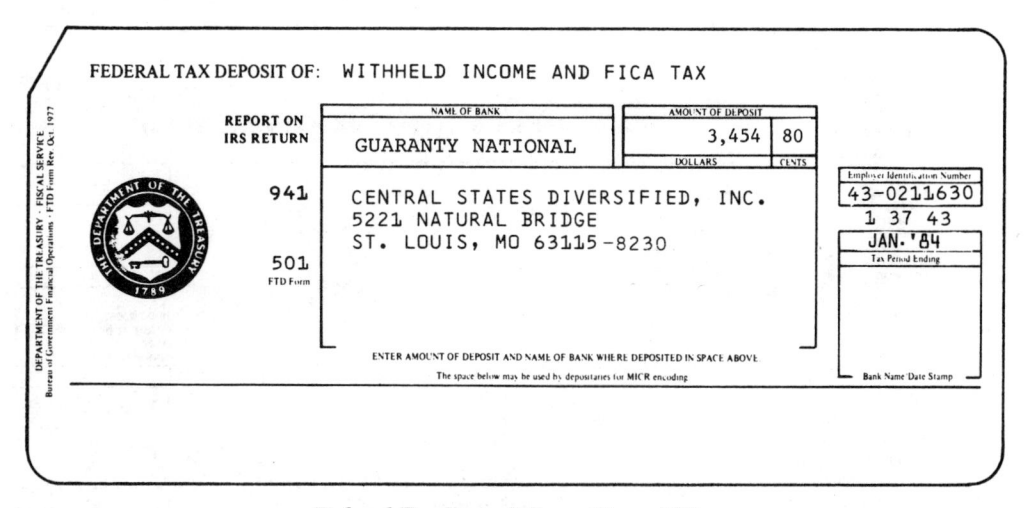

Federal Tax Deposit Form (Form 501)

Federal Tax Return which must be filed with the Internal Revenue Service during the month following the end of each quarter. A completed copy of Form 941 which would be used by Central States Diversified, Inc., on April 16, 1984, to file for the quarter ended March 31, 1984, is shown on page 110. This form summarizes employee FICA and federal income taxes withheld and employer FICA taxes due for the quarter. Portions of the information needed to complete Form 941 are obtained from the payroll register.

Responsibilities for State and Federal Unemployment Taxes. The amount of the tax imposed on employers under the state unemployment compensation laws must be remitted to the proper state office during the month following the close of each calendar quarter. Each state provides an official form to be used in making a return of the taxes due. To illustrate the accounting procedure for recording the payment of state unemployment taxes, assume that a check for $1,084.59 was issued on April 30 in payment of state unemployment compensation taxes on wages paid during the preceding quarter ended March 31. This transaction would be recorded properly with the following two-column journal entry:

Apr. 30	State Unemployment Tax Payable	1,084.59	
	Cash		1,084.59
	Paid state unemployment tax.		

Federal unemployment tax must be computed on a quarterly basis. If the amount of the employer's liability under the Federal Unemployment Tax Act during any quarter is more than $100, the

[¶ 208] 151 4-81	[Form 941]	1175

Form **941** (Rev. March 1981)
Department of the Treasury
Internal Revenue Service

Employer's Quarterly Federal Tax Return

T		
FF		
FD		
FP		
I		
T		

Your name, address, employer identification number, and calendar quarter of return. (If not correct, please change.)

Name (as distinguished from trade name): Central States Diversified, Inc.
Trade name, if any: Central States
Address and ZIP code: 5221 Natural Bridge, St. Louis, MO 63115-8230
Date quarter ended: March 31, 1984
Employer identification number: 43-0211630

If address is different from prior return, check here ▶ ☐

1	Number of employees (except household) employed in the pay period that includes March 12th (complete first quarter only)	8	
2	Total wages and tips subject to withholding, plus other compensation	36,675	00
3	Total income tax withheld from wages, tips, annuities, sick pay, gambling, etc.	6,084	70
4	Adjustment of withheld income tax for preceding quarters of calendar year	-0-	
5	Adjusted total of income tax withheld	6,084	70
6	Taxable FICA wages paid . . . $ 36,675.00 times 14.0% = TAX	5,134	50
7a	Taxable tips reported . . . $_____ times 7.0% = TAX	-0-	
b	Tips deemed to be wages (see instructions) . . $_____ times 7.0% = TAX	-0-	
8	Total FICA taxes (add lines 6, 7a, and 7b)	5,134	50
9	Adjustment of FICA taxes (see instructions)	-0-	
10	Adjusted total of FICA taxes	5,134	50
11	Total taxes (add lines 5 and 10)	11,219	20
12	Advance earned income credit (EIC) payments, if any (see instructions)	-0-	
13	Net taxes (subtract line 12 from line 11)	11,219	20

▶ ☐ Check if you are a first-time 3-banking-day depositor (see Specific Instructions on page 6).

Deposit period ending: Overpayment from previous quarter . .		a. Tax liability for period	b. Date of deposit	c. Amount deposited

I First month total	I	3,454.80	Feb. 15	3,454.80
1st through 3rd day	I			
4th through 7th day	J	863.10		
8th through 11th day	K			
12th through 15th day	L	863.00		
16th through 19th day	M			
20th through 22nd day	N	861.80		
23rd through 25th day	O			
26th through last day	P	862.40		
II Second month total	II	3,450.30	Mar. 15	3,450.30
III Third month total	III	4,314.10	Apr. 15	4,314.10
IV Total for quarter (add items I, II, and III)		11,219.20		11,219.20
V Final deposit made for quarter. (Enter 0 if included in item IV)				-0-
VI Total deposits for quarter. Add items IV and V. Enter here and on line 14 on next page				11,219.20

13a	Net taxes. Enter amount from line 13 on front	11,219	20
14	Total deposits for quarter. Enter amount from item VI on front	11,219	20
15	Undeposited taxes due (subtract line 14 from line 13a). Pay to Internal Revenue Service and enter here ▶	-0-	
16	If line 14 is more than line 13a, enter overpayment here ▶ $_____ and check if to be: ☐ Applied to next return, or ☐ Refunded.		
17	Number of Forms W-4 enclosed. Do not send originals. (See General and Specific Instructions.) ▶		
18	If you are not liable for returns in the future, write "FINAL" (see instructions) ▶ Date final wages paid ▶		

Under penalties of perjury, I declare that I have examined this return, including accompanying schedules and statements, and to the best of my knowledge and belief it is true, correct, and complete.

Date ▶ April 16, 1984   Signature ▶ *Sharon Sorensen*   Title ▶ Treasurer

Please file this form with your Internal Revenue Service Center (see instructions on "Where to File").

[¶ 208]

Employer's Quarterly Federal Tax Return and Quarterly Report (Form 941)

total must be paid to a Federal Reserve Bank or some other authorized depository by the last day of the first month following the close of the quarter. If the amount is $100 or less, no deposit is necessary, but this amount must be added to the amount subject to deposit for the next quarter. When a federal unemployment tax deposit is made, the employer should submit to the bank a completed copy of the Federal Tax Deposit form, Form 508. This form is similar to Form 501, which was illustrated on page 109.

In addition to these quarterly reports and deposits, employers are required to submit an annual report of federal unemployment tax on Form 940 to the District Director of Internal Revenue by the end of the month following the close of the calendar year. Form 940 is not illustrated here. Any federal unemployment tax due for the last quarter or for other periods during the year would be submitted with Form 940.

To illustrate the accounting procedure for payment of federal unemployment tax, assume that a check for $23.66 was issued on January 31 in payment of federal unemployment tax on wages paid during the preceding quarter ended December 31. This transaction would be recorded properly with the following two-column journal entry:

Jan. 31	FUTA Tax Payable	23.66	
	Cash		23.66
	Paid federal unemployment tax.		

BUILDING YOUR ACCOUNTING KNOWLEDGE

1. Why do employer payroll taxes represent an additional expense to the employer whereas, the various employee payroll taxes do not?
2. What is the purpose of the FUTA tax and who must pay it?
3. Why is most of the total amount of the tax levied under the FUTA program typically paid to the state governments?
4. Describe how a state merit-rating system works to reduce an employer's unemployment tax rate.
5. Identify all items that are debited or credited to the FICA Tax Payable account.
6. Explain why an employee whose gross salary is $16,000 costs an employer more than $16,000 to employ.
7. What is the purpose of the Employer's Quarterly Federal Tax Return Form 941?
8. What accounts are affected when employer payroll tax expenses are properly recorded?

Report No. 4-2

> Complete Report No. 4-2 in the study assignments and submit your working papers to the instructor for approval. After completing the report, you may continue with the textbook discussion in Chapter 5 until the next report is required.

EXPANDING YOUR BUSINESS VOCABULARY

What is the meaning of each of the following terms?

- additional withholding allowances (p. 87)
- automated systems (p. 90)
- direct deposit (p. 94)
- electronic system (p. 91)
- employee (p. 83)
- employee's earnings record (pp. 90, 94)
- employer's identification number (p. 98)
- fee (p. 83)
- FICA taxes (p. 85)
- FUTA tax (p. 102)
- gross pay (p. 85)
- independent contractor (p. 83)
- manual system (p. 90)
- mechanical system (p. 90)
- merit-rating system (p. 104)
- net pay (p. 85)
- payroll register (pp. 90, 92)
- salary (p. 84)
- service bureaus (p. 91)
- special withholding allowance (p. 87)
- State Unemployment Tax (p. 102)
- time sharing (p. 91)
- wage-bracket method (p. 88)
- wages (p. 84)
- withholding allowance (p. 87)
- write-it-once principle (p. 91)
- zero-bracket amounts (p. 87)

CHAPTERS 1-4

SUPPLEMENTARY PRACTICAL ACCOUNTING PROBLEMS

The following problems supplement those in Reports 1-1 through 4-2 of the study assignments. These problems are numbered to indicate the chapter of the textbook with which they correlate. For example, Problem 1-A, Problem 1-B, and Challenge Problem 1 correlate with Chapter 1. Loose-leaf stationery should be used in solving these problems. The paper required includes plain ruled paper, two-column journal paper, two-column and three-column statement paper, and ledger paper.

Problem 1-A Accounting elements — equation form

Sheila Reilly is a practicing physician. As of December 31, Reilly owned the following property that related to the practice: Cash, $2,961; professional equipment, $9,500; and an automobile, $7,560. At the same time Reilly owed practice creditors $860.

Required: **(1)** On the basis of the above information, compute the amounts of the accounting elements and show them in equation form. **(2)** Assume that during the following year there is an increase in Reilly's practice assets of $1,800 and a decrease in practice liabilities of $189. Indicate the changes in the accounting elements by showing them in equation form after the changes have occurred.

Problem 1-B T accounts; trial balance

George L. Runck who has been employed by a large national brokerage firm decides to go into business as an investment advisor. Runck's business transactions for the first month of operations were as follows:

- (a) Runck invested $20,000 cash in the business.
- (b) Paid office rent for one month, $800.
- (c) Purchased office equipment from the Von Brocken Office Equipment Co. (a supplier), $2,840 on account.
- (d) Paid telephone bill, $108.
- (e) Received $500 for services rendered to J. S. Marsden.
- (f) Paid $600 to the Von Brocken Office Equipment Co., on account.
- (g) Received $325 for services rendered to Marie Krebs.
- (h) Paid $1,100 salary to office secretary.

Required: **(1)** On a plain sheet of paper, rule eight T accounts and enter the following titles: Cash; Office Equipment; Accounts Payable; George L. Runck, Capital; Professional Fees; Rent Expense; Salary Expense; and Telephone Expense. **(2)** Record the foregoing transactions directly in the accounts. **(3)** Foot the accounts and enter the balances where necessary. **(4)** Prepare a trial balance of the accounts, using a sheet of two-column journal paper.

Challenge Problem 1

Gloria Larkin is the owner of the Larkin Advertising Agency. A trial balance of Larkin's accounts on January 31, 19-- follows:

THE LARKIN ADVERTISING AGENCY
Trial Balance
January 31, 19--

Cash	4,543	
Office Supplies	225	
Office Equipment	3,966	
Accounts Payable		918
Gloria Larkin, Capital		6,514
Advertising Fees		2,387
Rent Expense	1,000	
Telephone Expense	85	
	9,819	9,819

Required: **(1)** On a plain sheet of paper, prepare an income statement for the Larkin Advertising Agency showing the results of operations for the month of January. **(2)** Prepare a balance sheet in account form showing the financial condition of the agency as of

January 31. The assets should be shown on the left side of the sheet of paper, and the liabilities and owner's equity should be shown on the right side.

Problem 2-A Journal entries

Following is a narrative of the transactions completed by R. M. Brown, management consultant, during the first month of Brown's business operations:

June 1 Brown invested $25,000 cash in the business.
      1 Paid office rent, $925.
      3 Purchased office furniture for $1,975 cash.
      3 Paid $87.90 for installation of telephone and for one month's service.
      6 Received $225 from Larsen Clock Repairing Service for consulting services rendered.
      6 Purchased stationery and supplies on account from Van Atta Stationery Co., $189.64.
      7 Paid $10 for subscription to a professional management magazine. (Debit Miscellaneous Expense.)
      8 Paid $35 to Dr. Javier Banvelos, a dentist, for dental service performed for Brown. (Note: This is equivalent to a withdrawal of $35 by Brown for personal use. Debit Brown's drawing account.)
      9 Received $280 from Quality Insulation, Inc., for professional services rendered.
     13 Paid $98.63 for an airplane ticket for a business trip.
     14 Paid other traveling expenses, $140.50.
     20 Paid account of Van Atta Stationery Co. in full, $189.64.
     21 Received $265 from Wagner Electric Co. for professional services rendered.
     30 Paid $960 monthly salary to secretary.

Required: Journalize the foregoing transactions, using a sheet of two-column journal paper. Number the pages and use both sides of the sheet if necessary. Select the account titles from the chart of accounts shown below.

Chart of Accounts

Assets
   111 Cash
   112 Stationery and Supplies
   211 Office Furniture

Liabilities
   311 Accounts Payable

Owner's Equity
   511 R. M. Brown, Capital
   512 R. M. Brown, Drawing

Revenue
   611 Professional Fees

Expenses
   711 Miscellaneous Expense
   714 Rent Expense
   715 Salary Expense
   717 Telephone Expense
   718 Traveling Expense

After journalizing the transactions, prove the equality of the debits and credits by footing the amount columns. Enter the footings in pencil immediately under the line on which the last entry appears.

Problem 2-B Journalizing, posting, taking a trial balance

David E. Hess is a consulting psychologist engaged in practice. Following is the trial balance of Hess' business taken as of March 31, 19‑‑.

DAVID E. HESS CONSULTING PSYCHOLOGIST
Trial Balance
March 31, 19‑‑

Cash	111	4,526.56	
Office Equipment	211	2,525.00	
Automobile	221	7,200.00	
Accounts Payable	311		312.36
David E. Hess, Capital	511		14,207.98
David E. Hess, Drawing	512	6,200.00	
Professional Fees	611		15,600.00
Automobile Expense	801	392.70	
Charitable Contributions Expense	803	65.00	
Miscellaneous Expense	805	22.38	
Rent Expense	810	2,400.00	
Salary Expense	812	6,450.00	
Telephone Expense	815	338.70	
		30,120.34	30,120.34

A narrative of the transactions completed by Hess during the month of April follows below. Hess has two employees.

Narrative of Transactions for April

April   1   Paid one month's rent, $800.
        4   Paid telephone bill, $115.70.
        4   Gave the Salvation Army, $10.
        5   Received $1,325 from Associated Grocers for services rendered.
        7   Paid a garage bill, $89.80.
        8   Received $1,100 from the Midvale Board of Education for services rendered.
      12   Paid Franks' Department Store, $32.40. (Debit Hess' drawing account.)
      15   Hess withdrew $1,275 for personal use.
      18   Paid Lowell Office Supply Co. $90 on account.
      19   Received $1,220 from Maywood Hospital for services rendered.
      22   Gave the American Cancer Society, $15.
      26   Paid the American Psychological Association $150 for annual membership dues.
      28   Received $1,650 from the District Court, Monroe County, for

professional services.
April 29 Hess withdrew $900 for personal use.
     29 Paid April salaries, $2,200.

Required: (1) Journalize the April transactions, using a sheet of two-column journal paper. Number the pages and use both sides of the sheet if necessary. Foot the amount columns. (2) Open the necessary accounts, using the standard account form of ledger paper. Allow one page for each account. Record the April 1 balances as shown in the March 31 trial balance and post the journal entries for April. (3) Foot the ledger accounts and enter the balances. Prove the balances by taking a trial balance as of April 30. Use a sheet of two-column journal paper for the trial balance.

Problem 2-C Financial statements

The following is the trial balance of the The L. R. Gonzalez Agency.

THE L. R. GONZALEZ AGENCY
Trial Balance
January 31, 19--

Cash	111	3,953.84	
Stationery and Supplies	112	351.34	
Automobile	211	8,752.48	
Office Furniture	221	3,842.00	
Notes Payable	311		900.00
Accounts Payable	312		789.30
L. R. Gonzalez, Capital	511		14,516.91
L. R. Gonzalez, Drawing	512	1,630.40	
Professional Fees	611		6,018.00
Automobile Expense	701	118.35	
Miscellaneous Expense	711	29.25	
Rent Expense	715	900.00	
Salary Expense	718	2,200.00	
Stationery and Supplies Expense	720	48.43	
Telephone Expense	722	81.60	
Traveling Expense	725	316.52	
		22,224.21	22,224.21

Required: (1) Prepare an income statement for The L. R. Gonzalez Agency showing the results of the first month of operations, January. Use a sheet of two-column statement paper for the income statement. (2) Prepare a balance sheet in account form showing the financial condition of the agency as of January 31. Two sheets of two-column statement paper may be used for the balance sheet. List the assets on one sheet and the liabilities and owner's equity on the other sheet.

Challenge Problem 2

Philip Isabella is a manufacturers' agent selling machinery on commission for several machinery manufacturers. Isabella began the agency on January 2, 19--. A trial balance of the accounts as of March 31, 19-- follows:

PHILIP ISABELLA, MANUFACTURERS' AGENT
Trial Balance
March 31, 19--

Cash	111	3,982	
Office Supplies	115	428	
Office Equipment	121	3,750	
Automobile	131	10,115	
Accounts Payable	311		742
Philip Isabella, Capital	500		14,881
Philip Isabella, Drawing	505	4,178	
Commissions Earned	611		13,920
Automobile Expense	700	279	
Office Supplies Expense	705	280	
Rent Expense	710	3,000	
Salary Expense	715	3,300	
Telephone Expense	720	231	
		29,543	29,543

During the month of April the following selected transactions took place:

April 1   Paid April rent, $1,000.
     3   Paid telephone bill for month, $78.
     5   Purchased office supplies for cash, $71.
     8   Received commission from the Midwest Tool Company for machines sold by Isabella, $3,479.
   15   Paid assistant's salary for first half of month, $550.
   20   Paid part of accounts payable, $429.
   25   Purchased office equipment on account, $1,235.
   27   Paid garage bill, $84.
   29   Paid assistant's salary for second half of month, $550.
   29   Isabella withdrew $1,500 for personal use.
   29   By taking an inventory it was found that $105 of the office supplies were used during April.

Required: **(1)** On a plain sheet of paper draw up T accounts for the accounts in the trial balance as of March 31, 19-- and enter the balances in the accounts. **(2)** Using a sheet of two-column paper, journalize the foregoing transactions. Select the account titles from the March 31 trial balance. **(3)** Post the journal entries to the T accounts and figure the balance of the accounts where necessary. **(4)** Using a sheet of two-column paper, take a trial balance of the accounts as of April 30, 19--.

Chapters 1–4   Supplementary Practical Accounting Problems   **119**

Problem 3-A   Journalizing, posting, taking a trial balance

Angela Sartori is a management consultant. The only book of original entry for Sartori's business is a two-column journal. Sartori uses the standard form of account in the general ledger. Following is the trial balance of the business taken as of May 31:

ANGELA SARTORI, MANAGEMENT CONSULTANT
Trial Balance
May 31, 19--

Cash	111	3,634.28	
Automobile	211	8,750.00	
Office Equipment	221	2,800.00	
Accounts Payable	311		191.45
Angela Sartori, Capital	511		13,155.43
Angela Sartori, Drawing	512	5,000.00	
Professional Fees	611		19,990.00
Automobile Expense	701	537.80	
Charitable Contributions Expense	705	325.00	
Electricity Expense	708	127.80	
Miscellaneous Expense	710	124.80	
Rent Expense	715	5,500.00	
Salary Expense	718	6,000.00	
Telephone Expense	720	537.20	
		33,336.88	33,336.88

The following transactions were completed in the month of June:

June 1 Paid June office rent, $1,100.
     1 Paid electric bill, $24.32.
     2 Paid telephone bill, $109.18.
     2 Received a check from Wagner Electric Co. for $500 for services rendered.
     6 Received $1,400 from Fitzpatrick Grocery Co. for services rendered.
     7 Donated $25 to the Heart Association.
     7 Paid garage bill, $98.20.
     8 Received a check for $1,250 from Millette Corporation for consulting services.
    13 Sartori withdrew $550 for personal use.
    15 Paid secretary's salary for the half month, $600.
    16 Purchased office furniture on credit from Union Furniture Co., $1,600.
    20 Paid $3 for a messenger fee.
    20 Received $1,200 from Associated General Contractors for services rendered.
    22 Paid traveling expenses while on business, $32.25.
    23 Donated $30 to the United Fund.
    27 Paid Union Furniture Co. $200 on account.
    28 Sartori withdrew $500 for personal use.
    30 Paid secretary's salary for the half month, $600.

Required: (1) Journalize the June transactions. For the journal, use two-column journal paper and number the page 1. (2) Open the necessary ledger accounts. Allow one page for each account and number the accounts. Record the June 1 balances and post the journal entries. Foot the ledger accounts and enter the balances. (3) Take a trial balance. Use a sheet of two-column journal paper for the trial balance.

Problem 3-B Reconciliation of bank statement

Mark Sloneker, a plumber, completed the following transactions with the Kenton Bank during the month of July:

July	1 Balance in bank per record kept on check stubs....	$4,500.00	July 12 Check No. 118....	$ 190.00
	1 Deposit	1,500.00	12 Check No. 119....	45.90
	1 Check No. 108....	788.20	13 Check No. 120....	447.75
	5 Check No. 109....	30.00	14 Check No. 121....	41.80
	5 Check No. 110....	1,475.00	14 Check No. 122....	457.32
	5 Check No. 111....	110.00	14 Deposit	1,381.43
	5 Check No. 112....	350.00	18 Check No. 123....	125.00
	6 Check No. 113....	90.00	18 Check No. 124....	265.01
	7 Check No. 114....	280.70	21 Check No. 125....	97.45
	7 Check No. 115....	50.00	21 Deposit	971.00
	7 Check No. 116....	346.00	25 Check No. 126....	131.42
	7 Deposit	1,268.45	25 Check No. 127....	227.89
	8 Check No. 117....	454.32	27 Check No. 128....	277.97
			28 Check No. 129....	183.00
			29 Check No. 130....	547.63
			29 Deposit	1,825.14

Required: (1) Prepare a record of the bank account as it would appear on the check stubs. (2) Prepare a reconciliation of the bank statement for July which indicated a balance of $5,639.41 on July 29, with Checks Nos. 116, 126, 129, and 130 outstanding, and a service charge of $2.30.

Problem 3-C Petty cash disbursements record

Saul Polanski, a general contractor, had a balance of $125 in the petty cash fund as of April 1. During April the following petty cash transactions were completed:

April 1 Paid $17.50 for typewriter repairs. Petty Cash Voucher No. 45.
      4 Reimbursed Polanski $3.25 for a long distance telephone call made from a booth. Petty Cash Voucher No. 46.
      8 Gave $10 to the United Fund. Petty Cash Voucher No. 47.

April 8 Paid garage for washing car, $5.75. Petty Cash Voucher No. 48.
11 Gave Polanski's son $3. (Debit Saul Polanski, Drawing.) Petty Cash Voucher No. 49.
14 Paid for postage stamps, $20. Petty Cash Voucher No. 50.
18 Paid for newspaper for the month, $6. Petty Cash Voucher No. 51.
22 Paid for window washing, $10. Petty Cash Voucher No. 52.
28 Paid $15 to the Parent-Teachers Association for dues. (Debit Saul Polanski, Drawing.) Petty Cash Voucher No. 53.
28 Paid for car lubrication, $4.50. Petty Cash Voucher No. 54.
29 Donated $15 to the American Red Cross. Petty Cash Voucher No. 55.
29 Rendered report of petty cash expenditures for the month and received the amount needed to replenish the petty cash fund.

Required: **(1)** Record the foregoing transactions in a petty cash disbursements record, distributing the expenditures as follows:

Saul Polanski, Drawing   Donations Expense
Automobile Expense   Miscellaneous Expense
Telephone Expense

(2) Prove the petty cash disbursements record by footing the amount columns and proving the totals. Enter the totals and rule the amount columns with single and double lines. **(3)** Prepare a statement of the petty cash disbursements for April. **(4)** Bring down the balance of the petty cash fund below the ruling in the Description column. Enter the amount received to replenish the fund and record the total.

Challenge Problem 3

Leona Raymond owns an executive recruiting company. The balance in the petty cash fund on August 1 was $125. During August the following petty cash transactions were completed:

Aug. 1 Paid $7.10 for office supplies. Petty Cash Voucher No. 57.
5 Paid $5.50 for cab fare. Petty Cash Voucher No. 58.
8 Paid for newspapers for month of July, $7.00. Petty Cash Voucher No. 59.
11 Paid for gasoline and oil for car, $15.82. Petty Cash Voucher No. 60.
16 Gave $12.00 to the American Red Cross. Petty Cash Voucher No. 61.
22 Paid $27.00 for typewriter repairs. Petty Cash Voucher No. 62.
26 Paid $20.00 for postage stamps. Petty Cash Voucher No. 63.
30 Gave Raymond's daughter $5.00. (Debit Leona Raymond, Drawing.) Petty Cash Voucher No. 64.
31 The cash in the petty cash drawer was counted and was found to be $27.12.

Aug. 31 Rendered report of petty cash expenditures for month and received the amount needed to replenish the petty cash fund.

Required: (1) Record the foregoing transactions in a petty cash disbursements record, distributing the expenditures as follows:

    Leona Raymond, Drawing   Office Supplies Expense
    Automobile Expense   Postage Expense
    Charitable Contributions Expense   Repairs Expense
    Miscellaneous Expense

Also include a column at the right end of the petty cash disbursements record headed Account and a column headed Amount. (2) As the last item in the petty cash disbursements record, enter the cash overage on August 31 by placing the amount of the overage in the total column and drawing a circle around it. Also enter the account title Cash Short and Over in the Account column and the dollar amount of the overage in the Amount column with a circle around the figures. The circle around the amount of the overage in the Total column means that it is a debit to Cash. The overage should be subtracted from the other figures in the column. The circle around the figures in the Amount column at the right end of the petty cash disbursements record means that the overage is a credit to Cash Short and Over. (3) Prove the petty cash disbursements record by footing the amount columns and proving the totals. Enter the totals and rule the amount columns with single and double lines. (4) Prepare a statement of the petty cash disbursements for August including the overage. (5) Prepare a compound journal entry on a piece of two-column paper for the transactions in the petty cash disbursements record. (6) Assuming that the balance in the fund was found to be $23.33, prepare a statement of the petty cash disbursements for August including the shortage. (7) Prepare a compound journal entry on a piece of two-column paper for the transactions in the petty cash disbursements record.

Problem 4-A   Payroll register

Following is a summary of the hours worked, rates of pay, and other relevant information concerning the employees of The Rogers Machine Tool Co., M. L. Rogers, owner, for the week ended Saturday, December 2. Employees are paid at the rate of time and one half for all hours worked in excess of 8 in any day or 40 in any week.

Chapters 1–4 Supplementary Practical Accounting Problems **123**

No.	Name	Allowances Claimed	Hours Worked M T W T F S	Regular Hourly Rate	Cumulative Earnings Jan. 1–Nov. 25
1	Case, Ralph E.	3	8 8 8 8 8 6	$10.00	$18,679
2	Eiler, Ruth A.	4	8 9 8 8 8 4	16.00	30,810
3	Markland, Marilyn E.	3	8 8 8 8 8 0	9.50	17,860
4	Nolan, Louis C.	1	8 8 8 9 8 4	8.35	15,434
5	Stevens, Carolyn R.	2	8 8 8 8 0 4	9.40	17,872
6	Turner, Henry T.	1	8 8 8 8 0 0	12.00	22,922

Case and Nolan each have $3 withheld this payday for group life insurance. Eiler and Turner each have $20 withheld this payday for health insurance. Stevens has $5 withheld this payday as a contribution to the United Fund.

Required: (1) Using plain ruled paper size 8½" by 11", rule a payroll register form similar to that reproduced on pages 92 and 93 and insert the necessary columnar headings. Enter on this form the payroll for the week ended Saturday, December 2. Refer to the Weekly Income Tax Table on page 89 to determine the amounts to be withheld from the wages of each employee for income tax purposes. All of Rogers' employees are married. Seven percent of the taxable wages of all of the employees except Eiler should be withheld for FICA tax. Checks Nos. 511 through 516 were issued to the employees. Complete the payroll record by footing the amount columns, proving the footings, entering the totals, and ruling. (2) Assuming that the wages were paid on December 5, record the payment on a sheet of two-column journal paper.

Problem 4-B Payroll taxes

The O'Leary Store employs twelve people. They are paid by checks on the day nearest to the 15th and last day of each month. The entry to record each payroll includes the liabilities for the amounts withheld. The expense and liabilities arising from the employer's payroll taxes are recorded on each payday.

Following is a narrative of the transactions completed during the month of January that relate to payrolls and payroll taxes.

Jan. 5 Paid $5,009.72 for December's payroll taxes:
FICA tax, $2,627.68.
Employees' income tax withheld, $2,382.04.

14 Payroll for first half of month:
Total salaries $9,331.00
Less amounts withheld:
FICA tax .... $ 653.17
Employees' income tax 1,190.40   1,843.57
Net amount paid $7,487.43

Jan. 14 Social security taxes imposed on employer:
FICA tax, 7%.
State unemployment tax, 2%.
FUTA tax, 0.7%.

28 Paid state unemployment tax for quarter ended December 31, $93.42.

28 Paid FUTA tax for quarter ended December 31, $32.69.

31 Payroll for last half of month:
Total salaries		$9,528.00
Less amounts withheld:		
FICA tax	$ 666.96	
Employees' income tax	1,201.80	1,868.76
Net amount paid		$7,659.24

31 Social security taxes imposed on employer:
All salaries taxable; rates same as on January 14.

Required: **(1)** Journalize the foregoing transactions, using two-column journal paper. **(2)** Foot the debit and credit amount columns as a means of proof.

Challenge Problem 4

Margaret Koester, Lawrence Skirvin, and Frank Cosgrove are employed by Midstates Sales Co. Their monthly salaries are $1,500, $1,650, and $1,375 respectively. All of the employees are entitled to time and one half for all hours worked in excess of 40 hours a week. During the week ended March 19, 1983, the employees worked the following hours:

Margaret Koester	43 hours
Lawrence Skirvin	48 hours
Frank Cosgrove	47 hours

Required: Calculate the wages earned by each of the three employees in the week ended March 19, 1983.

5

ACCOUNTING FOR PERSONAL SERVICE (ATTORNEYS)

CHAPTER OBJECTIVES

> The objectives of this chapter are to enable you:
> ▶ To explain and use the cash basis of accounting.
> ▶ To understand the special characteristics of accounting for attorneys.
> ▶ To perform the tasks involved in accounting for attorneys.

In contrast to a **manufacturing enterprise** which manufactures and sells merchandise or a **mercantile enterprise** which buys merchandise for resale, a **personal service enterprise** is one in which service is rendered to a company or a person. There are two types of personal service enterprises:

(1) Professional enterprises
(2) Business enterprises

Professional enterprises include public accountants, attorneys, physicians, dentists, engineers, architects, artists, educators, and other professionals whose income is earned chiefly by performing personal services.

Business enterprises of the personal service type include insurance, brokerage, advertising, real estate, entertainment, storage, transportation, and dry cleaning.

This chapter relates to personal services performed by an attorney. An attorney may represent either a plaintiff or a defendant. A person or company instituting a suit against someone else is called the **plaintiff**. The person or company being sued is called the **defendant**.

In a personal service firm such as that conducted by attorneys, the most valuable asset the attorney has is "time." The significance of time to a professional firm cannot be overemphasized. Adequate **time records** must be maintained by each attorney, including the sole practitioner. Many legal firms believe that it is desirable for each attorney to account for a working day by analyzing the activities that cannot be charged to clients. An analysis of nonchargeable time will disclose the amount of time the firm is devoting to community affairs, research, and other desirable activities.

Time records may be kept in various ways; some attorneys maintain a daily diary, and the chargeable time is posted daily to the clients' records. In a large law firm, weekly reports of work for each client may be used to reduce paperwork. Another method of time reporting is to use a consolidated weekly report of all attorney time. Thus, a secretary posts the billable time to the clients' records on a weekly rather than a daily basis.

THE CASH BASIS OF ACCOUNTING FOR A PERSONAL SERVICE ENTERPRISE

Most law firms use the **cash basis of accounting** which means that revenue is not recognized until cash is received and expenses are not recorded until paid. Thus, services may be performed in one month, and the revenue may be accounted for the following month or several months later. The cash basis of accounting violates the **matching principle** which holds that revenues earned and expenses incurred during a period should be matched against each other in order to arrive at as accurate a figure of net income or net loss for the period as possible. In many cases, however, expenses such as rent or telephone bills may be approximately the same each month, so that only a slight distortion is caused by paying and recording an expense in November which actually was incurred in October. The cash basis of accounting is acceptable for federal and state income tax purposes.

It should be noted that accounting cannot be based completely on cash transactions. Property or service accepted in lieu of cash must be recorded as revenue at the fair market value of the property or service at the time it is received. Also, if revenue such as interest on a savings account is available for withdrawal by the owner of the account, the revenue is said to be **constructively received** and must be reported as revenue even though no cash is withdrawn from the account.

Another exception to the cash basis of accounting is made when depreciation is recorded. Assets which provide benefits for several years, such as automobiles or office equipment, will wear out or **depreciate** with the passage of time. When such assets are purchased, they must be debited to asset accounts. As the asset is used, expense is incurred which should be allocated over the estimated life of the asset. The purpose of depreciation is to charge the expense to the period in which it is actually incurred, in accordance with the matching principle explained on page 126. The portion of cost assigned to each period is called **depreciation expense**.

For example, an automobile, possibly the largest item in the balance sheet of a legal firm, must be debited to the asset account Automobile. Depreciation of the automobile is based on the cost, less any residual or scrap value, and the estimated life of the automobile. Since the residual value and the expected useful life are estimates, the amount charged to depreciation expense each period is not entirely accurate; but an allocation of cost over the expected useful life of an asset results in a more equitable profit or loss measurement than charging such an asset to expense in the period it is purchased.

When an entry is made at the end of the period debiting Depreciation Expense, the credit is usually to an account called **Accumulated Depreciation**, such as Accumulated Depreciation — Automobile. Accumulated depreciation accounts are **contra accounts** (meaning "opposite" or "offsetting" accounts) and should be deducted from the related asset accounts in the balance sheet. The difference between the asset account and the accumulated depreciation account is known as the **book value** of the asset. Adjustments for depreciation will be explained further in Chapter 7.

Chart of Accounts

To illustrate the cash basis of accounting for an attorney, a chart of accounts for Karl F. Andersen, Attorney at Law, is reproduced on page 128. Note that asset accounts have account numbers beginning with 1 and 2; liability accounts begin with 3; owner's equity accounts begin with 5; revenue accounts begin with 6; and expense accounts begin with 7. New accounts may be added as needed without disturbing the numerical order of the existing accounts.

KARL F. ANDERSEN, ATTORNEY AT LAW
CHART OF ACCOUNTS

Assets*

- 111 Cash
- 112 Petty Cash Fund
- 121 Clients' Trust Account
- 131 Advances on Behalf of Clients
- 211 Automobile
- 212 Accumulated Depreciation — Automobile
- 221 Office Equipment
- 222 Accumulated Depreciation — Office Equipment

Liabilities

- 321 Liability for Trust Funds
- 331 Employees Income Tax Payable
- 341 FICA Tax Payable
- 351 FUTA Tax Payable
- 361 State Unemployment Tax Payable

Owner's Equity

- 511 Karl F. Andersen, Capital
- 512 Karl F. Andersen, Drawing
- 521 Expense and Revenue Summary

Revenue

- 611 Legal Fees Revenue
- 621 Collection Fees Revenue

Expenses

- 701 Automobile Expense
- 703 Charitable Contributions Expense
- 705 Depreciation Expense
- 708 Law Library Expense
- 709 Miscellaneous Expense
- 710 Office Supplies Expense
- 712 Payroll Taxes Expense
- 715 Rent Expense
- 718 Salary Expense
- 720 Telephone Expense

*Words in bold type represent headings and not account titles.

Many of the accounts in the preceding list have been explained and their uses illustrated in the previous chapters. Accounts appearing for the first time in this chapter will be discussed before the records of Andersen are presented.

Advances on Behalf of Clients, Account No. 131. Payments for items such as court filing fees, fees charged by accountants for making audits, and the cost of obtaining depositions are sometimes made for clients. Absorption of these expenses by the attorney would be equivalent to lowering fees for certain clients. To avoid unethical "fee cutting," payments made for clients are debited to the account Advances on Behalf of Clients and then billed to the clients on a monthly or quarterly basis. A record of the payments made and remittances received is also made in the client's account on an office docket (an auxiliary record which provides a complete record of each legal case). A minimum amount, usually 50 cents to $1, can be established below which the firm will absorb the expense to save clerical work.

Expense and Revenue Summary Account, Account No. 521. The expense and revenue summary account is a clearing account which is used only when the books are closed at the end of the accounting period. Use of this account will be explained further in Chapter 8.

Legal Fees Revenue, Account No. 611. Legal Fees Revenue is a revenue account that is credited for cash received from clients in payment of legal work performed. When the accounts are kept on the cash basis, revenue is not recorded in the account until cash is received or until a note or other property is accepted in lieu of cash.

Since legal fees are usually not collected until they are billed, billing is very important. The more frequent the billing, the more frequent the collection. If bills are collected frequently, the firm can operate with a smaller cash investment, and in some cases may collect a larger total fee without impairing the client relationship than would be possible if the entire amount were billed at one time. Many clients of a law firm prefer to be billed on a monthly or quarterly basis even though the legal work is not completed, rather than to receive one large bill at the end of the engagement.

Clients' Trust Account, Account No. 121, Liability for Trust Funds, Account No. 321, and Collection Fees Revenue, Account No. 621. Funds received or collected by an attorney and held for a client must be deposited in a separate bank account promptly.[1] If money is collected on an account owed to a client, the lawyer will deduct a commission or fee before the money is deposited for the client in the special bank account. This transaction is then recorded as follows: Cash (Account No. 111) is debited for the lawyer's commission; Clients' Trust Account (Account No. 121) is debited for the amount that is in the special bank account; Liability for Trust Funds (Account No. 321) is credited to indicate the amount owed to the client; and Collection Fees Revenue (Account No. 621) is credited to indicate the commission or fee earned by the lawyer. The balance in Account No. 121 and in Account No. 321 will always be equal. When the amount in the special bank account is paid to the client, Liability for Trust Funds (Account No. 321) is debited, and Clients' Trust Account (Account No. 121) is credited.

To illustrate, Andersen undertakes to collect an account amounting to $300 for the City Department Store on a commission basis of

---

[1] For example, Rule 8-101 of the California Business and Professions Code entitled "Preserving Identity of Funds and Property of a Client," reads in part as follows:

(A) All funds received or held for the benefit of clients by a member of the State Bar or firm of which he is a member, including advances for costs and expenses, shall be deposited in one or more identifiable bank accounts labeled "Trust Account," "Client's Funds Account" or words of similar import. West's Annotated California Codes, Volume 3B (St. Paul, Minn. West Publishing Co. 1978) p. 91.

33⅓%. When cash is received in payment of the account, the following entry should be made:

May 16	Cash..	100	
	Clients' Trust Account	200*	
	Liability for Trust Funds..		200
	Collection Fees Revenue		100
	Collected an account in the amount of $300 on behalf of the City Department Store and recorded fee of $100.		
	*The $200 is deposited in a special checking account.		

When the amount collected for the City Department Store ($200) is paid to them by the attorney, an entry should be made as follows:

May 17	Liability for Trust Funds...	200	
	Clients' Trust Account...		200*
	Payment to City Department Store of collection made for them.		
	*At this time a check is written for $200 from the special checking account and sent to City Department Store.		

Books of Account

Andersen uses the following books of account:

(1) General books
    (a) Combination journal
    (b) General ledger
(2) Auxiliary records
    (a) Petty cash disbursements record
    (b) Lawyer's office docket
    (c) Lawyer's collection docket
    (d) Employee's earnings record
    (e) Checkbook used with Account No. 111
    (f) Checkbook used with Account No. 121

Combination Journal. Andersen uses only one book of original entry — a **combination journal**. Such a journal is sometimes called a special column journal because there are special columns for specific items. Special columns for accounts in which frequent entries are made will save time and labor in the bookkeeping process. Andersen's combination journal, reproduced on pages 142–145 contains eight amount columns, two on the left side of the Description column and six on the right. The columnar arrangement follows:

(1) Cash
    (a) Deposits 111 Dr.
    (b) Checks 111 Cr.

(2) General
   (a) Debit
   (b) Credit
(3) Revenue
   (a) Legal Fees Revenue 611 Cr.
   (b) Collection Fees Revenue 621 Cr.
(4) Wage Deductions
   (a) Employees Income Tax Payable 331 Cr.
   (b) FICA Tax Payable 341 Cr.

The account numbers in the headings are an aid in completing the summary posting at the end of the month. The combination journal contains a Check Number column to the right of the Checks 111 Cr. column to account for the law firm's cash account and a Check Number column to the right of the General Credit column to account for the clients' cash.

A narrative of transactions completed by Andersen during the month of December is given on pages 135–145. These transactions are recorded in the combination journal on pages 142–145. Note that before any transactions were recorded in this journal, the bank balance at the start of the month, $20,164.36, was entered in the Description column beside the words "Amounts Forwarded." Accounts No. 121 and No. 321 have no balance on December 1.

General Ledger. Andersen uses an account form, called a **balance-column-account form**, which has four amount columns: a debit column, a credit column, and two balance columns — one for debit and one for credit. Although the standard two-column account form illustrated to this point is still favored by some, the four-column form of balance-column account has the advantage of providing a place to record the balance of the account. The balance may be determined and recorded after each transaction or only at the end of the month.

The ledger is reproduced on pages 146–151. In each case, the balance as of December 1 has been entered. The accounts in the **general ledger** are arranged in the order given in the chart of accounts shown on page 128. All posting to the general ledger accounts is from the combination journal. A trial balance is taken at the end of each month to prove the equality of the general ledger account balances. The trial balance as of December 31 appears on page 150.

Auxiliary Records. **Auxiliary records** are used to record information not recorded in the regular accounting records. Anderson uses a petty cash disbursements record, an office docket, a collection docket, and two checkbooks as auxiliary records. An employee's earnings record, similar to the one illustrated in Chapter 4 on pages 96–97, is maintained for each employee.

Petty Cash Disbursements Record. Andersen maintains a petty cash fund in the amount of $75. The petty cash disbursements record is similar to that illustrated on pages 60–61.

Lawyer's Office Docket. An office docket is a form used to maintain a memorandum record of each legal case with a client. A model filled-in office docket (reproduced on page 133) shows the history of the case of Acme Products Co., plaintiff, vs. Anne Murchison, defendant. The legal information that may be needed in handling the case is recorded on the upper part of the form, and a memorandum account of the charges and credits to the account of the client is kept on the lower part of the form.

When an attorney's accounts are kept on the cash basis, there is no general ledger account for the client, but the information must be kept on the office docket. The client's account, as recorded on the office docket, should be charged for:

(1) Fees for services rendered.
(2) Disbursements on behalf of the client, such as filing fees and other expenses paid for the client.

The client's account should be credited for:

(1) Payments received for services.
(2) Reimbursements for advances made on behalf of the client.

In the illustration on page 133, the client, Acme Products Co., is charged for the following:

November 24   Amount of the fee agreed upon at the time the case was taken, $750.
November 29   Amount advanced in payment of suit fee, $10.

The account is credited for the following:

December 1   Amount received as a retainer, $200.
December 27 Amount received in payment of balance due on account, $560.

Lawyer's Collection Docket. Lawyers who collect accounts for clients may use a form known as a collection docket to keep a record of the necessary information pertaining to collections. A model filled-in copy of a collection docket is shown on page 134.

The docket provides a record of the case of the Newton Department Store, creditor, vs. John N. Holland, debtor. It also furnishes a record of the amounts collected from the debtor and the amounts paid to the creditor.

Chapter 5   Accounting for Personal Service (Attorneys)

Lawyer's Office Docket

CLIENT	ACME PRODUCTS CO.	ADDRESS 250 E. Fourth St., City	NO. 215

IN RE: ACME PRODUCTS CO. vs. ANNE MURCHISON

COURT	Common Pleas, Butler County	19 83
COURT FILE NO.	29836	
CALENDAR NO.	912	ATTORNEY FOR Plaintiff
OTHER ATTORNEYS		

NATURE OF MATTER Lawsuit

REMARKS

DATE	SERVICES RENDERED	FEES AND DISBURSEMENTS	MONEYS RECEIVED PURPOSE	AMOUNT	BALANCE DUE
Nov. 24	Fee for preparing case	750 00			750 00
29	Suit fee	10 00			760 00
Dec. 1			Retainer	200 00	560 00
27			Balance due	560 00	-0-
	CARRIED FORWARD				

DEBTOR	John N. Holland	DATE CLAIM REC'D	12-5-83	NO. 36
ADDRESS	750 Hudson Avenue, City	DATE DISPOSED OF	1-31-84	
BUSINESS		TOTAL AMOUNT	$ 360	
CREDITOR	Newton Department Store	AMOUNT COLLECTED	$ 360	
ADDRESS	Main and Baum St., City	FEE	$ 120	
REC'D CLAIM FROM		EXPENSE	$	
ATTORNEY FOR DEBTOR		AMOUNT REMITTED	$ 240	
CALLS ON DEBTOR		CHECK NO.	59 & 64	

RECEIVED FROM CREDITOR

DATE	FOR	AMOUNT
12-21	Com.	100 00
1-15	Com.	20 00

CORRESPONDENCE

RECEIVED FROM DEBTOR		PAID TO CREDITOR	
DATE	AMOUNT	CHECK NO.	AMOUNT
12 21	300 00	59	200 00
1 15	60 00	64	40 00

REMARKS: Statement of account. Collection fee 33 1/3%.
No suit without further instructions.

Lawyer's Collection Docket

Attorneys usually take most collection cases on a percentage basis. Any expenses incurred in making collections should be charged to the expense accounts of the attorney and not to the client. If, however, a client has agreed to pay any expenses incident to a lawsuit, such as court costs, the amounts paid by the attorney should be charged to the client's account just the same as payments made for clients in handling other legal cases.

In the illustration, the following transactions were recorded on the collection docket for the Newton Department Store:

December 21 Collected $300 from John N. Holland, debtor.
December 28 Paid $200 to the Newton Department Store.
January   15 Collected $60 from John N. Holland, debtor.
January   31 Paid $40 to the Newton Department Store.

The amount of the commission of 33⅓% is deducted from the amounts collected from the debtor and is entered on the collection docket as follows:

December 21 $100.
January   15 $20.

Employee's Earnings Record. The employee's earnings record was discussed in Chapter 4.

Following is a narrative of transactions completed by Karl F. Andersen during the month of December. These transactions are recorded in the combination journal on pages 142–145.

KARL F. ANDERSEN, ATTORNEY AT LAW
NARRATIVE OF TRANSACTIONS

Thursday, December 1

Issued Check No. 720 for $900, payable to Robert Nehring, for the December rent.

Received $200 from Acme Products Co. as a retainer in the lawsuit of Acme Products Co. against Anne Murchison. Case No. 215.

The amount received as a retainer constitutes revenue realized on the cash basis. Office Docket No. 215 is reproduced on page 133. This docket is an auxiliary record designed to supplement the information recorded in the regular accounting records and to facilitate the handling of the case.

The transaction was recorded in the combination journal by debiting Cash, Account No. 111, and by crediting Legal Fees Revenue, Account No. 611. Since this entry was recorded in special columns, individual posting is not required, and a check mark was placed in the Posting Reference column.

Friday, December 2

Issued Check No. 721 for $55.25 to the Centerville Electric Co. for electricity consumed during November.

Debit Miscellaneous Expense, Account No. 709.

Received $250 from Rachael Shipley for services rendered in preparation of a trust agreement.

Monday, December 5

Issued Check No. 722 for $63.89 to the Bell Telephone Co. for November service.

Received a check for $1,500 from E. A. Elbrecht in payment of the balance due on Case No. 210.

Received for collection from the Newton Department Store, Main and Baum Street, City, a statement of its account with John N. Holland, 750 Hudson Avenue, City, for $360. Holland's account is over 18 months past due. Collection fee, 33⅓%; no suit without further instructions. Collection No. 36.

> Inasmuch as Andersen's books are kept on the cash basis, no entry in the regular accounting records is required for this transaction. Collection Docket No. 36 is reproduced on page 134. This docket is an auxiliary record of information designed to supplement the information recorded in the regular accounting records and to facilitate handling the account.

Tuesday, December 6

Received a check for $1,540 from the Polinsky Manufacturing Company in full payment of Case No. 212.

Issued Check No. 723 for $158.82 to the Riley Service Station in payment of the December 1 statement for gasoline, oil, and services rendered during November.

Received a check for $400 from R. E. Coughlin for participating in an estate planning conference with Coughlin's accountant and with his insurance agent.

Wednesday, December 7

Received a check for $250 from Reichert and Sullivan, certified public accountants, for drafting a partnership agreement.

Thursday, December 8

Andersen has been engaged to represent the Patricia Herzog Advertising Agency, Inc., in the purchase of a building owned by Russell Craig at a minimum fee of $825. Case No. 216. Received a check for $150 as a retainer.

Received an invoice for $98.22 from the Kaderli Stationery Company, 1011 Fifth Avenue, City, for stationery and supplies.

> Since Andersen's books are kept on the cash basis, invoices for expenses are not recorded until they are paid. When expense invoices are received, they are filed in an invoice file until they are paid. When payment is made, the proper entry is made in the combination journal.

Friday, December 9

Received a check for $528.15 from Barbara A. Newell in payment of the amount due on Collection No. 34.

The collection docket shows that Andersen had agreed to handle this collection on a 33⅓% commission basis. The transaction was entered in the combination journal by debiting Cash, Account No. 111, for $176.05, and by debiting Clients' Trust Account, Account No. 121, for $352.10, for the amount due to the Walter Schadler Co. Liability for Trust Funds, Account No. 321, was credited for $352.10, and Collection Fees Revenue, Account No. 621, was credited for $176.05, the amount of the commission earned. A memorandum entry was also made in the collection docket for the amount received from the debtor.

END-OF-WEEK WORK

(1) Proved the footings of the combination journal. **(2)** Compared the balance in Account No. 111 in the combination journal with the balance in the checkbook ($23,452.45). Deposits of cash receipts have been made in the First National Bank in Accounts No. 111 and No. 121 on the day of receipts and the amounts of the deposits have been entered in the checkbook kept for each account. **(3)** Completed the individual postings from the General Debit and Credit columns of the combination journal to the ledger accounts. As each item was posted, the account number was entered in the Posting Reference column of the combination journal and the page number of the combination journal was entered in the Posting Reference column of the account.

Monday, December 12

Issued Check No. 724 for $729.28 to the National Law Book Company for law books.

Tuesday, December 13

Issued Check No. 725 for $50 to the Christmas Bureau Fund.

The check is recorded in the combination journal by debiting Charitable Contributions Expense, Account No. 703, and crediting Cash, Account No. 111.

Received $100 from the Zeisler and Young Supply Co. for preparing and filing a mechanic's lien on the property of Dwight L. Lindner.

Wednesday, December 14

Issued Check No. 726 for $100 to the State Bar Association for annual dues.

The amount of this check was debited to Miscellaneous Expense, Account No. 709.

Received $125 from Rose Chan for preparing a lease on office space in a building owned by Chan.

Issued Check No. 727 for $652.92 to the First National Bank in payment of the following payroll taxes based on wages paid during the month of November:

Employees' income tax withheld from wages		$336.80
FICA tax:		
Withheld from employees' wages	$158.06	
Imposed on employer	158.06	316.12
Amount of check		$652.92

A Federal Tax Deposit, Form No. 501, was filled out and sent with the check. Andersen will not be required to pay the balance in the FUTA tax payable account until January.

Andersen telephoned the First National Bank and learned that the check for $528.15 received from Barbara A. Newell had cleared. Issued Check No. 58 to the Walter Schadler Co. in the amount of $352.10 which represents the full amount of Collection No. 34 ($528.15 less a 33⅓% collection fee, $176.05).

The transaction was recorded in the combination journal by debiting Liability for Trust Funds, Account No. 321, for $352.10, and by crediting Clients' Trust Account, Account No. 121, for the same amount. The collection fee had been recorded at the time the remittance was received from the debtor. A memorandum entry, however, was made in the collection docket to record the amount paid to the creditor. Since the claim was settled in full, the following information was entered in the upper right-hand corner of the collection docket: (1) the date the case was disposed of, (2) the total amount collected, (3) the total amount of the attorney's fees, (4) the amount sent to the client, and (5) the check number.

Thursday, December 15

Issued the following checks in payment of salaries for the first half of the month:

No. 728 for $411.44 to Gertrude Ryan, part-time law clerk, in payment of her salary in the amount of $528.00, less $79.60 withheld for income tax and $36.96 withheld for FICA tax.

No. 729 for $487.65 to Patricia Stearns, the office secretary, in payment of her salary in the amount of $625.00, less $93.60 withheld for income tax and $43.75 withheld for FICA tax.

Received a check for $2,225 from Hubbard Tool Company, 415 Sage Avenue, City, in full payment of Case No. 209.

This remittance is in payment of the balance due for legal fees, $2,000, and $225 for payment for work done by an accountant paid by Andersen on November 10 and debited to Advances on Behalf of Clients.

The check was recorded in the combination journal by debiting Cash, Account No. 111, for $2,225, by crediting Advances on Behalf of Clients, Account No. 131, for $225, and by crediting Legal Fees Revenue, Account No. 611, for $2,000.

Friday, December 16

Andersen withdrew $2,000 for personal use. Check No. 730.

The check was recorded in the combination journal by debiting Karl F. Andersen, Drawing, Account No. 512, and by crediting Cash.

END-OF-WEEK WORK

(1) Proved the footings of the combination journal. **(2)** Compared the cash balance in Account No. 111 in the combination journal with the balance in the checkbook ($21,471.16). **(3)** Completed the individual postings from the General Debit and Credit columns of the combination journal to the ledger accounts.

Monday, December 19

Issued Check No. 731 for $98.22 to the Kaderli Stationery Company in payment of the invoice received on December 8.

Office Supplies Expense is debited.

Andersen completed the work he had been doing on the settlement of the estate of Charles R. Rolfsen, deceased, and received a check for $8,500 in payment of his services. Case No. 198.

Tuesday, December 20

Received $75 from Louise Haines for drawing a will.

Wednesday, December 21

Andersen has been engaged to represent the Santini Manufacturing Co. in the purchase of a building owned by Harris Jergens at a minimum fee of $1,500. Case No. 217. Received a check for $100 as a retainer and also received a check for $4,000 as a deposit on the purchase price of the building.

This transaction was recorded by debiting Cash, Account No. 111, for $100, and by crediting Legal Fees Revenue, Account No. 611, for $100. Also, Clients' Trust Account, Account No. 121, was debited for $4,000, and Liability for Trust Funds, Account No. 321, was credited for $4,000.

Issued Check No. 732 for $839.54 to Montague Office Equipment Company in payment for a new electric typewriter.

This transaction was recorded in the combination journal by debiting Office Equipment, Account No. 221, and crediting Cash, Account No. 111.

Received a check for $300 from John N. Holland to apply on his account with the Newton Department Store. Collection No. 36.

> This transaction was recorded in the combination journal by debiting Cash, Account No. 111, for $100, and by debiting Clients' Trust Account, Account No. 121, for $200 for the amount due the Newton Department Store. Liability for Trust Funds, Account No. 321, was credited for $200, and Collection Fees Revenue, Account No. 621, was credited for $100, the amount of the commission earned. A memorandum entry was also made in the collection docket for the amount received from the debtor.

Thursday, December 22

Received a check for $675 from the Patricia Herzog Advertising Agency, Inc., in payment of the balance due for legal work done in connection with the purchase of a building. Case No. 216.

Friday, December 23

Frieda Klein, 3415 Lawrence Avenue, City, has engaged Andersen to handle the incorporation of an insurance agency. Minimum fee, $750. A check for $100 was received as a retainer. Case No. 218.

Received an invoice for $84.70 from the Legal Supply Co., 220 Fifth Avenue, New York City, for legal forms.

> Legal forms used by an attorney are an expense, and invoices for expenses are recorded only when paid in cash.

END-OF-WEEK WORK

(1) Proved the footings of the combination journal. **(2)** Compared the cash balance in Account No. 111 in the combination journal with the balance in the checkbook ($30,083.40). **(3)** Completed the individual postings from the General Debit and Credit columns of the combination journal to the ledger accounts.

Tuesday, December 27

Received a check for $560 from the Acme Products Co. in payment of the balance due on account. Case No. 215.

> The check was recorded in the combination journal by debiting Cash, Account No. 111, for $560, by crediting Advances on Behalf of Clients, Account No. 131, for $10, and by crediting Legal Fees Revenue, Account No. 611, for $550.

Andersen directed that Check No. 733 for $110.83 be issued to the Jordan Department Store in payment of his personal account.

> Since this transaction is a disbursement in payment of a personal account of Andersen, it was recorded in the combination journal by debiting Karl F. Andersen, Drawing, Account No. 512, and by crediting Cash, Account No. 111.

Received a check for $200 from Wilma Peterson for a title search of a house Peterson wishes to buy.

Wednesday, December 28

Issued Check No. 734 for $375 to S. A. Justice, CPA, in payment of her statement covering accounting services rendered to Andersen's client, W. J. Broderick. Case No. 213.

Received a check in the amount of $250 from A. J. Colina in settlement of account. Case No. 211.

Issued Check No. 59 for $200 to the Newton Department Store to remit a partial collection from John N. Holland in the amount of $300, less a 33⅓% collection fee. Collection No. 36.

> The transaction was recorded in the combination journal by debiting Liability for Trust Funds, Account No. 321, for $200, and by crediting Clients' Trust Account, Account No. 121, for $200. A memorandum entry was made in the collection docket to record the amount paid to the creditor.

Thursday, December 29

Andersen withdrew $2,500 for personal use. Check No. 735.

Friday, December 30

Issued the following checks in payment of salaries for the second half of the month:

No. 736 for $376.40 to Gertrude Ryan, part-time law clerk, in payment of her salary in the amount of $480.00, less $70.00 withheld for income tax and $33.60 withheld for FICA tax.

No. 737 for $487.65 to Patricia Stearns, the office secretary, in payment of her salary in the amount of $625.00, less $93.60 withheld for income tax and $43.75 for FICA tax.

Issued Check No. 738 for $64.31 to replenish the petty cash fund.

The following statement provided the information needed in recording this transaction in the combination journal:

STATEMENT OF PETTY CASH DISBURSEMENTS FOR DECEMBER	
Advances on Behalf of Clients	$10.00
Karl F. Andersen, Drawing	11.57
Automobile Expense	19.94
Charitable Contributions Expense	10.00
Miscellaneous Expense	6.85
Office Supplies Expense	5.95
Total disbursements	$64.31

Made an entry in the combination journal for the employer's portion of the FICA tax for the month of December by debiting Payroll Taxes Expense and by crediting FICA Tax Payable for $158.06.

Accounting for Personal Service (Attorneys) — Chapter 5

PAGE 42 — COMBINATION JOURNAL

#	Cash Deposits 111 Dr.	Cash Checks 111 Cr.	Ck. No.	Day	Description	Post. Ref.	#
1					Amounts Forwarded 20,164.36		1
2		900 00	720	1	Rent Expense	715	2
3	200 00			1	Acme Products Co. - Case #215	✓	3
4		55 25	721	2	Miscellaneous Expense	709	4
5	250 00			2	R. Shipley - Trust Agreement	✓	5
6		63 89	722	5	Telephone Expense	720	6
7	1500 00			5	E. A. Elbrecht - Case #210	✓	7
8	1540 00			6	Polinsky Mfg. Co. - Case #212	✓	8
9		158 82	723	6	Automobile Expense	701	9
10	400 00			6	R. E. Coughlin - Estate Plan. Conf.	✓	10
11	250 00			7	Reichert & Sullivan - Partnership Agree.	✓	11
12	150 00			8	P. Herzog Advt. - Case #216	✓	12
13	176 05			9	Clients' Trust Account - Coll. #34	121	13
14					Liability for Trust Funds 23,452.45	321	14
15	4466 05	1177 96					15
		729 28	724	12	Law Library Expense	708	
16		50 00	725	13	Charitable Contributions Exp.	703	16
17	100 00			13	Zeisler & Young Supply Co. - Mech. Lien	✓	17
18		100 00	726	14	Miscellaneous Expense	709	18
19	125 00			14	R. Chan - Lease	✓	19
20		652 92	727	14	Employees Inc. Tax Payable	331	20
21					FICA Tax Payable	341	21
22				14	Liability for Trust Funds	321	22
23					Clients' Trust Account - Coll. #34	121	23
24		411 44	728	15	Salary Expense	718	24
25		487 65	729	15	Salary Expense	718	25
26	2225 00			15	Hubbard Tool Co. - Case #209	✓	26
27					Advances on Behalf of Clients	131	27
28		2000 00	730	16	Karl F. Andersen, Drawing 21,471.16	512	28
29	6916 05	5609 25					29
		98 22	731	19	Office Supplies Expense	710	
30	8500 00			19	C. R. Roljsen - Case #198	✓	30
31	75 00			20	L. Haines - Will	✓	31
32	100 00			21	Clients' Trust Account - Case #217	121	32
33					Liability for Trust Funds	321	33
34		839 54	732	21	Office Equipment	221	34
35	100 00			21	Clients' Trust Account - Coll. #36	121	35
36					Liability for Trust Funds	321	36
37	675 00			22	P. Herzog Advt. Agency - Case #216	✓	37
38	100 00			23	F. Klein - Case #218 30,083.40	✓	38
39	16466 05	6547 01					39

Karl F. Andersen — Combination Journal (left page)
(continued)

Chapter 5 Accounting for Personal Service (Attorneys) 143

FOR MONTH OF December 19 83   PAGE 42

	GENERAL DEBIT	GENERAL CREDIT	CK. NO.	LEGAL FEES 611 CR.	COLLECTION FEES 621 CR.	EMP. INC. TAX PAY. 331 CR.	FICA TAX PAY. 341 CR.	
1								1
2	900.00							2
3				200.00				3
4	55.25							4
5				250.00				5
6	63.89							6
7				1500.00				7
8				1540.00				8
9	158.82							9
10				400.00				10
11				250.00				11
12				150.00				12
13	352.10				176.05			13
14		352.10						14
15	1530.06 / 729.28	352.10		4290.00	176.05			15
16	50.00							16
17				100.00				17
18	100.00							18
19				125.00				19
20	336.80							20
21	316.12							21
22	352.10							22
23		352.10	58					23
24	528.00					79.60	36.96	24
25	625.00					93.60	43.75	25
26				2000.00				26
27		225.00						27
28	2000.00							28
29	6567.36 / 98.22	929.20		6515.00	176.05	173.20	80.71	29
30				8500.00				30
31				75.00				31
32	4000.00			100.00				32
33		4000.00						33
34	839.54							34
35	200.00				100.00			35
36		200.00						36
37				675.00				37
38				100.00				38
39	11705.12	5129.20		15965.00	276.05	173.20	80.71	39

Karl F. Andersen — Combination Journal (right page)
(continued)

PAGE 43			COMBINATION JOURNAL		
CASH DEPOSITS 111 DR.	CASH CHECKS 111 CR.	CK. NO.	DAY	DESCRIPTION	POST. REF.
16466 05	6547 01			AMOUNTS FORWARDED 30,083.40	
560 00			27	Acme Products Co. – Case #215	✓
				Advances on Behalf of Clients	131
	110 83	733	27	Karl F. Andersen, Drawing	512
200 00			27	W. Peterson – Title Search	✓
	375 00	734	28	Advances on Behalf of Clients – Case #213	131
250 00			28	A. J. Colina – Case #211	✓
			28	Liability for Trust Funds	321
				Clients' Trust Account – Case #36	121
	2500 00	735	29	Karl F. Andersen, Drawing	512
	376 40	736	30	Salary Expense	718
	487 65	737	30	Salary Expense	718
	64 31	738	30	Advances on Behalf of Clients – Case #218	131
				Karl F. Andersen, Drawing	512
				Automobile Expense	701
				Charitable Contributions Expense	703
				Miscellaneous Expense	709
				Office Supplies Expense	710
			30	Payroll Taxes Expense	712
			30	Payroll Taxes Expense	712
				FUTA Tax Payable	351
				State Unemployment Tax Payable	361
17476 05	10461 20			27,179.21	
17476 05	10461 20				
(111)	(111)				

Karl F. Andersen — Combination Journal (left page)
(concluded)

Made an entry in the combination journal for the FUTA tax in the amount of $7.06 and for the state unemployment tax in the amount of $27.22 on Ryan's December salary. Stearns' salary has exceeded $6,000 in the current year and there is no expense in the month of December for federal or state unemployment taxes on her salary.

END-OF-MONTH WORK

(1) Proved the footings, entered the totals, and ruled the combination journal. (2) Compared the bank balance in the combination

Chapter 5 Accounting for Personal Service (Attorneys) **145**

GENERAL DEBIT	GENERAL CREDIT	CK. NO.	LEGAL FEES 611 CR.	COLLECTION FEES 621 CR.	EMP. INC. TAX PAY. 331 CR.	FICA TAX PAY. 341 CR.
1170512	51 29 20		15965 00	276 05	173 20	80 71
			550 00			
	10 00					
110 83						
			200 00			
375 00						
			250 00			
200 00						
	200 00	59				
2500 00						
480 00					70 00	33 60
625 00					93 60	43 75
10 00						
11 57						
19 94						
10 00						
6 85						
5 95						
158 06						158 06
34 28						
	7 06					
	27 22					
1625260	537348		1696500	276 05	336 80	316 12
(✓)	(✓)		(611)	(621)	(331)	(341)

FOR MONTH OF *December* 1983   PAGE 43

Karl F. Andersen — Combination Journal (right page)
(concluded)

journal with the balance in the checkbook ($27,179.21). **(3)** Completed the individual postings from the General Debit and Credit columns of the combination journal to the ledger accounts.

Since this was the end of the month, the summary posting was completed, and the account numbers were written immediately below the totals of the columns in the combination journal. Compared the bank balance in Account No. 121, Clients' Trust Account ($4,000) with the balance in the checkbook maintained for that account.

A trial balance of the general ledger accounts which have balances on December 31 appears on page 150.

ACCOUNT Cash — ACCOUNT NO. 111

DATE	ITEM	POST. REF.	DEBIT	CREDIT	BALANCE DEBIT	BALANCE CREDIT
1983 Dec. 1	Balance	✓			2016436	
30		CJ43	1747605			
30		CJ43		1046120	2717921	

ACCOUNT Petty Cash Fund — ACCOUNT NO. 112

DATE	ITEM	POST. REF.	DEBIT	CREDIT	BALANCE DEBIT	BALANCE CREDIT
1983 Dec. 1	Balance	✓			7500	

ACCOUNT Clients' Trust Account — ACCOUNT NO. 121

DATE	ITEM	POST. REF.	DEBIT	CREDIT	BALANCE DEBIT	BALANCE CREDIT
1983 Dec. 9		CJ42	35210			
14		CJ42		35210		
21		CJ42	400000			
21		CJ42		20000		
28		CJ43		20000	400000	

ACCOUNT Advances on Behalf of Clients — ACCOUNT NO. 131

DATE	ITEM	POST. REF.	DEBIT	CREDIT	BALANCE DEBIT	BALANCE CREDIT
1983 Dec. 1	Balance	✓			34500	
15		CJ42		22500		
27		CJ43		1000		
28		CJ43	37500			
30		CJ43	1000		49500	

ACCOUNT Automobile — ACCOUNT NO. 211

DATE	ITEM	POST. REF.	DEBIT	CREDIT	BALANCE DEBIT	BALANCE CREDIT
1983 Dec. 1	Balance	✓			965028	

ACCOUNT Accumulated Depreciation—Automobile — ACCOUNT NO. 212

DATE	ITEM	POST. REF.	DEBIT	CREDIT	BALANCE DEBIT	BALANCE CREDIT
1983 Dec. 1	Balance	✓				361886

General Ledger Accounts (continued)

Chapter 5 — Accounting for Personal Service (Attorneys) — 147

ACCOUNT Office Equipment   **ACCOUNT NO. 221**

DATE	ITEM	POST. REF.	DEBIT	CREDIT	BALANCE DEBIT	BALANCE CREDIT
1983 Dec. 1	Balance	✓			4982 73	
21		CJ42	839 54		5822 27	

ACCOUNT Accumulated Depreciation - Office Equipment   **ACCOUNT NO. 222**

DATE	ITEM	POST. REF.	DEBIT	CREDIT	BALANCE DEBIT	BALANCE CREDIT
1983 Dec. 1	Balance	✓				1494 81

ACCOUNT Liability for Trust Funds   **ACCOUNT NO. 321**

DATE	ITEM	POST. REF.	DEBIT	CREDIT	BALANCE DEBIT	BALANCE CREDIT
1983 Dec. 9		CJ42		352 10		
14		CJ42	352 10			
21		CJ42		4000 00		
21		CJ42		200 00		
28		CJ43	200 00			4000 00

ACCOUNT Employees Income Tax Payable   **ACCOUNT NO. 331**

DATE	ITEM	POST. REF.	DEBIT	CREDIT	BALANCE DEBIT	BALANCE CREDIT
1983 Dec. 1	Balance	✓				336 80
14		CJ42	336 80			—0—
30		CJ43		336 80		336 80

ACCOUNT FICA Tax Payable   **ACCOUNT NO. 341**

DATE	ITEM	POST. REF.	DEBIT	CREDIT	BALANCE DEBIT	BALANCE CREDIT
1983 Dec. 1	Balance	✓				316 12
14		CJ42	316 12			—0—
30		CJ43		316 12		316 12

ACCOUNT FUTA Tax Payable   **ACCOUNT NO. 351**

DATE	ITEM	POST. REF.	DEBIT	CREDIT	BALANCE DEBIT	BALANCE CREDIT
1983 Dec. 1	Balance	✓				105 84
30		CJ43		7 06		112 90

General Ledger Accounts (continued)

ACCOUNT State Unemployment Tax Payable — ACCOUNT NO. 361

DATE	ITEM	POST. REF.	DEBIT	CREDIT	BALANCE DEBIT	BALANCE CREDIT
1983 Dec. 1	Balance	✓				54 43
30		CJ43		27 22		81 65

ACCOUNT Karl F. Andersen, Capital — ACCOUNT NO. 511

DATE	ITEM	POST. REF.	DEBIT	CREDIT	BALANCE DEBIT	BALANCE CREDIT
1983 Dec. 1	Balance	✓				18542 39

ACCOUNT Karl F. Andersen, Drawing — ACCOUNT NO. 512

DATE	ITEM	POST. REF.	DEBIT	CREDIT	BALANCE DEBIT	BALANCE CREDIT
1983 Dec. 1	Balance	✓			54760 68	
16		CJ42	2000 00			
27		CJ43	110 83			
29		CJ43	2500 00			
30		CJ43	11 57		59383 08	

ACCOUNT Expense and Revenue Summary — ACCOUNT NO. 521

DATE	ITEM	POST. REF.	DEBIT	CREDIT	BALANCE DEBIT	BALANCE CREDIT

ACCOUNT Legal Fees Revenue — ACCOUNT NO. 611

DATE	ITEM	POST. REF.	DEBIT	CREDIT	BALANCE DEBIT	BALANCE CREDIT
1983 Dec. 1	Balance	✓				109908 00
30		CJ43		16965 00		126873 00

ACCOUNT Collection Fees Revenue — ACCOUNT NO. 621

DATE	ITEM	POST. REF.	DEBIT	CREDIT	BALANCE DEBIT	BALANCE CREDIT
1983 Dec. 1	Balance	✓				4731 99
30		CJ43		276 05		5008 04

General Ledger Accounts (continued)

Chapter 5 — Accounting for Personal Service (Attorneys)

ACCOUNT Automobile Expense **ACCOUNT NO. 701**

DATE	ITEM	POST. REF.	DEBIT	CREDIT	BALANCE DEBIT	BALANCE CREDIT
1988 Dec. 1	Balance	✓			3534 37	
6		CJ42	158 82			
30		CJ43	19 94		3713 13	

ACCOUNT Charitable Contributions Expense **ACCOUNT NO. 703**

DATE	ITEM	POST. REF.	DEBIT	CREDIT	BALANCE DEBIT	BALANCE CREDIT
1988 Dec. 1	Balance	✓			934 00	
13		CJ42	50 00			
30		CJ43	10 00		994 00	

ACCOUNT Depreciation Expense **ACCOUNT NO. 705**

DATE	ITEM	POST. REF.	DEBIT	CREDIT	BALANCE DEBIT	BALANCE CREDIT

ACCOUNT Law Library Expense **ACCOUNT NO. 708**

DATE	ITEM	POST. REF.	DEBIT	CREDIT	BALANCE DEBIT	BALANCE CREDIT
1988 Dec. 1	Balance	✓			3375 00	
12		CJ42	729 28		4104 28	

ACCOUNT Miscellaneous Expense **ACCOUNT NO. 709**

DATE	ITEM	POST. REF.	DEBIT	CREDIT	BALANCE DEBIT	BALANCE CREDIT
1988 Dec. 1	Balance	✓			502 38	
2		CJ42	55 25			
14		CJ42	100 00			
30		CJ43	6 85		664 48	

ACCOUNT Office Supplies Expense **ACCOUNT NO. 710**

DATE	ITEM	POST. REF.	DEBIT	CREDIT	BALANCE DEBIT	BALANCE CREDIT
1988 Dec. 1	Balance	✓			2859 42	
19		CJ42	98 22			
30		CJ43	5 95		2963 59	

General Ledger Accounts *(continued)*

Payroll Taxes Expense — Account No. 712

DATE	ITEM	POST. REF.	DEBIT	CREDIT	BALANCE DEBIT	BALANCE CREDIT
1983 Dec. 1	Balance	✓			2266.18	
30		CJ43	158.06			
30		CJ43	34.28		2458.52	

Rent Expense — Account No. 715

DATE	ITEM	POST. REF.	DEBIT	CREDIT	BALANCE DEBIT	BALANCE CREDIT
1983 Dec. 1	Balance	✓			9900.00	
1		CJ42	900.00		10800.00	

General Ledger Accounts *(continued)*

KARL F. ANDERSEN, ATTORNEY AT LAW
Trial Balance
December 31, 1983

Account	No.	Debit	Credit
Cash	111	27,179.21	
Petty Cash Fund	112	75.00	
Clients' Trust Account	121	4,000.00	
Advances on Behalf of Clients	131	495.00	
Automobile	211	9,650.28	
Accumulated Depreciation — Automobile	212		3,618.86
Office Equipment	221	5,822.27	
Accumulated Depreciation — Office Equipment	222		1,494.81
Liability for Trust Funds	321		4,000.00
Employees Income Tax Payable	331		336.80
FICA Tax Payable	341		316.12
FUTA Tax Payable	351		112.90
State Unemployment Tax Payable	361		81.65
Karl F. Andersen, Capital	511		18,542.39
Karl F. Andersen, Drawing	512	59,383.08	
Legal Fees Revenue	611		126,873.00
Collection Fees Revenue	621		5,008.04
Automobile Expense	701	3,713.13	
Charitable Contributions Expense	703	994.00	
Law Library Expense	708	4,104.28	
Miscellaneous Expense	709	664.48	
Office Supplies Expense	710	2,963.59	
Payroll Taxes Expense	712	2,458.52	
Rent Expense	715	10,800.00	
Salary Expense	718	27,288.00	
Telephone Expense	720	793.73	
		160,384.57	160,384.57

Chapter 5   Accounting for Personal Service (Attorneys)

ACCOUNT: Salary Expense						ACCOUNT NO. 718	
DATE	ITEM	POST. REF.	DEBIT	CREDIT	BALANCE DEBIT	BALANCE CREDIT	
1983 Dec. 1	Balance	✓			25 030 00		
15		CJ42	528 00				
15		CJ42	625 00				
30		CJ43	480 00				
30		CJ43	625 00		27 288 00		

ACCOUNT: Telephone Expense						ACCOUNT NO. 720	
DATE	ITEM	POST. REF.	DEBIT	CREDIT	BALANCE DEBIT	BALANCE CREDIT	
1983 Dec. 1	Balance	✓			729 84		
5		CJ42	63 89		793 73		

General Ledger Accounts *(concluded)*

BUILDING YOUR ACCOUNTING KNOWLEDGE

1. Why is time the most valuable asset an attorney has?
2. What is meant by nonchargeable time?
3. Why does the cash basis of accounting violate the matching principle?
4. Why cannot accounting be based completely on cash transactions?
5. What is meant by constructive receipt of revenue?
6. What is the purpose of depreciation?
7. Will the balance in the Clients' Trust Account, Account No. 121, and the balance in Account No. 321, Liability for Trust Funds, always be the same?
8. Why will special columns for specific items in a special column journal save time and labor in the bookkeeping process?

Report No. 5-1

> Complete Report No. 5-1 in the study assignments and submit your working papers to the instructor for approval. After completing the report, you may continue with the textbook discussion in Chapter 6 until the next report is required.

EXPANDING YOUR BUSINESS VOCABULARY

What is the meaning of each of the following terms:

accumulated depreciation (p. 127)
auxiliary records (p. 131)
balance-column account form (p. 131)
book value (p. 127)
business enterprises (p. 125)
cash basis of accounting (p. 126)
collection docket (p. 132)
combination journal (p. 130)
constructively received (p. 127)
contra accounts (p. 127)
defendant (p. 126)

depreciate (p. 127)
depreciation expense (p. 127)
general ledger (p. 131)
manufacturing enterprise (p. 125)
matching principle (p. 126)
mercantile enterprise (p. 125)
office docket (p. 132)
personal service enterprise (p. 125)
plaintiff (p. 126)
professional enterprises (p. 125)
time records (p. 126)

APPENDIX

THE PROFESSIONAL CORPORATION

Organizing a Professional Corporation

In Chapter 5, Andersen's legal practice is operated as a sole proprietorship, but he could have incorporated his practice. The designation of the corporate practice will vary with the state in which the practice is conducted. In one state the name of the corporation might be Karl F. Andersen, P.S.C. The letters P.S.C. stand for Professional Service Corporation. If attorneys John Woods, Nancy Cartwright, and Ralph Steiger decided to form a corporation for the practice of law in another state, the firm might be known as Woods, Cartwright, and Steiger Co. LPA. The letters LPA stand for Lawyers Professional Association.

In 1819 in the Dartmouth College case, John Marshall, then Chief Justice of the United States Supreme Court, described a corporation as follows:

> "A corporation is an artificial being, invisible, intangible, and existing only in contemplation of law."

The definition draws attention to the fact that corporations possess legal entity which means that they are separate and distinct from their owners. All corporations operate under a grant of authority from a state or other political unit in the form of articles of incorporation. The articles of incorporation is the document prepared by the person or persons establishing a corporation in the United States and filed with state authorities. One copy, returned with a certificate of incorporation, becomes the corporate charter, and enables the corporation to function. In the United States, each of the states, territories, and possessions has its own general- or business-corporation act and also an act which permits some or all licensed professional persons to form professional associations or corporations.

In many states the form of the certificate of incorporation for a professional corporation is essentially the same as that required for a business corporation, but in other states specific forms are required for professional corporations. In all states, the articles of incorporation must spell out the corporation's purpose, and in most states a professional corporation can be created only for the purpose of conducting a specific professional practice. Usually, a law corporation cannot carry on an engineering practice, and a medical practice cannot operate an accounting practice. Most states require that a professional corporation be incorporated in the state in which it is to carry on its practice. A business corporation, however, may be incorporated under the laws of one state and operate exclusively in another state.

The articles of incorporation must indicate the location of the corporate office and must designate the corporate name which in professional corporations usually includes the name of one or more of the professionals involved. In many states, the use of fictitious names by professional corporations is prohibited. Before the articles of incorporation are filed with the state, the corporate name should be checked, because the name must not be the same as the name used by any other business organization.

Another item that must be included in the articles of incorporation is the number of shares of capital stock that the corporation is authorized to issue. Ownership of a corporation is represented by shares of capital stock each share of which might be assigned a par value such as $100 or there might be no par value at the time the corporation is formed. Authorization of more shares than will be issued immediately upon formation of the corporation may be requested. The unissued shares can be held in the corporate treasury for future use.

A small corporation with one or two or three stockholders does not need a board of directors, but the articles of incorporation of a large medical practice, for example, should provide that a board of directors is to be responsible for the management of the affairs of the corporation. The board of directors is a group of persons elected by the stockholders to determine corporate policies and select the officers who will manage the corporation.

In some states cumulative voting by the stockholders for directors of the corporation is mandatory and even if it is not required, it may be provided for in the articles of incorporation. Under cumulative voting, a stockholder is permitted to cast all of his or her votes for a single director. For example, if a stockholder has 100 shares of stock and there are seven directors to be elected, he or she can cast 700 votes for just one director. An advantage of cumulative voting is that it may enable a minority stockholder to elect a director. A minority stockholder is one who owns less than a majority of the number of shares of stock of the corporation.

The articles of incorporation should list the basic powers of the corporation. Among those usually stated are that the corporation will have the power to conduct its business or practice and carry on its operations; to elect or appoint officers and fix compensation; to sue and be sued; and to make and alter bylaws.

A professional corporation may have bylaws, but they may not be required by state law. The authority to adopt or amend bylaws may be given to the board of directors by the certificate of incorporation. In other cases, the bylaws must be adopted or amended by the stockholders.

The purpose of bylaws is to provide details concerning how the practice is to be operated. Some items such as the location of the principal office will be included in both the articles of incorporation and in the bylaws but such items as the date and location of the annual stockholders' meeting will be found only in the bylaws. The bylaws should identify the officers of the corporation and state their qualifications. If the corporation consists of only one person, he or she may serve as the president and treasurer of the corporation. A small corporation having more than one stockholder may need only a president, secretary, and treasurer. A larger corporation may have a chairman of the board of directors, one or more vice presidents, a recording secretary, a controller, and an attorney who serves as general counsel.

The certificate of incorporation which has been approved by the state granting it is a matter of public record, and if it later becomes necessary to change the certificate, approval must be given by the state. The bylaws of the corporation are private records and any of the details in them can be changed or repealed through the use of a procedure usually stated in the bylaws themselves.

Characteristics of the Corporate Form of Organization

Some of the characteristics of the corporate form of organization are described in the following paragraphs.

Limited Liability of Owners. The owners of a corporation invest in the corporation by purchasing shares of stock. The stockholders cannot be compelled to contribute additional capital to the corporation if the stock is fully paid for at the time of issuance. The stockholders have no personal liability for the debts of the corporation. A sole proprietor such as Karl F. Andersen has unlimited personal liability for the debts of his legal practice.

Transferable Ownership Units. In a business corporation any stockholder can usually transfer stock to another person or company without the knowledge or the consent of the other stockholders and without disturbing the normal activities of the corporation. In most states, however, trading of the capital stock of a professional corporation is strictly limited. The limitations are necessary to permit the stockholders to control their future associates and to insure that no stockholder will sell his or her stock to an individual who is not a licensed member of the profession. An engineer or a certified public accountant, for example, would not be permitted to buy the capital stock of the firm incorporated as Woods, Cartwright, and Steiger Co., LPA.

Unlimited Life. Most corporations are chartered either with a perpetual life or with provision for renewal if the charter specifies a limit, irrespective of the deaths of any stockholders or disposal of their stock. In some states, the duration of a professional corporation is limited; in others the duration may be perpetual. If the duration of the corporation is to be perpetual, this should be stated in the articles of incorporation.

Suitability for Large Scale Operations. Certain businesses such as large manufacturing companies must be operated on a large scale. The corporate form of organization makes it possible to secure substantial amounts of capital through the sale of stock. Large numbers of investors in the stock of corporations provide much of the capital required for their operation. The corporate form of organization is also suitable in many cases for persons who desire to form professional corporations.

Access to Stockholder and Employee Fringe Benefits. Some of the benefits that a professional person or persons may obtain by incorporating are being able to obtain group term life insurance, health and accident insurance, wage continuation, and medical reimbursement plans.

Taxation of Corporate Earnings. With regard to income taxes, there are advantages and disadvantages in the corporate form of organization. Corporations must pay income taxes on their earnings, and the individual stockholders of corporations are subject to personal income tax on the dividends they receive from their companies. A dividend is usually paid in cash and, in most cases, represents taxable income. A tax advantage of a corporation is that dividends do not have to be declared and paid and the earnings may be allowed to accumulate in the corporation within certain limits. Sole proprietorships and partnerships, as such, do not pay income taxes. Instead, the owner or partner reports his or her share of the net income or the net loss from the business or practice in his or her personal income tax return.

Lack of the Drawing Account. In accounting for a sole proprietorship the owner has both a capital account and a drawing account. In lieu of a salary paid by the enterprise, the owner can withdraw funds from the business or practice at will. Since the corporation is a legal entity separate from the owner or owners, professional persons who incorporate their practices become employees of the corporation. They are paid salaries which are subject to all the payroll taxes to which an employee who is not a stockholder is subject. If a professional person wishes to withdraw funds from the practice in excess of his or her salary, the transaction would have to be either in the form of a loan or of a sale of all or a part of the individual's stock in the practice. The sale of the stock in a professional corporation would be subject to the legal requirements of the state in which the corporation is located.

Government Regulation. A further disadvantage of the corporate form of organization is the restriction of freedom to act. Federal, state, and local governments may restrict the corporation's ownership of real property, the purchase of its own stock, and the excessive retention of its earnings.

The following paragraphs are presented to illustrate the accounting for a firm of three attorneys who have chosen to operate their practice as a professional corporation.

Attorneys John Woods, Nancy Cartwright, and Ralph Steiger combined their individual practices and applied for a certificate of incorporation. The certificate was received from the state on January 4, 1982, and permits them to practice law as a professional corporation to be known as Woods, Cartwright, and Steiger Co., LPA. At a meeting on January 2, 1982, it was agreed that John Woods would be president of the corporation; Nancy Cartwright would be the treasurer; and Ralph Steiger would be the secretary. The fiscal year will be the calendar year. The firm will operate on the cash basis of accounting with the following exceptions. Property or service received in lieu of cash will be recorded at the fair market value of the property or service at the time it is received. Revenue constructively received will be reported as revenue in the period in which it is earned even though no cash is withdrawn from the account, and long-term assets will be depreciated.

The authorized capital stock of the firm on January 4, 1982, consists of 2,500 shares with a value of $25 each for a total of $62,500. The following number of shares have been issued to the incorporators:

John Woods	800 shares at $25 = $20,000
Nancy Cartwright	700 shares at $25 = 17,500
Ralph Steiger	500 shares at $25 = 12,500
	2,000 $50,000

The remaining 500 shares are unissued and do not appear in the firm's accounts.

Accounts used only in a corporation are discussed in the following paragraphs.

Dividends Payable, Account No. 371. Earnings of a corporation are transmitted to the stockholders through the declaration of dividends. The declaration must state the amount of dividend per share to be paid. Payment may be made immediately upon declaration, or it may be deferred until a later date. When the payment is deferred, a current liability called Dividends Payable is created.

Corporation Income Tax Payable, Account No. 381. If a corporation operates at a profit, it must pay a tax on its earnings. Unpaid corporation income taxes are a liability of the corporation.

Common Stock, Account No. 511. All corporations operated for profit have capital stock. If there is only one class of stock, it is called common. Note that even though there are three stockholders in the firm of Woods, Cartwright, and Steiger Co., LPA, there is only one common stock account. The firm keeps a subsidiary ledger which contains an account for each stockholder in number of shares only. John Woods' account is shown on page 158.

STOCKHOLDERS LEDGER

STOCKHOLDER: John Woods
ADDRESS: 1225 Oakland Avenue, City

DATE	CERTIFICATE NOS. OLD	CERTIFICATE NOS. NEW	RECEIVED FROM	TRANSFERRED TO	NO. OF SHARES	BALANCE
1982 Jan. 2		1	Original Issue		800	800

Retained Earnings, Account No. 512. At the end of the fiscal year, the earnings of the corporation are determined and credited in the retained earnings account. When dividends are declared, the retained earnings account is debited. The account is also debited for a net loss.

Income Tax Expense, Account No. 706. The 1981 Economic Recovery Tax Act requires that corporations make quarterly estimated tax payments totaling at least 80 percent of the tax due for the year or face penalties for underpayments. Woods, Cartwright, and Steiger Co., LPA, has estimated the 1983 earnings and has paid three-fourths of the amount prior to December 1, 1983.

Following is a narrative of selected transactions completed by Woods, Cartwright, and Steiger Co., LPA, during the months of January 1982 and March 1983. These transactions are recorded in the combination journal shown below and on pages 159–161.

WOODS, CARTWRIGHT, AND STEIGER CO., LPA
Narrative of Transactions
Monday, January 4, 1982

Received cash from the incorporators as follows: John Woods, $20,000; Nancy Cartwright, $17,500; Ralph Steiger, $12,500.

The transaction was recorded in the combination journal by debiting Cash, Account No. 111, for $50,000, and crediting Common Stock, Account No. 511, for $50,000.

COMBINATION JOURNAL

PAGE 1

CASH DEPOSITS 111 DR.	CASH CHECKS 111 CR.	CK. NO.	DAY	DESCRIPTION	POST. REF.
				AMOUNTS FORWARDED	
50000 00			4	Common Stock	511

Combination Journal (left page)

Monday, March 4, 1983

The firm voted to pay a cash dividend of $5 per share to be paid on March 25 to stockholders of record on March 15.

The entry was recorded in the combination journal by debiting Retained Earnings, Account No. 512, for $10,000 and crediting Dividends Payable, Account No. 371, for $10,000. There are 2,000 shares in the hands of the stockholders and 2,000 × $5 = $10,000. The record date, March 15, means that the dividend will be paid to the persons who own the stock on that date. Dividends may also be paid on the date of declaration.

Friday, March 25, 1983

Issued the following checks in payment of the dividend declared on March 4:

No. 531 for $4,000 to John Woods (800 shares × $5).
No. 532 for $3,500 to Nancy Cartwright (700 shares × $5).
No. 533 for $2,500 to Ralph Steiger (500 shares × $5).

The checks were recorded in the combination journal by debiting Dividends Payable, Account No. 371, and crediting Cash, Account No. 111.

Tuesday, March 29, 1983

Received $2,500 from John Woods for the purchase of 100 of the 500 shares of unissued stock at $25 a share.

This transaction was recorded in the combination journal by debiting Cash, Account No. 111, for $2,500 and by crediting Common Stock, Account No. 511, for $2,500. One hundred shares was entered in Woods' account in the stockholders' ledger.

Thursday, March 31, 1983

Issued the following checks in payment of salaries for the month of March:

No. 534 for $1,042.70 to Jane Adams in the amount of $1,300.00 less $91.00 withheld for FICA tax and $166.30 withheld for income tax.

No. 535 for $896.70 to Laura Jahnke in the amount of $1,100.00

Combination Journal (right page)

PAGE 29 — COMBINATION JOURNAL

Cash Deposits 111 DR.	Cash Checks 111 CR.	CK. NO.	DAY	DESCRIPTION	POST. REF.
				AMOUNTS FORWARDED	
			4	Retained Earnings	512
				Dividends Payable	371
	4 000 00	531	25	Dividends Payable	371
	3 500 00	532	25	Dividends Payable	371
	2 500 00	533	25	Dividends Payable	371
2 500 00			29	Common Stock	511
	1 042 70	534	31	Salary Expense	718
	896 70	535	31	Salary Expense	718
	780 40	536	31	Salary Expense	718
	1 600 40	537	31	Salary Expense	718
	1 321 50	538	31	Salary Expense	718
	1 117 70	539	31	Salary Expense	718
2 500 00	16 759 40				
(111)	(111)				

Combination Journal (left page)

less $77.00 withheld for FICA tax and $126.30 withheld for income tax.

No. 536 for $780.40 to Carla Wagner in the amount of $1,000.00 less $70.00 withheld for FICA tax and $149.60 withheld for income tax.

No. 537 for $1,600.40 to John Woods in the amount of $2,000.00 less $140.00 withheld for FICA tax and $259.60 withheld for income tax.

ACCOUNT Cash — ACCOUNT NO. 111

DATE	ITEM	POST. REF.	DEBIT	CREDIT	BALANCE DEBIT	BALANCE CREDIT
1982 Jan. 4		CJ1	50 000 00		50 000 00	
1983 Mar. 1	Balance	✓			48 862 92	
31		CJ29	2 500 00			
31		CJ29		16 759 40	34 603 52	

General Ledger (continued)

Combination Journal (right page)

No. 538 for $1,321.50 to Nancy Cartwright in the amount of $1,800.00 less $126.00 withheld for FICA tax and $352.50 withheld for income tax.

No. 539 for $1,117.70 to Ralph Steiger in the amount of $1,500.00 less $105.00 withheld for FICA tax and $277.30 withheld for income tax.

General Ledger (continued)

Dividends Payable — Account No. 371

DATE	ITEM	POST. REF.	DEBIT	CREDIT	BALANCE DEBIT	BALANCE CREDIT
1983 Mar. 4		CJ29		1000000		1000000
25		CJ29	400000			
		CJ29	350000			
		CJ29	250000			0

Common Stock — Account No. 511

DATE	ITEM	POST. REF.	DEBIT	CREDIT	BALANCE DEBIT	BALANCE CREDIT
1982 Jan. 4		CJ1		5000000		5000000
1983 Mar. 29		CJ29		250000		5250000

Retained Earnings — Account No. 512

DATE	ITEM	POST. REF.	DEBIT	CREDIT	BALANCE DEBIT	BALANCE CREDIT
1983 Mar. 1	Balance	✓				2052138
4		CJ29	1000000			1052138

Salary Expense — Account No. 718

DATE	ITEM	POST. REF.	DEBIT	CREDIT	BALANCE DEBIT	BALANCE CREDIT
1983 Mar. 31		CJ29	130000			
		CJ29	110000			
		CJ29	100000			
		CJ29	200000			
		CJ29	180000			
		CJ29	150000		870000	

General Ledger (concluded)

6

ACCOUNTING FOR PERSONAL SERVICE (PHYSICIANS AND DENTISTS)

CHAPTER OBJECTIVES

The objectives of this chapter are to enable you:
▶ To define terms used in accounting for a physician or dentist who uses the cash basis of accounting.
▶ To understand the special characteristics of accounting for physicians and dentists.
▶ To perform the tasks involved in accounting for physicians and dentists.

Accounting for physicians and dentists has much in common with accounting for attorneys. Indeed there are many similarities in accounting for any type of personal service whether professional or business; but each type of service also has its own peculiarities. Some of the items peculiar to accounting for physicians or dentists will be explained in this chapter.

As with attorneys, the most valuable asset the physician or dentist has is time. A **daily service record** should be kept showing as a minimum the name of the patient, the kind of service, and the charge to the patient's account or the amount of cash received.

THE CASH BASIS OF ACCOUNTING FOR PHYSICIANS AND DENTISTS

Most physicians and dentists use the cash basis of accounting. Usually income is not recognized until cash is received and expenses are not recorded until they are paid. The revenue for services performed in one month may be accounted for in a later month, and expenses incurred in one month may be paid in the following month, or sometimes several months later.

Chart of Accounts

As a means of explaining some of the peculiarities of accounting for persons in the medical and dental professions, a system of accounts for James Kennedy and Erica Weiss, physicians and surgeons, is presented. The chart of accounts appears on page 165. All asset accounts have numbers beginning with 1; liability accounts begin with 2; owners' equity accounts begin with 3; revenue accounts begin with 4; and expense accounts begin with 5. If new accounts are needed, they may be added without disturbing the numerical order of the existing accounts.

New accounts which appear in the chart of accounts are discussed in the following paragraphs.

Prepaid Insurance, Account No. 161. The balance in the prepaid insurance account includes automobile insurance, fire and casualty insurance on the equipment, and medical liability insurance. **Prepaid insurance** is similar to the equipment items in that as time passes, both become expense.

Professional Fees, Account No. 411. Kennedy and Weiss use only one general ledger account in which to record their professional fees. In the daily service record there are columns headed Office Calls and Surgery. The totals of these columns at the end of the month will show the amounts entered for office calls and for surgery. If it is desired, separate revenue accounts could be kept for as many types of service as are rendered. For example, office calls might be assigned the number 411, surgery the number 412, and laboratory work the number 413. A dentist could use one account for professional fees, or separate accounts could be used for different types of service rendered to patients.

Medical Library Expense, Account No. 515. The number of reference books a professional person may have in a personal library will vary according to the person's needs. For example, a lawyer may require quick and easy access to a large number of references and

Chapter 6   Accounting for Personal Service (Physicians and Dentists)   165

KENNEDY AND WEISS, PHYSICIANS AND SURGEONS
CHART OF ACCOUNTS

Assets*
- 111   Cash
- 112   Petty Cash Fund
- 121   Automobiles
- 122   Accumulated Depreciation — Automobiles
- 131   Laboratory Equipment
- 132   Accumulated Depreciation — Laboratory Equipment
- 141   Medical Equipment
- 142   Accumulated Depreciation — Medical Equipment
- 151   Office Equipment
- 152   Accumulated Depreciation — Office Equipment
- 161   Prepaid Insurance

Liabilities
- 211   Employees Income Tax Payable
- 221   FICA Tax Payable
- 231   FUTA Tax Payable
- 241   State Unemployment Tax Payable

Owners' Equity
- 311   James Kennedy, Capital
- 312   James Kennedy, Drawing
- 321   Erica Weiss, Capital
- 322   Erica Weiss, Drawing
- 331   Expense and Revenue Summary

Revenue
- 411   Professional Fees

Expenses
- 501   Automobile Expense
- 503   Charitable Contributions Expense
- 505   Depreciation Expense
- 506   Dues and Subscriptions Expense
- 508   Electricity Expense
- 510   Insurance Expense
- 512   Laundry Expense
- 513   Legal Expense
- 515   Medical Library Expense
- 516   Medical Supplies Expense
- 518   Miscellaneous Expense
- 519   Office Supplies Expense
- 520   Payroll Taxes Expense
- 522   Postage Expense
- 525   Rent Expense
- 527   Repairs and Maintenance Expense
- 529   Salary Expense
- 530   Surgical Instruments Expense
- 532   Surgical Supplies Expense
- 535   Telephone Expense
- 538   Traveling and Meetings Expense

*Words in bold type represent headings and not account titles.

thus would need an extensive library. A physician, on the other hand, may have a limited number of references in a personal library if there happens to be a complete reference library at a nearby hospital. In this illustration, medical reference books are charged to expense when paid for.

Medical Supplies Expense, Account No. 516; Office Supplies Expense, Account No. 519; Surgical Instruments Expense, Account No. 530; Surgical Supplies Expense, Account No. 532. Supplies and instruments are charged to expense when paid for since they frequently need to be restocked or replaced.

Books of Account

Kennedy and Weiss use the following books of account:

(1) General books
    (a) Combination journal
    (b) General ledger
(2) Auxiliary records
    (a) Petty cash disbursements record
    (b) Daily service record
    (c) Patients ledger
    (d) Employee's earnings record
    (e) Checkbook.

Combination Journal. Kennedy and Weiss use one book of original entry, a combination journal. The combination journal, reproduced on pages 180–183, contains two money columns to the left of the Description column and six to the right of the Description column. The column headings are as listed below.

(1) Cash
    (a) Deposits 111 Dr.
    (b) Checks 111 Cr.
(2) General
    (a) Debit
    (b) Credit
(3) Professional Fees 411 Cr.
(4) Salary Expense 529 Dr.
(5) Wage Deductions
    (a) Employees Income Tax Payable 211 Cr.
    (b) FICA Tax Payable 221 Cr.

General Ledger. Kennedy and Weiss use a four-column account form for the general ledger accounts. The ledger is reproduced on pages 180 to 189. In each case, the balance as of July 1 has been entered. The accounts in the general ledger are arranged in the order given in the chart of accounts on page 165. Posting to the general ledger is from the combination journal. A trial balance is taken at the end of each month to prove the equality of the general ledger balances. The trial balance as of July 31 appears on page 190.

Auxiliary Records. Kennedy and Weiss use a petty cash disbursements record, a daily service record, a patients ledger, employees' earnings record and a checkbook as **auxiliary records**. The employee's earnings record kept for each employee is similar to the one illustrated on pages 96 and 97.

Petty Cash Disbursements Record. A petty cash fund of $100 is maintained. The petty cash disbursements record is similar to that illustrated on pages 60 and 61.

Daily Service Record. A portion of the daily service record is illustrated on page 167. Note that the daily service record is not set up as a double entry record. There is nothing to offset the Payments

Chapter 6   Accounting for Personal Service (Physicians and Dentists)   **167**

DAILY SERVICE RECORD FOR MONTH OF July 1983

Day	Name of Patient	Office Calls	Surgery	Charges	Payments	Cash Services
	Amounts Forwarded					
1	James Crowell		75 00	75 00		
1	Douglas Schacht	25 00				25 00
1	Angela Daly — S. Carl	20 00				20 00
1	Kathy Huneke		1,700 00	1,700 00		
1	Linda Russell	25 00		25 00		
5	Blue Shield — R. Skidmore				1,500 00	
5	Dan Lauber — D. Ruth		1,750 00	1,750 00		
5	Lena O'Reilly	30 00				30 00
5	Paul Drago	25 00				25 00
6	Alice Wachs	20 00				20 00
6	Robert Wyler		1,250 00	1,250 00	250 00	
6	Aetna Ins. Co. — P. Battista				1,750 00	
6	Evelyn Pratt		625 00	625 00		
6	Lucille Sartori	20 00				20 00
7	Medicare — J. Antonelli				852 00	
7	James Wu		2,000 00	2,000 00		
7	Rita Luebbe — D. Jane	25 00				25 00
7	Blue Shield — L. Strong				1,250 00	
7	David Dugan	25 00				25 00
8	Daniel Goldstein		1,300 00	1,300 00		
8	Patricia Mullaney	20 00				20 00
8	Blue Shield — M. Chen				3,100 00	
8	Raymond Barton	25 00				25 00
8	Timothy Strauss				250 00	
11	Prudential Ins. Co. — R. Wyler				1,000 00	
11	Roberta Baker		800 00	800 00		
11	Ann Lucas — S. John	30 00				30 00
11	Francis St. John				100 00	
12	Louis Massarelli	25 00		25 00		
12	Mary Smith	20 00		20 00		
12	Margaret Brown		1,300 00	1,300 00		
12	Prudential Ins. Co. — J. Wu				1,700 00	
13	Rachael Silvers	25 00				25 00
13	Margaret Auerbach		100 00	100 00		
29	Col. Penn Ins. Co.—D. Grigsby				2,100 00	
29	Ruth Bernstein	30 00				30 00
29	Medicare — R. Zimmer				180 00	
29	Cecilia Fugate		60 00	60 00		
		1,120 00	37,900 00	38,185 00	36,232 00	835 00

Daily Service Record for Month of July

column under Patients' Accounts, but the total of the Office Calls and Surgery columns must equal the total of the Patients' Charges and the Cash Services columns as shown below:

Office calls	$ 1,120	Patients' accounts charges	$38,185
Surgery	37,900	Cash services	835
	$39,020		$39,020

Each entry in the appropriate Kind of Service Column must also be entered in either the Patients' Accounts Charges or the Cash Services column. The amounts in the Charges column are posted to the Charges column in the appropriate patients ledger accounts, and the amounts in the Payments column are posted to the Payments column in the patients ledger accounts. The total cash received should be recorded in the combination journal in the Cash Deposits Dr. column and the Professional Fees Cr. column.

Patients Ledger. The patients' accounts are kept in a file known as the **patients' ledger**, rather than in a bound book to permit using a copying machine to reproduce the accounts as monthly statements. Information in the Charges column of the daily service record is posted to the individual patients' accounts. Credits to the patients' accounts are posted from the Payments column of the daily service record. Information in the Cash Services column of the daily service record is posted to the patients' accounts in both the Charges and Payments columns to show that service has been rendered and immediately paid for. A model **patient's account** for Louise Strong is reproduced on page 169.

Payment for Services

In the last few years much of the burden of payment for services rendered by physicians and surgeons has shifted from the patient to private organizations such as **Blue Cross**, **Blue Shield**, **commercial insurance companies**, **company health insurance plans**, and to government programs such as **Medicare** and **Medicaid**. As a result, keeping the accounts in the patients' ledger has become much more complex.

Some physicians and surgeons accept an **assignment** of the amounts due them which means that the patient will pay only those amounts due which are not covered by insurance. The balance is paid by the insurance companies to the physicians.

Kennedy and Weiss have agreed to accept assignments and fill out insurance forms necessary to collect the amounts due them. The office personnel has to handle a wide variety of insurance forms and be familiar with coverage under many different plans. There are about 1,000 insurance companies offering health care insurance in the United States plus health plans such as Blue Cross and Blue Shield and the government programs. A standardized claim form has been developed by the Health Insurance Council and the American Medical Association for private carriers. Special forms are still required by Blue Cross, Blue Shield, and the government programs.

Chapter 6 Accounting for Personal Service (Physicians and Dentists) 169

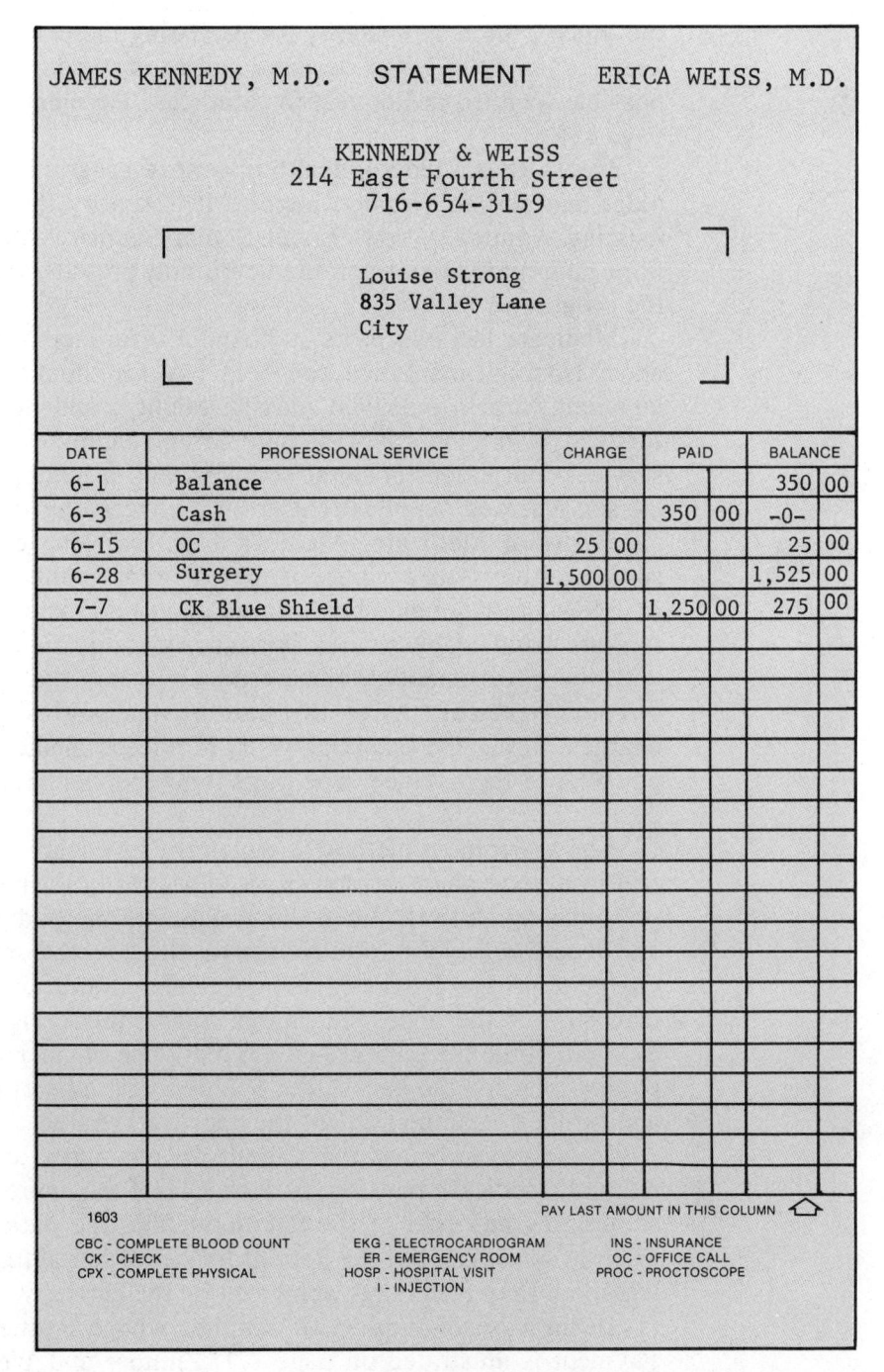

```
JAMES KENNEDY, M.D.      STATEMENT      ERICA WEISS, M.D.

                    KENNEDY & WEISS
                  214 East Fourth Street
                      716-654-3159

                  Louise Strong
                  835 Valley Lane
                  City
```

DATE	PROFESSIONAL SERVICE	CHARGE	PAID	BALANCE
6-1	Balance			350 00
6-3	Cash		350 00	-0-
6-15	OC	25 00		25 00
6-28	Surgery	1,500 00		1,525 00
7-7	CK Blue Shield		1,250 00	275 00

1603   PAY LAST AMOUNT IN THIS COLUMN

CBC - COMPLETE BLOOD COUNT   EKG - ELECTROCARDIOGRAM   INS - INSURANCE
CK - CHECK   ER - EMERGENCY ROOM   OC - OFFICE CALL
CPX - COMPLETE PHYSICAL   HOSP - HOSPITAL VISIT   PROC - PROCTOSCOPE
                              I - INJECTION

Illustration of Patient's Account

In order to process the insurance claims as efficiently as possible, Kennedy and Weiss have assigned Rita Strobel, a secretary in the office, the responsibility for preparing the claims forms. Strobel keeps a supply of forms on hand and uses standard forms whenever possible. A filled in Request for Medicare Payment is reproduced on page 171.

Medicare is a federal health insurance program for people 65 and older and certain disabled people. It is run by the Health Care Financing Administration. Local Social Security Administration offices take applications for Medicare and provide information about the program.

Medicare has two parts — hospital insurance and medical insurance. Hospital insurance can help pay for inpatient hospital care, inpatient care in a skilled nursing facility, and home health care. Medical insurance can help pay for medically necessary doctors' services, outpatient hospital services, and a number of other medical services and supplies that are not covered by the hospital insurance part of Medicare. Medical insurance also can help pay for some health services when hospital insurance cannot pay for them.

Medicare payments for hospital stays and for treatments by doctors are handled by private insurance organizations under contract with the government. Medicare does not pay the full cost of some covered services. After the patient has paid $75 in reasonable charges during the calendar year, Medicare medical insurance will pay 80% of the balance. The patient is responsible for the remaining 20%.

The assignment method in which the physician receives the medical insurance payment can be used only if both the patient and the physician agree to it. When the assignment method is used, the physician agrees that the total charge for the covered service will be the charge approved by the Medicare carrier. Medicare pays the physician 80% of the approved charge after subtracting any part of the $75 deductible the patient has not met. The physician can charge the patient only for the part of the $75 deductible he or she has not met and for the remaining 20% of the approved charge.

If the physician or the patient do not agree to the assignment method, Medicare pays the patient 80% of the approved charge after subtracting any part of the $75 deductible the patient has not met. The physician can bill the patient for his or her actual charge even if it is more than the charge approved by the carrier.

In the case of Raphael J. Zimmer whose Request for Medicare Payment is illustrated on page 171, Zimmer and Weiss have agreed to use the assignment method. It is assumed that Zimmer has previously paid more than $75 in medical bills before this illness. It is also assumed that the insurance carrier has approved the charges of

Chapter 6 Accounting for Personal Service (Physicians and Dentists) 171

REQUEST FOR MEDICARE PAYMENT

MEDICAL INSURANCE BENEFITS—SOCIAL SECURITY ACT (See Instructions on Back—Type or Print Information)

Form Approved
Budget Bureau No.
72-RO730

NOTICE—Anyone who misrepresents or falsifies essential information requested by this form may upon conviction be subject to fine and imprisonment under Federal Law.

PART I—PATIENT TO FILL IN ITEMS 1 THROUGH 6 ONLY

Send completed form to:
METROPOLITAN LIFE INSURANCE CO.
MEDICARE OFFICE
1218 HARRODSBURG ROAD
LEXINGTON, KENTUCKY 40504
Do Not Write In This Space

Copy from YOUR OWN HEALTH INSURANCE CARD (See example on back)

1 Name of patient (First name, Middle initial, Last name)
Raphael J. Zimmer

2 Health insurance claim number
269-09-3509-A

[X] Male [ ] Female

3 Patient's mailing address / City, State, ZIP code
47 Sunnymeade, City

Telephone Number
341-8774

4 Describe the illness or injury for which you received treatment (Always fill in this item if your doctor does not complete Part II below).
Appendicitis

Was your illness or injury connected with your employment?
[ ] Yes [X] No

5 If any of your medical expenses will be or could be paid by another insurance organization or government agency, show below.

Name and address of organization or agency | Policy or Identification Number

Note: If you Do Not want information about this Medicare claim released to the above upon its request, check (X) the following block [ ]

6 I authorize any holder of medical or other information about me to release to the Social Security Administration or its intermediaries or carriers any information needed for this or a related Medicare claim. I permit a copy of this authorization to be used in place of the original, and request payment of medical insurance benefits either to myself or to the party who accepts assignment below.

Signature of patient (See instructions on reverse where patient is unable to sign)
SIGN HERE X *Raphael J. Zimmer*

Date Signed
7/21/83

PART II—PHYSICIAN OR SUPPLIER TO FILL IN 7 THROUGH 14

7

A. Date of each service	B. Place of service (*See Codes below)	C. Fully describe surgical or medical procedures and other services or supplies furnished for each date given	Procedure Code	Nature of illness or injury requiring services or supplies	E. Charges (If related to unusual circumstances explain in 7C)	Leave Blank
7/12/83	O	Examination	1	Appendicitis	$ 25.00	
7/13/83	IH	Appendectomy	2	Appendicitis	200.00	

8 Name and address of physician or supplier (Number and street, city, State, ZIP code)
Erica Weiss, M.D.
214 East Fourth Street
City

Telephone No.
654-8863

Physician or supplier code
18903

9 Total charges $ 225.00
10 Amount paid $ -0-
11 Any unpaid balance due $ 225.00

12 Assignment of patient's bill
[X] I accept assignment (See reverse)
[ ] I do not accept assignment

13 Show name and address of facility where services were performed (If other than home or office visits)
General Hospital
1525 Ridge Road, City

14 Signature of physician or supplier (A physician's signature certifies that physician's services were personally rendered by him or under his personal direction) *Erica Weiss*

Date signed
7/21/83

*O—Doctor's Office
IL—Independent Laboratory
H—Patient's Home (If portable X-ray services, identify the supplier)
IH—Inpatient Hospital
SNF—Skilled Nursing Facility
OH—Outpatient Hospital
OL—Other Locations
NH—Nursing Home

FORM SSA-1490D   BE SURE TO FILL IN ITEM **4** AND SIGN ITEM **6**

Request for Medicare Payment

$225 as being reasonable. A check for $180 was received by Kennedy and Weiss on July 29 and was entered as a credit in Zimmer's account, leaving a balance due of $45.

Computer-Based Accounting Systems. A manual accounting system such as that illustrated in this chapter is the most common system found in physicians' offices. The manual system is a good one if properly set up and maintained. The development of **minicomputers** and their relatively low cost in the last few years has made it possible for physicians and dentists to computerize their accounting systems or to make use of a **computer service bureau**. In most cases, computers are used in some type of **accounts receivable system**. Many **computer programs** will produce a daily service record, a summary of the amounts owed the physician or dentist, a patients ledger, collection letters, and monthly billing statements. There are also programs which will reduce the paperwork in the physician's office by preparing the insurance reports. Basically, what is needed for a computerized accounting system in a physician's or dentist's office is a small computer with the necessary storage capacity, a printer, and computer programs designed to produce the desired records.

Accounting Procedure

Following is a narrative of transactions completed by Kennedy and Weiss during the month of July. These transactions are recorded in the combination journal on pages 180–183.

KENNEDY AND WEISS, PHYSICIANS AND SURGEONS
NARRATIVE OF TRANSACTIONS

Friday, July 1

Issued Check No. 714 for $2,500 payable to Johnson Realtors for rent of the office for the month of July.

The transaction was recorded in the combination journal by debiting Rent Expense, Account No. 525, in the General Dr. column and crediting Cash, Account No. 111.

Tuesday, July 5

Issued Check No. 715 for $227.30 payable to the Hostetter Garage for the garage bill for June.

This transaction was recorded in the combination journal by debiting Automobile Expense, Account No. 501, and crediting Cash, Account No. 111.

Issued Check No. 716 for $150.37 to the Centerville Electric Co. for electricity consumed during June.

<small>This transaction was recorded in the combination journal by debiting Electricity Expense, Account No. 508, and by crediting Cash, Account No. 111.</small>

Issued Check No. 717 for $89.70 to the Bell Telephone Co. for June service.

Wednesday, July 6

Issued Check No. 718 for $185.30 to the Acme Laundry for laundry service for the month of June.

Issued Check No. 719 for $120.02 to the Physicians' Supply Corporation for medical supplies purchased in June.

Thursday, July 7

Issued Check No. 720 for $48.90 to the Medical Equipment Co. for equipment repair.

<small>This transaction was recorded in the combination journal by debiting Repairs and Maintenance Expense, Account No. 527, and by crediting Cash, Account No. 111.</small>

Issued Check No. 721 for $5,516 to the Seymour Insurance Agency for a physicians' liability insurance policy for Kennedy and Weiss.

<small>This transaction was recorded in the combination journal by debiting Prepaid Insurance, Account No. 161, and by crediting Cash, Account No. 111.</small>

Friday, July 8

Issued Check No. 722 for $175.42 to the Stevens Surgical Supply Co. for surgical instruments purchased in June.

<small>This transaction was recorded in the combination journal by debiting Surgical Instruments Expense, Account No. 530, and by crediting Cash, Account No. 111.</small>

Weiss has given the account of Martha Bothwell in the amount of $1,800 and the account of Paul Schoenhoft in the amount of $630 to Karl F. Andersen, an attorney, for collection. If Andersen collects all or part of these accounts, the fee will be 33⅓%. No entry is needed at this time.

Footed the amount columns in the daily service record and obtained the following totals:

Kind of service:	
Office calls	$ 260
Surgery	8,700
Total	$8,960

Patients' accounts — charges	$8,750
Cash services	210
Total	$8,960

Posted all entries in the Patients' Accounts Charges and Payments columns to the appropriate individual accounts in the patients ledger.

The total cash received from patients for the week was found to be:

Payments	$8,952
Cash services	210
Total	$9,162

Recorded the total cash received ($9,162) in the combination journal by entering the words "Total receipts" in the Description column and the amount in both the Cash Deposits Dr. column and the Professional Fees Cr. column.

Footed the amount columns of the combination journal and checked the cash balance in the checkbook ($67,848.52) by starting with the checkbook balance on July 1 ($67,699.53) and adding the total of the Cash Dr. column and subtracting the total of the Cash Cr. column.

Completed the individual postings from the General Dr. and Cr. columns of the combination journal. As each item was posted, the account number was entered in the Posting Reference column of the combination journal. The page number of the combination journal was entered in the Posting Reference column of the accounts to which items from the combination journal were posted.

Monday, July 11

Issued Check No. 723 for $15 to the American Medical Association for a subscription to a professional journal.

Tuesday, July 12

Issued Check No. 724 to the Johnson Supply Co. for surgical supplies, $65.20.

Thursday, July 14

Issued Check No. 725 for $37.80 to the Scientific Publishing Co. for medical books.

This transaction was recorded by debiting Medical Library Expense, Account No. 515, and by crediting Cash.

Issued Check No. 726 for $52.75 to the Perkins Department Store in payment of Weiss' personal account.

Since this transaction is a personal expense, it was recorded in the combination journal by debiting Erica Weiss, Drawing, Account No. 322, and by crediting Cash.

Issued Check No. 727 to the Centerville National Bank in payment of the following payroll taxes based on wages paid during the month of June:

Employees income tax withheld from wages		$ 654.60
FICA tax:		
Withheld from employees' wages	$336.00	
Imposed on employer	336.00	672.00
Amount of check		$1,326.60

Form 501 accompanied this deposit to the Centerville National Bank. Form 501 had also been sent to the bank in May and June in payment of the employees income tax and the FICA tax payable for the months of April and May. Since all taxes have been deposited when due, Form 941, the Quarterly Return of Withheld Income Tax and FICA taxes, does not have to be filed with the Internal Revenue Service until August 10.

Friday, July 15

Kennedy withdrew $3,750 for personal use. Check No. 728.

Weiss withdrew $3,000 for personal use. Check No. 729.

Issued the following checks in payment of salaries for the first half of the month:

Check No. 730 for $487.65 to Kathleen Reilly, R.N. in payment of salary in the amount of $625.00, less $93.60 withheld for federal income tax and $43.75 withheld for FICA tax.

Check No. 731 for $523.17 to Ellen Jones, secretary-bookkeeper, in payment of salary in the amount of $651.90, less $83.10 withheld for federal income tax and $45.63 withheld for FICA tax.

Check No. 732 for $456.70 to Rita Strobel, secretary, in payment of salary in the amount of $550.00, less $54.80 withheld for federal income tax and $38.50 withheld for FICA tax.

Check No. 733 for $477.45 to David Blackburn, laboratory technologist, in payment of salary in the amount of $625.00, less $103.80 withheld for federal income tax and $43.75 withheld for FICA tax.

Kennedy and Weiss are subject to the tax imposed under federal unemployment tax and to the state unemployment tax. These taxes are collected entirely from the employer on the first $6,000 of each employee's earnings during the year. No deductions are made from the salaries of the employees for unemployment taxes.

Footed the amount columns in the daily service record and obtained the following totals:

Kind of service:	
Office calls	$ 275
Surgery	9,800
Total	$10,075

Patients' accounts — charges	$ 9,925
Cash services	150
Total	$10,075

Posted all entries in the Patients' Accounts Charges and Payments columns to the appropriate individual accounts in the patients ledger.

The total cash received from patients for the week was found to be:

Payments	$8,943
Cash services	150
Total	$9,093

Recorded the total cash recieved ($9,093) in the combination journal by entering the words "Total receipts" in the Description column and the amount in both the Cash Deposits Dr. column and the Professional Fees Cr. column.

Footed the amount columns of the combination journal and checked the cash balance in the checkbook ($66,749.20) by adding the total of the Cash Dr. column to the checkbook balance on July 1 ($67,699.53) and subtracting the total of the Cash Cr. column.

Completed the individual postings from the General Dr. and Cr. columns of the combination journal.

Monday, July 18

Issued Check No. 734 for $171.30 to the Burke Office Furniture Co. in payment for a new filing cabinet.

Tuesday, July 19

Issued Check No. 735 for $35.18 to the Kaderli Stationery Co. for stationery and office supplies.

Issued Check No. 736 for $165.38 to the Physicians Supply Co. for medical supplies.

Wednesday, July 20

Issued Check No. 737 for $50 to the Red Cross.

This transaction was recorded in the combination journal by debiting Charitable Contributions Expense, Account No. 503, and by crediting Cash.

Thursday, July 21

Issued Check No. 738 for $429.70 to the Cook Insurance Agency in payment of the renewal premium on an insurance policy on Kennedy's car.

Since the car is used exclusively for business purposes, the cost of the policy is debited to Prepaid Insurance, Account No. 161.

Friday, July 22

Issued Check No. 739 for $20 to the Centerville National Bank in payment of the annual rental of a safe deposit box for use of the partnership.

This transaction was recorded by debiting Miscellaneous Expense, Account No. 518, and by crediting Cash.

Footed the amount columns in the daily service record and obtained the following totals:

Kind of service:	
Office calls	$ 290
Surgery	9,650
Total	$9,940
Patients' accounts — charges	$9,775
Cash services	165
Total	$9,940

Posted all entries in the Patients' Accounts Charges and Payments columns to the appropriate individual accounts in the patients ledger.

The total cash received from patients for the week was found to be:

Payments	$9,250
Cash services	165
Total	$9,415

Recorded the total cash received ($9,415) in the combination journal.

Footed the amount columns of the combination journal and checked the balance in the checkbook ($75,292.64).

Completed the individual postings from the General Dr. and Cr. columns of the combination journal.

Monday, July 25

Issued Check No. 740 for $500 to the American Cancer Society.

Tuesday, July 26

Issued Check No. 741 for $2,137.47 to the C. & D. Medical Equipment Co. for medical equipment.

Received $420 from Karl F. Andersen representing collection of the account of Paul Schoenhoft in the amount of $630. Andersen deducted the fee of $210 and remitted the balance ($420).

This transaction was recorded in the combination journal by debiting Cash for $420 and Legal Expense, Account No. 513, for $210, and by crediting Professional Fees, Account No. 411, for $630. In order to avoid a duplication of the $630 credit to Professional Fees, this payment was not entered in the daily service record. An entry was made, however, in Schoenhoft's account in the patients ledger crediting the account for $630.

Wednesday, July 27

Issued Check No. 742 for $25.30 to the Wilson Office Equipment Co. for typewriter repairs.

Issued Check No. 743 for $579.72 to Weiss for reimbursement of expenses incurred in attending a medical convention earlier this month.

This transaction was recorded in the combination journal by debiting Traveling and Meetings Expense, Account No. 538, for $579.72 and by crediting Cash.

Thursday, July 28

Received $400 from Karl F. Andersen to apply on the account of Martha Bothwell. Andersen collected $600 from Bothwell and remitted $400 after deducting the fee of $200.

This transaction was recorded in the combination journal by debiting Cash for $400 and Legal Expense, Account No. 513, for $200, and by crediting Professional Fees, Account No. 411, for $600. An entry was also made in Bothwell's account in the patients ledger crediting the account for $600.

Friday, July 29

Kennedy withdrew $3,750 for personal use. Check No. 744.

Weiss withdrew $3,000 for personal use. Check No. 745.

Issued the following checks in payment of salaries for the second half of the month:

Check No. 746 for $487.65 to Kathleen Reilly, R.N., in payment of salary, $625.00, less $93.60 withheld for federal income tax and $43.75 withheld for FICA tax.

Check No. 747 for $482.90 to Ellen Jones, secretary-bookkeeper, in payment of salary in the amount of $600.00, less $75.10 withheld for federal income tax and $42.00 withheld for FICA tax.

Check No. 748 for $479.26 to Rita Strobel, secretary, in payment of salary in the amount of $578.56, less $58.80 withheld for federal income tax and $40.50 withheld for FICA tax.

Check No. 749 for $477.45 to David Blackburn, laboratory technologist, in payment of salary in the amount of $625.00, less $103.80 withheld for federal income tax and $43.75 for FICA tax.

Issued Check No. 750 for $259.20 to the State Unemployment Bureau for the state unemployment tax for the second quarter. (Since the balance in FUTA Tax Payable, $67.20, is less than $100.00, payment may be delayed until January 31.)

Footed the amount columns in the daily service record and obtained the following totals:

Kind of service:	
Office calls	$ 295
Surgery	9,750
Total	$10,045
Patients' accounts — charges	$ 9,735
Cash services	310
Total	$10,045

Posted all entries in the Patients' Charges and Payments columns to the individual accounts in the patients ledger.

The total cash received from patients for the week was found to be:

Payments	$8,562
Cash services	310
Total	$8,872

Recorded the total cash received ($8,872) in the combination journal.

Made an entry in the combination journal for the payroll taxes imposed on Kennedy and Weiss for the month of July by debiting Payroll Taxes Expense, Account No. 520, for $341.63 and by crediting FICA Tax Payable, Account No. 221. All of the employees have earned more than $6,000 prior to July 1, so no further FUTA tax or state unemployment tax is owed for the balance of the year.

Issued Check No. 751 for $91.34 to replenish the petty cash fund. The following statement provided the information needed in recording this transaction in the combination journal:

STATEMENT OF PETTY CASH DISBURSEMENTS FOR JULY

James Kennedy, Drawing	$13.25
Erica Weiss, Drawing	12.30
Automobile Expense	6.50
Office Supplies Expense	4.29
Postage Expense	40.00
Traveling and Meetings Expense	15.00
Total disbursements	$91.34

Footed the amount columns of the combination journal and checked the cash balance in the checkbook ($72,714.35).

Completed the individual postings from the general columns of the combination journal. Since this was the end of the month, the summary posting was completed and the account numbers were written immediately below the totals of the columns in the combination journal. A trial balance of the general ledger accounts which have balances on July 31 appears on page 190.

Kennedy & Weiss Combination Journal (left page)
(continued)

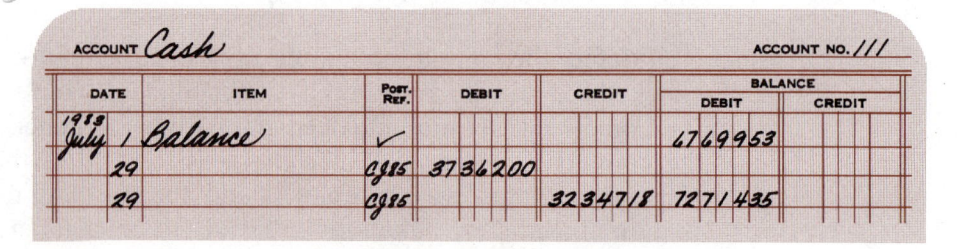

PAGE 84 — COMBINATION JOURNAL

	CASH		CK. NO.	DAY	DESCRIPTION	POST. REF.	
	DEPOSITS 111 DR.	CHECKS 111 CR.					
1					AMOUNTS FORWARDED Balance 67,699.53		1
2		2500 00	714	1	Rent Expense	525	2
3		227 30	715	5	Automobile Expense	501	3
4		150 37	716	5	Electricity Expense	508	4
5		89 70	717	5	Telephone Expense	535	5
6		185 30	718	6	Laundry Expense	512	6
7		120 02	719	6	Medical Supplies Expense	516	7
8		48 90	720	7	Repairs & Maintenance Expense	527	8
9		5516 00	721	7	Prepaid Insurance	161	9
10		175 42	722	8	Surgical Instruments Expense	530	10
11	9162 00			8	Total receipts	✓	11
12	9162 00	9013 01			67,848.52		12
12		15 00	723	11	Dues & Subscript. Expense	506	12
13		65 20	724	12	Surgical Supplies Expense	532	13
14		37 80	725	14	Medical Library Expense	515	14
15		52 75	726	14	Erica Weiss, Drawing	322	15
16		1326 60	727	14	Employees Income Tax Payable	211	16
17					FICA Tax Payable	221	17
18		3750 00	728	15	James Kennedy, Drawing	312	18
19		3000 00	729	15	Erica Weiss, Drawing	322	19
20		487 65	730	15	Kathleen Reilly	✓	20
21		523 17	731	15	Ellen Jones	✓	21
22		456 70	732	15	Rita Strobel	✓	22
23		477 45	733	15	David Blackburn	✓	23
24	9093 00			15	Total receipts	✓	24
25	18255 00	19205 33			66,749.20		
25		171 30	734	18	Office Equipment	151	25
26		35 18	735	19	Office Supplies Expense	519	26
27		165 38	736	19	Medical Supplies Expense	516	27
28		50 00	737	20	Charitable Contributions Exp.	503	28
29		429 70	738	21	Prepaid Insurance	161	29
30	18255 00	20056 89			Carried Forward 65,897.64		30

13735

General Ledger *(continued)*

ACCOUNT Cash — ACCOUNT NO. 111

DATE	ITEM	POST. REF.	DEBIT	CREDIT	BALANCE DEBIT	BALANCE CREDIT
1988 July 1	Balance	✓			67699 53	
29		CJ85	37362 00			
29		CJ85		32347 18	72714 35	

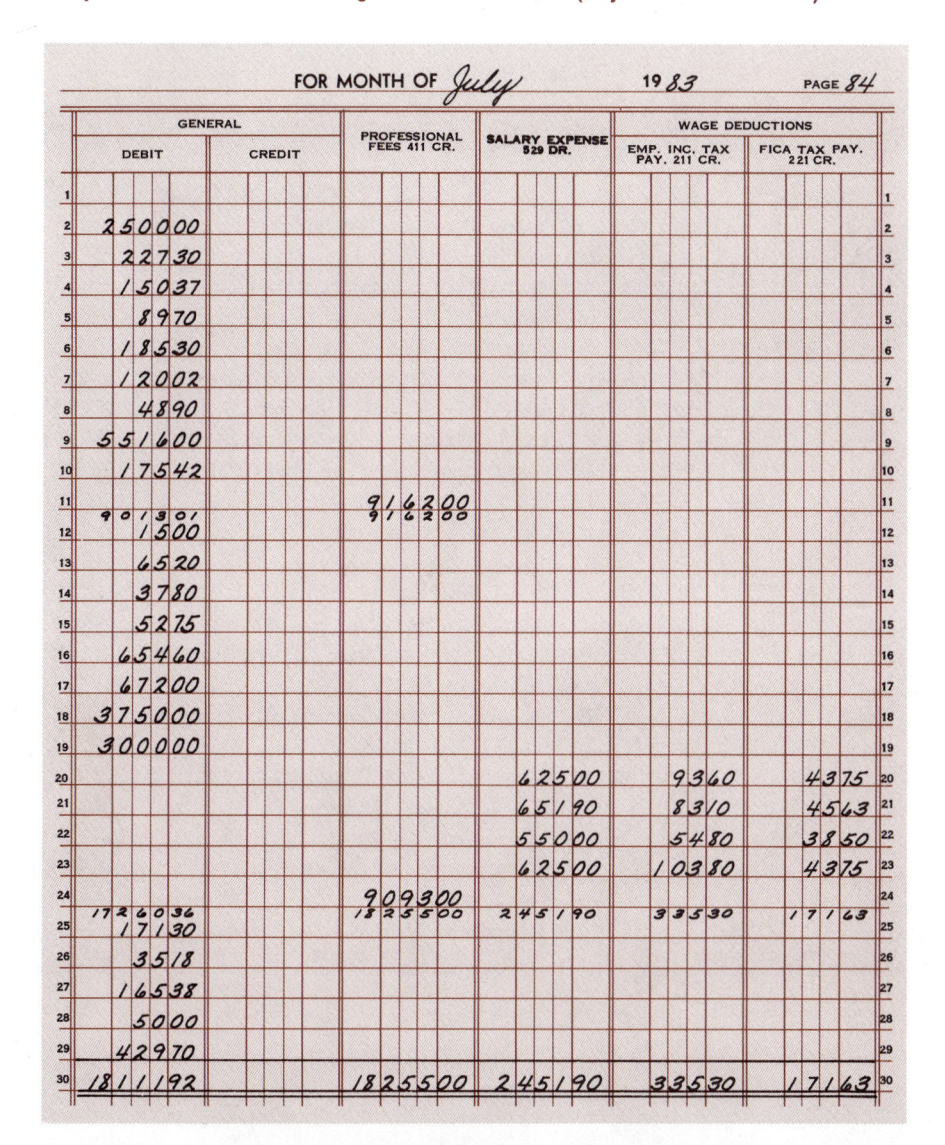

Chapter 6 — Accounting for Personal Service (Physicians and Dentists)

FOR MONTH OF July 19 83   PAGE 84

	GENERAL		PROFESSIONAL FEES 411 CR.	SALARY EXPENSE 529 DR.	WAGE DEDUCTIONS	
	DEBIT	CREDIT			EMP. INC. TAX PAY. 211 CR.	FICA TAX PAY. 221 CR.
1						
2	2500 00					
3	227 30					
4	150 37					
5	89 70					
6	185 30					
7	120 02					
8	48 90					
9	5516 00					
10	175 42					
11	901 30√		9162 00			
12	15 00		9162 00			
13	65 20					
14	37 80					
15	52 75					
16	654 60					
17	672 00					
18	3750 00					
19	3000 00					
20				625 00	93 60	43 75
21				651 90	83 10	45 63
22				550 00	54 80	38 50
23				625 00	103 80	43 75
24			9093 00			
25	17260 36	171 30	18255 00	2451 90	335 30	171 63
26	35 18					
27	165 38					
28	50 00					
29	429 70					
30	18111 92		18255 00	2451 90	335 30	171 63

Kennedy & Weiss Combination Journal (right page)
(continued)

ACCOUNT Petty Cash Fund   ACCOUNT NO. 112

DATE	ITEM	POST. REF.	DEBIT	CREDIT	BALANCE DEBIT	BALANCE CREDIT
1983 July 1	Balance	✓			100 00	

General Ledger *(continued)*

182 Accounting for Personal Service (Physicians and Dentists) — Chapter 6

COMBINATION JOURNAL — PAGE 85

CASH DEPOSITS 111 DR.	CASH CHECKS 111 CR.	CK. NO.	DAY	DESCRIPTION	POST. REF.	
18,255.00	2,005.6.89			AMOUNTS FORWARDED Balance 65,897.64		1
	20.00	739	22	Miscellaneous Expense	518	2
9,415.00			22	Total receipts	✓	3
27,670.00	20,076.89 500.00	740	25	Charitable Contributions Exp. 75,292.64	503	4
	2,137.47	741	26	Medical Equipment	141	5
420.00			26	Legal Expense — Paul Schoenhoft	513	6
	25.30	742	27	Repairs & Maintenance Expense	527	7
	579.72	743	27	Travel & Meetings Expense	538	8
400.00			28	Legal Expense — Martha Bothwell	513	9
	3,750.00	744	29	James Kennedy, Drawing	312	10
	3,000.00	745	29	Erica Weiss, Drawing	322	11
	487.65	746	29	Kathleen Reilly	✓	12
	482.90	747	29	Ellen Jones	✓	13
	479.26	748	29	Rita Strobel	✓	14
	477.45	749	29	David Blackburn	✓	15
	259.20	750	29	State Unemployment Tax Payable	241	16
8,872.00			29	Total receipts	✓	17
			29	Payroll Taxes Expense	520	18
				FICA Tax Payable	✓	19
	91.34	751	29	James Kennedy, Drawing	312	20
				Erica Weiss, Drawing	322	21
				Automobile Expense	501	22
				Office Supplies Expense	519	23
				Postage Expense	522	24
				Traveling & Meetings Expense 72,714.35	538	25
37,362.00	32,347.18					26
(111)	(111)					27

Kennedy & Weiss Combination Journal (left page)
(concluded)

ACCOUNT: Automobiles   ACCOUNT NO. 121

DATE	ITEM	POST. REF.	DEBIT	CREDIT	BALANCE DEBIT	BALANCE CREDIT
1953 July 1	Balance	✓			18,402.98	

ACCOUNT: Accumulated Depreciation — Automobiles   ACCOUNT NO. 122

DATE	ITEM	POST. REF.	DEBIT	CREDIT	BALANCE DEBIT	BALANCE CREDIT
1953 July 1	Balance	✓				6,901.12

General Ledger *(continued)*

Chapter 6 — Accounting for Personal Service (Physicians and Dentists)

FOR MONTH OF July 19 83   PAGE 85

GENERAL DEBIT	GENERAL CREDIT	PROFESSIONAL FEES 411 CR.	SALARY EXPENSE 529 DR.	EMP. INC. TAX PAY. 211 CR.	FICA TAX PAY. 221 CR.
18 111 92		18 255 00	2451 90	335 30	171 63
	20 00				
13 131 92		9415 00	2451 90	335 30	171 63
	500 00	27670 00			
	2137 47				
	210 00		630 00		
	25 30				
	579 72				
	200 00		600 00		
3750 00					
3000 00					
			625 00	93 60	43 75
			600 00	75 10	42 00
			578 56	58 80	40 50
			625 00	103 80	43 75
259 20					
			8872 00		
341 63					
					341 63
	13 25				
	12 30				
	6 50				
	4 29				
	40 00				
	15 00				
29226 58	3777 200	4880 46	666 60	683 26	
(✓)	(✓)	(411)	(529)	(211)	(221)

Kennedy & Weiss Combination Journal (right page)
(concluded)

ACCOUNT: Laboratory Equipment — ACCOUNT NO. 131

DATE	ITEM	POST. REF.	DEBIT	CREDIT	BALANCE DEBIT	BALANCE CREDIT
1983 July 1	Balance	✓			15219 62	

ACCOUNT: Accumulated Depreciation — Laboratory Equip't — ACCOUNT NO. 132

DATE	ITEM	POST. REF.	DEBIT	CREDIT	BALANCE DEBIT	BALANCE CREDIT
1983 July 1	Balance	✓				3077 88

General Ledger (continued)

Account: Medical Equipment — Account No. 141

DATE	ITEM	POST. REF.	DEBIT	CREDIT	BALANCE DEBIT	BALANCE CREDIT
1983 July 1	Balance	✓			21188 35	
25		CJ85	2137 47		23326 32	

Account: Accumulated Depreciation—Medical Equip. — Account No. 142

DATE	ITEM	POST. REF.	DEBIT	CREDIT	BALANCE DEBIT	BALANCE CREDIT
1983 July 1	Balance	✓				8641 64

Account: Office Equipment — Account No. 151

DATE	ITEM	POST. REF.	DEBIT	CREDIT	BALANCE DEBIT	BALANCE CREDIT
1983 July 1	Balance	✓			10129 77	
18		CJ84	171 30		10301 07	

Account: Accumulated Depreciation—Office Equip. — Account No. 152

DATE	ITEM	POST. REF.	DEBIT	CREDIT	BALANCE DEBIT	BALANCE CREDIT
1983 July 1	Balance	✓				3038 94

Account: Prepaid Insurance — Account No. 161

DATE	ITEM	POST. REF.	DEBIT	CREDIT	BALANCE DEBIT	BALANCE CREDIT
1983 July 1	Balance	✓			15732 84	
7		CJ84	5516 00			
21		CJ84	429 70		21678 54	

Account: Employees Income Tax Payable — Account No. 211

DATE	ITEM	POST. REF.	DEBIT	CREDIT	BALANCE DEBIT	BALANCE CREDIT
1983 July 1	Balance	✓				654 60
14		CJ84	654 60			—0—
29		CJ85		666 60		666 60

General Ledger (continued)

ACCOUNT FICA Tax Payable — ACCOUNT NO. 221

DATE	ITEM	POST. REF.	DEBIT	CREDIT	BALANCE DEBIT	BALANCE CREDIT
1983 July 1	Balance	✓				672 00
14		CJ84	672 00			—0—
29		CJ85		683 26		683 26

ACCOUNT FUTA Tax Payable — ACCOUNT NO. 231

DATE	ITEM	POST. REF.	DEBIT	CREDIT	BALANCE DEBIT	BALANCE CREDIT
1983 July 1	Balance	✓				67 20

ACCOUNT State Unemployment Tax Payable — ACCOUNT NO. 241

DATE	ITEM	POST. REF.	DEBIT	CREDIT	BALANCE DEBIT	BALANCE CREDIT
1983 July 1	Balance	✓				259 20
29		CJ85	259 20			—0—

ACCOUNT James Kennedy, Capital — ACCOUNT NO. 311

DATE	ITEM	POST. REF.	DEBIT	CREDIT	BALANCE DEBIT	BALANCE CREDIT
1983 July 1	Balance	✓				20437 85

ACCOUNT James Kennedy, Drawing — ACCOUNT NO. 312

DATE	ITEM	POST. REF.	DEBIT	CREDIT	BALANCE DEBIT	BALANCE CREDIT
1983 July 1	Balance	✓			45089 50	
15		CJ84	3750 00			
29		CJ85	3750 00			
29		CJ85	13 25		52602 75	

ACCOUNT Erica Weiss, Capital — ACCOUNT NO. 321

DATE	ITEM	POST. REF.	DEBIT	CREDIT	BALANCE DEBIT	BALANCE CREDIT
1983 July 1	Balance	✓				21027 14

General Ledger (continued)

Accounting for Personal Service (Physicians and Dentists) — Chapter 6

ACCOUNT: Erica Weiss, Drawing — ACCOUNT NO. 322

DATE	ITEM	POST. REF.	DEBIT	CREDIT	BALANCE DEBIT	BALANCE CREDIT
1983 July 1	Balance	✓			3632580	
14		CJ84	5275			
15		CJ84	300000			
29		CJ85	300000			
29		CJ85	1230		4239085	

ACCOUNT: Expense and Revenue Summary — ACCOUNT NO. 331

DATE	ITEM	POST. REF.	DEBIT	CREDIT	BALANCE DEBIT	BALANCE CREDIT

ACCOUNT: Professional Fees — ACCOUNT NO. 411

DATE	ITEM	POST. REF.	DEBIT	CREDIT	BALANCE DEBIT	BALANCE CREDIT
1983 July 1	Balance	✓				22543800
29		CJ85		3777200		26321000

ACCOUNT: Automobile Expense — ACCOUNT NO. 501

DATE	ITEM	POST. REF.	DEBIT	CREDIT	BALANCE DEBIT	BALANCE CREDIT
1983 July 1	Balance	✓			131526	
5		CJ84	22730			
29		CJ85	650		154906	

ACCOUNT: Charitable Contributions Expense — ACCOUNT NO. 503

DATE	ITEM	POST. REF.	DEBIT	CREDIT	BALANCE DEBIT	BALANCE CREDIT
1983 July 1	Balance	✓			57500	
20		CJ84	5000			
25		CJ85	50000		112500	

ACCOUNT: Depreciation Expense — ACCOUNT NO. 505

DATE	ITEM	POST. REF.	DEBIT	CREDIT	BALANCE DEBIT	BALANCE CREDIT

General Ledger *(continued)*

Dues and Subscription Expense — Account No. 506

DATE	ITEM	POST. REF.	DEBIT	CREDIT	BALANCE DEBIT	BALANCE CREDIT
1953 July 1	Balance	✓			1527.00	
11		CJ84	15.00		1542.00	

Electricity Expense — Account No. 508

DATE	ITEM	POST. REF.	DEBIT	CREDIT	BALANCE DEBIT	BALANCE CREDIT
1953 July 1	Balance	✓			1047.60	
5		CJ84	150.37		1197.97	

Insurance Expense — Account No. 510

DATE	ITEM	POST. REF.	DEBIT	CREDIT	BALANCE DEBIT	BALANCE CREDIT

Laundry Expense — Account No. 512

DATE	ITEM	POST. REF.	DEBIT	CREDIT	BALANCE DEBIT	BALANCE CREDIT
1953 July 1	Balance	✓			1078.50	
6		CJ84	185.30		1263.80	

Legal Expense — Account No. 513

DATE	ITEM	POST. REF.	DEBIT	CREDIT	BALANCE DEBIT	BALANCE CREDIT
1953 July 1	Balance	✓			500.00	
26		CJ85	210.00			
28		CJ85	200.00		910.00	

Medical Library Expense — Account No. 515

DATE	ITEM	POST. REF.	DEBIT	CREDIT	BALANCE DEBIT	BALANCE CREDIT
1953 July 1	Balance	✓			337.50	
14		CJ84	37.80		375.30	

General Ledger (continued)

Medical Supplies Expense — Account No. 516

DATE	ITEM	POST. REF.	DEBIT	CREDIT	BALANCE DEBIT	BALANCE CREDIT
1983 July 1	Balance	✓			1795.69	
6		CJ84	120.02			
19		CJ84	165.38		2081.09	

Miscellaneous Expense — Account No. 518

DATE	ITEM	POST. REF.	DEBIT	CREDIT	BALANCE DEBIT	BALANCE CREDIT
1983 July 1	Balance	✓			121.64	
22		CJ85	20.00		141.64	

Office Supplies Expense — Account No. 519

DATE	ITEM	POST. REF.	DEBIT	CREDIT	BALANCE DEBIT	BALANCE CREDIT
1983 July 1	Balance	✓			169.80	
19		CJ84	35.18			
29		CJ85	4.29		209.27	

Payroll Taxes Expense — Account No. 520

DATE	ITEM	POST. REF.	DEBIT	CREDIT	BALANCE DEBIT	BALANCE CREDIT
1983 July 1	Balance	✓			2843.36	
29		CJ85	341.63		3184.99	

Postage Expense — Account No. 522

DATE	ITEM	POST. REF.	DEBIT	CREDIT	BALANCE DEBIT	BALANCE CREDIT
1983 July 1	Balance	✓			257.20	
29		CJ85	40.00		297.20	

Rent Expense — Account No. 525

DATE	ITEM	POST. REF.	DEBIT	CREDIT	BALANCE DEBIT	BALANCE CREDIT
1983 July 1	Balance	✓			15000.00	
1		CJ84	2500.00		17500.00	

General Ledger (continued)

Account: Repairs and Maintenance Expense — Account No. 527

DATE	ITEM	POST. REF.	DEBIT	CREDIT	BALANCE DEBIT	BALANCE CREDIT
1953 July 1	Balance	✓			596 83	
7		CG84	48 90			
27		CG85	25 30		671 03	

Account: Salary Expense — Account No. 529

DATE	ITEM	POST. REF.	DEBIT	CREDIT	BALANCE DEBIT	BALANCE CREDIT
1953 July 1	Balance	✓			28962 26	
29		CG85	4880 46		33842 72	

Account: Surgical Instruments Expense — Account No. 530

DATE	ITEM	POST. REF.	DEBIT	CREDIT	BALANCE DEBIT	BALANCE CREDIT
1953 July 1	Balance	✓			1032 47	
8		CG84	175 42		1207 89	

Account: Surgical Supplies Expense — Account No. 532

DATE	ITEM	POST. REF.	DEBIT	CREDIT	BALANCE DEBIT	BALANCE CREDIT
1953 July 1	Balance	✓			342 75	
12		CG84	65 20		407 95	

Account: Telephone Expense — Account No. 535

DATE	ITEM	POST. REF.	DEBIT	CREDIT	BALANCE DEBIT	BALANCE CREDIT
1953 July 1	Balance	✓			475 32	
5		CG84	89 70		565 02	

Account: Traveling and Meetings Expense — Account No. 538

DATE	ITEM	POST. REF.	DEBIT	CREDIT	BALANCE DEBIT	BALANCE CREDIT
1953 July 1	Balance	✓			2348 50	
27		CG85	579 72			
29		CG85	15 00		2943 22	

General Ledger (concluded)

KENNEDY AND WEISS, PHYSICIANS AND SURGEONS
Trial Balance
July 31, 1983

Account	No.	Debit	Credit
Cash	111	72,714.35	
Petty Cash Fund	112	100.00	
Automobiles	121	18,402.98	
Accumulated Depreciation — Automobiles	122		6,901.12
Laboratory Equipment	131	15,219.62	
Accumulated Depr. — Laboratory Equipment	132		3,077.88
Medical Equipment	141	23,326.32	
Accumulated Depr. — Medical Equipment	142		8,641.64
Office Equipment	151	10,301.07	
Accumulated Depr. — Office Equipment	152		3,038.94
Prepaid Insurance	161	21,678.54	
Employees Income Tax Payable	211		666.60
FICA Tax Payable	221		683.26
FUTA Tax Payable	231		67.20
James Kennedy, Capital	311		20,437.85
James Kennedy, Drawing	312	52,602.75	
Erica Weiss, Capital	321		21,027.14
Erica Weiss, Drawing	322	42,390.85	
Professional Fees	411		263,210.00
Automobile Expense	501	1,549.06	
Charitable Contributions Expense	503	1,125.00	
Dues and Subscriptions Expense	506	1,542.00	
Electricity Expense	508	1,197.97	
Laundry Expense	512	1,263.80	
Legal Expense	513	910.00	
Medical Library Expense	515	375.30	
Medical Supplies Expense	516	2,081.09	
Miscellaneous Expense	518	141.64	
Office Supplies Expense	519	209.27	
Payroll Taxes Expense	520	3,184.99	
Postage Expense	522	297.20	
Rent Expense	525	17,500.00	
Repairs and Maintenance Expense	527	671.03	
Salary Expense	529	33,842.72	
Surgical Instruments Expense	530	1,207.89	
Surgical Supplies Expense	532	407.95	
Telephone Expense	535	565.02	
Traveling and Meetings Expense	538	2,943.22	
		327,751.63	327,751.63

BUILDING YOUR ACCOUNTING KNOWLEDGE

1. What is meant by the cash basis of accounting?
2. In what respect are prepaid insurance and office equipment similar?
3. Why must the total of the Kind of Service Columns equal the total of the Patients' Charges and Cash Services columns?

Chapter 6　Accounting for Personal Service (Physicians and Dentists)　　191

4. In handling insurance claims, what is meant by an assignment?
5. What percentage of an approved charge will Medicare insurance pay?
6. If a physician does not accept assignment of a Medicare claim, may he or she charge the patient more than Medicare approves?
7. What dollar amount per year must a patient who holds a Medicare card pay for treatment by a physician before Medicare insurance becomes effective?

Report No. 6-1

> *Complete Report No. 6-1 in the study assignments and submit your working papers to the instructor for approval. After completing the report, you will then be given instructions as to the work to be done next.*

EXPANDING YOUR BUSINESS VOCABULARY

What is the meaning of each of the following terms:

accounts receivable system (p. 172)
assignment (p. 168)
auxiliary records (p. 166)
Blue Cross (p. 168)
Blue Shield (p. 168)
commercial insurance companies (p. 168)
company health insurance plans (p. 168)

computer programs (p. 172)
computer service bureau (p. 172)
daily service record (p. 163)
Medicaid (p. 168)
Medicare (p. 168)
minicomputers (p. 172)
patient's account (p. 168)
patients ledger (p. 168)
prepaid insurance (p. 164)

7

THE PERIODIC SUMMARY

CHAPTER OBJECTIVES

The objectives of this chapter are to enable you:
▶ To prepare a ten-column end-of-year work sheet for an attorney.
▶ To prepare the financial statements for an attorney.

One of the major reasons for keeping accounting records is to accumulate information that will make it possible to prepare periodic summaries of both (1) the revenue and expenses of the business during a specified period and (2) the assets, liabilities, and owner's equity of the business at a specified date. A trial balance of the general ledger accounts will provide most of the information that is required for these summaries (the income statement and the balance sheet). However, the trial balance does not supply the data in a form that is easily interpreted, nor does it reflect changes in the accounting elements that have not been represented by ordinary business transactions. Therefore, at the end of a fiscal period it is necessary **(1)** to determine the kind and amounts of changes that the accounts do not reflect and to adjust the accounts accordingly and **(2)** to recast the information into the form of an income statement and a balance sheet. These two steps are often referred to as the **periodic summary**.

END-OF-PERIOD WORK SHEET

An end-of-period **work sheet** is a device that assists the accountant in three ways. It facilitates **(1)** the preparing of the financial statements, **(2)** the making of needed adjustments in the accounts, and **(3)** the closing of the temporary owner's equity accounts. When a number of adjustments are to be made at the end of a period **end-of-period adjustments**, a work sheet is especially helpful in determining the balance of the accounts after adjustment.

Work sheets are not financial statements; they are devices used to assist the accountant in performing certain tasks. Ordinarily, it is only the accountant who uses or even sees a work sheet.

A Work Sheet for an Attorney

Although an end-of-period work sheet can be in any of several forms, a common and widely used arrangement involves ten amount columns. The amount columns are used in pairs. The first pair of amount columns is for the trial balance. The data to be recorded consist of the name, number, and debit or credit balance of each account. Debit balances should be entered in the left-hand column and credit balances in the right-hand column. The second pair of amount columns is used to record needed end-of-period adjustments. The third pair of amount columns is used to show that the debit and credit account balances as adjusted are equal in amount. The fourth pair of amount columns is for the adjusted balances of the expense and revenue accounts. This pair of columns is headed "Income Statement" since the amounts shown will be reported in that statement. The fifth, and last, pair of amount columns is headed "Balance Sheet" and shows the adjusted account balances that will be reported in that statement.

To illustrate the preparation and use of the end-of-period work sheet, the example of the accounts of Karl F. Andersen, Attorney at Law, will be continued. The journal and ledger for Andersen for the month of December were reproduced in Chapter 5. In this chapter, the income statement for the year and the balance sheet at the end of the year will be reproduced, showing the use of a work sheet as a device for summarizing the data to be presented in those statements.

The end-of-year work sheet for Andersen is reproduced on page 195. Following is a description and discussion of the steps that were followed in the preparation of the work sheet. Each step should be studied carefully with frequent reference to the work sheet.

Trial Balance Columns. The trial balance of the general ledger accounts as of December 31 was entered in the first pair of amount columns. This trial balance is the same as the one shown on page 150 except that all of the account titles were included in the work sheet list even though certain of the accounts had no balance at this point.

The Trial Balance Debit and Credit columns were totaled. The totals should be equal. If not, the cause of any discrepancy must be found and corrected before the preparation of the work sheet can proceed.

Adjustments Columns. The second pair of amount columns on the work sheet was used to record certain entries necessary to reflect the depreciation that had occurred during the year.

Two entries were made in the Adjustments columns to reflect these changes. When the account was debited, the amount was entered in the Adjustments Debit column on the same horizontal line as the name of the account. Amounts credited were entered in the Credit column. Each entry made on the work sheet was identified by a small letter in parentheses to facilitate cross-reference. Following is an explanation of each of the entries.

Entry (a): This entry recorded the depreciation expense on the automobile by debiting Depreciation Expense, Account No. 705, for $2,412.57 and crediting Accumulated Depreciation — Automobile, Account No. 212, for the same amount.

The automobile has been owned for the entire year. The original cost of the automobile was $9,650.28. The depreciation rate is 25 percent; therefore, the depreciation expense is $2,412.57 ($9,650.28 × .25).

Entry (b): This entry recorded the depreciation expense for the year on office equipment by debiting Depreciation Expense, Account No. 705, for $498.27 and by crediting Accumulated Depreciation — Office Equipment, Account No. 222, for the same amount.

Chapter 7   The Periodic Summary

Karl F. Andersen, Attorney at Law
Work Sheet
For the Year Ended December 31, 1983

	ACCT. NO.	TRIAL BALANCE DEBIT	TRIAL BALANCE CREDIT	ADJUSTMENTS DEBIT	ADJUSTMENTS CREDIT	ADJUSTED TRIAL BALANCE DEBIT	ADJUSTED TRIAL BALANCE CREDIT	INCOME STATEMENT DEBIT	INCOME STATEMENT CREDIT	BALANCE SHEET DEBIT	BALANCE SHEET CREDIT
Cash	111	2717 92				2717 92				2717 92	
Petty Cash Fund	112	75 00				75 00				75 00	
Clients' Trust Account	121	4000 00				4000 00				4000 00	
Advances on Behalf of Clients	131	495 00				495 00				495 00	
Automobile	211	9650 28				9650 28				9650 28	
Accum. Depr.—Automobile	212		3618 86		(a) 2412 57		6031 43				6031 43
Office Equipment	221	5822 27				5822 27				5822 27	
Accum. Depr.—Office Equip.	222		1494 81		(b) 498 27		1993 08				1993 08
Liability on Trust Funds	321		4000 00				4000 00					4000 00
Employers' Income Tax Pay.	331		336 80				336 80					336 80
FICA Tax Payable	341		316 12				316 12					316 12
FUTA Tax Payable	351		11 290				11 290					11 290
State Unemp. Tax Payable	361		81 65				81 65					81 65
Karl F. Andersen, Capital	511		18542 39				18542 39					18542 39
Karl F. Andersen, Drawing	512	5938 308				5938 308				5938 308	
Expense & Revenue Summary	521										
Legal Fees Revenue	611		12873 00				12873 00		12873 00		
Collection Fees Revenue	621		500 804				500 804		500 804		
Automobile Expense	701	3713 13				3713 13	3713 13				
Charitable Contrib. Expense	703	994 00				994 00	994 00				
Depreciation Expense	705			(a) 2412 57 (b) 498 27		2412 57 498 27		2412 57 498 27				
Law Library Expense	708	4104 28				4104 28	4104 28				
Miscellaneous Expense	709	644 48				644 48	644 48				
Office Supplies Expense	710	2963 59				2963 59	2963 59				
Payroll Taxes Expense	712	2458 52				2458 52	2458 52				
Rent Expense	715	10800 00				10800 00	10800 00				
Salary Expense	718	27288 00				27288 00	27288 00				
Telephone Expense	720	793 73				793 73	793 73				
		108384 57	108384 57	2910 84	2910 84	143295 41	143295 41	56690 57	13188 104	106604 84	31444 37
Net Income								75190 47			75190 47
								13188 104	13188 104	106604 84	106604 84

Karl F. Andersen — Work Sheet

Office Equipment, Account No. 221, shows that an electric typewriter was purchased on December 21 at a cost of $839.54. Andersen follows the practice of not taking depreciation on assets that have been owned for less than a month. The debit to Depreciation Expense is therefore based on the December 1 balance of $4,982.73 in Account No. 221. The depreciation rate used for office equipment is 10 percent; therefore the depreciation expense is $498.27 ($4,982.73 × .10).

After making the required entries in the Adjustments columns of the work sheet, the columns were totaled to prove the equality of the debit and credit entries.

Adjusted Trial Balance Columns. The third pair of amount columns of the work sheet was used for the **adjusted trial balance**. To determine the balance of each account after making the required adjustments, it was necessary to take into consideration the amounts recorded in the first two pairs of amount columns. When an account balance was not affected by entries in the Adjustments columns, the amount in the Trial Balance columns was extended directly to the Adjusted Trial Balance columns. When an account balance was affected by an entry in the Adjustments columns, the balance recorded in the Trial Balance columns was increased or decreased, as the case might be, by the amount of the adjusting entry.

For example, Accumulated Depreciation — Office Equipment was listed in the Trial Balance Credit column as $1,494.81. Since there was an entry of $498.27 in the Adjustments Credit column, the amount extended to the Adjusted Trial Balance Credit column was the total of $1,494.81 and $498.27, or $1,993.08.

A rule which can always be followed in combining figures in the Trial Balance columns and the Adjustments columns is that if there are debits in both columns or credits in both columns, the two amounts are added and the total is carried to the Adjusted Trial Balance columns. If there is a debit in one column and a credit in the other, the smaller amount is subtracted from the larger and the difference will be either a debit or a credit depending on whether the debit or the credit is the larger amount. If the debit is the larger amount, the amount carried to the Adjusted Trial Balance columns will be placed in the Debit Column. If the credit is the larger amount, the difference will be placed in the Adjusted Trial Balance Credit column. The Adjusted Trial Balance columns were totaled to prove the equality of the debits and credits.

Income Statement Columns. The fourth pair of amount columns in the work sheet was used to show the amounts that will be reported in the income statement. The amounts for legal fees revenue and collection fees revenue were extended to the Income Statement Credit column from the Adjusted Trial Balance Credit column. The amounts of the expenses were extended to the Income Statement Debit column from the Adjusted Trial Balance Debit column.

The Income Statement columns were totaled. The difference between the totals of these columns is the amount of the increase or the decrease in owner's equity due to net income or net loss during the accounting period. If the total of the credits exceeds the total of the debits, the difference represents the increase in owner's equity due to net income; if the total of the debits exceeds the total of the credits, the difference represents the decrease in owner's equity due to net loss.

Reference to the Income Statement columns of Andersen's work sheet will show that the total of the credits amounted to $131,881.04 and the total of the debits amounted to $56,690.57. The difference, amounting to $75,190.47, was the amount of the net income for the year.

Balance Sheet Columns. The fifth pair of amount columns of the work sheet was used to show the amounts that will be reported in the balance sheet. The amounts were extended to the Balance Sheet Debit and Credit columns from the Adjusted Trial Balance columns. The Balance Sheet columns were totaled. The difference between the totals of these columns also is the amount of the net income or the net loss for the accounting period. If the total of the debits exceeds the total of the credits, the difference represents a net income for the accounting period; if the total of the credits exceeds the total of the debits, the difference represents a net loss for the period. The difference should be the same as the difference between the totals of the Income Statement columns.

Reference to the Balance Sheet columns of the work sheet will show that the total of the debits amounted to $106,604.84 and the total of the credits amounted to $31,414.37. The difference of $75,190.47 represented the amount of the net income for the year.

Completing the Work Sheet. The difference between the totals of the Income Statement columns and the totals of the Balance Sheet columns should be recorded on the next horizontal line below the column totals. If the difference represents net income, it should be so designated and recorded in the Income Statement Debit and in the Balance Sheet Credit columns. If, instead, a net loss has been the result, the amount should be so designated and entered in the Income Statement Credit and in the Balance Sheet Debit columns.

Finally, the totals of the Income Statement and Balance Sheet columns, after the net income (or net loss) has been recorded, are entered, and a double line is ruled immediately below the totals.

Proving the Work Sheet. The fact that the difference between the Income Statement columns and the difference between the Balance Sheet columns are the same amount is not a coincidence. This occurs because an excess of revenue over expenses results in net income. Likewise, an excess of expenses over revenue results in a net loss. It is also true, but not quite so obvious, that if there is a net income, it will result in an increase in assets in the Balance Sheet columns in the form of additional cash, accounts receivable, or other assets. Sometimes cash received is used to pay liabilities, so that the assets at the end of the period may not have increased in total, but the liabilities have decreased. The increase in owner's equity, however, which results from profitable operations has not yet been recorded in the permanent owner's equity account at the time the work sheet is prepared. The balance of the owner's capital account is the amount of owner's equity at the beginning of the period, because the day by day changes are recorded in the temporary owner's equity accounts — the revenue and expense accounts.

When the amount of the net income is added to the Income Statement Debit column, the total of expenses and net income is equal to the revenue items in the Income Statement Credit column; and when the amount of net income is added to the Balance Sheet Credit column, the total assets equal the total liabilities and owner's equity, which is the accounting equation presented on page 6. After the temporary accounts are closed at the end of the period and the net amount of income for the period has been transferred to the owner's capital account, that account includes the net income for the period.

BUILDING YOUR ACCOUNTING KNOWLEDGE

1. In what three ways does an end-of-period work sheet assist the accountant?
2. Explain the purpose of each of the two adjustments on Andersen's work sheet.

3. State the rule for combining figures in the Trial Balance columns and the Adjustment columns.
4. What is the difference called if the total of the Income Statement Debit column is greater than the total of the Income Statement Credit column?
5. Why must the difference between the totals of the Income Statement columns and the totals of the balance sheet columns always be the same?

Report No. 7-1

Complete Report No. 7-1 in the study assignments and submit your working papers to the instructor for approval. After completing the report, continue with the following textbook discussion until the next report is required.

THE FINANCIAL STATEMENTS

The financial statements usually consist of **(1)** an income statement and **(2)** a balance sheet.

The Income Statement

An **income statement** is a formal statement of the results of the operation of an enterprise during an accounting period. Other titles sometimes used for this statement include **profit and loss statement**, **income and expense statement**, **revenue and expense statement**, **operating statement**, and **report of earnings**. Whatever the title, the purpose of the statement or report is to show the types and amounts of revenue and expenses that the business had during the period involved, and the resulting net income or net loss for this accounting period.

Importance of the Income Statement. The income statement is generally considered to be one of the most important financial statements of a business. A business cannot exist indefinitely unless it has profit or net income. The income statement is essentially a "report card" of the enterprise. The statement provides a basis for judging the overall effectiveness of the management. Decisions as to whether to continue a business, to expand it, or to contract it are often based upon the results as reported in the income statement. Actual and potential creditors are interested in income statements because one of the best reasons for extending credit or for making a loan is that the business is profitable.

Various government agencies are interested in income statements of businesses for a variety of reasons. Regulatory bodies are concerned with the earnings of the enterprises they regulate, because a part of the regulation usually relates to the prices, rates, or fares that may be charged. If the enterprise is either exceptionally profitable or unprofitable, some change in the allowed prices or rates may be needed. Income tax authorities, both federal and local, have an interest in business income statements. Net income determination for tax purposes differs somewhat from the calculation of net income for other purposes; but, for a variety of reasons, the tax authorities are interested in both sets of calculations.

Form of the Income Statement. The form of the income statement depends in part upon the type of enterprise. For a professional practice, the professional revenue is listed first, the professional expenses are listed next, and the total of the professional expenses is subtracted from the professional revenue to determine the net professional income. The amounts of any revenue from other sources, such as dividend revenue from investments, are added to, and the amounts of any other expenses, such as interest on a loan from the bank, are subtracted from, the net professional income to arrive at the final amount of net income or net loss.

It is essential that the income statement be properly headed. The name of the business (or of the individual if the enterprise is a professional practice or if the business is operated in the owner's name) should be shown first. The name of the statement is placed on the second line, and the period of time that the statement covers appears on the third line. An income statement always covers a period of time, and if the period is a year, it may be stated, for example, "For the Year Ended December 31, 19--."

The income statement presented to the owner (or owners) of an enterprise and to potential creditors or other interested parties is usually typewritten. The income statement for Andersen for the year ended December 31, 1983, is shown at the top of page 201. The information needed to prepare the statement was obtained from the work sheet shown on page 195.

KARL F. ANDERSEN, ATTORNEY AT LAW
Income Statement
For the Year Ended December 31, 1983

Professional revenue:		
Legal fees revenue...		$126,873.00
Collection fees revenue..		5,008.04
Total professional revenue		$131,881.04
Professional expenses:		
Automobile expense...	$ 3,713.13	
Charitable contributions expense	994.00	
Depreciation expense...	2,910.84	
Law library expense...	4,104.28	
Miscellaneous expense	664.48	
Office supplies expense	2,963.59	
Payroll taxes expense...	2,458.52	
Rent expense..	10,800.00	
Salary expense...	27,288.00	
Telephone expense...	793.73	
Total professional expenses............................		56,690.57
Net income		$ 75,190.47

Karl F. Andersen, Attorney at Law — Income Statement

The Balance Sheet

A formal statement of the assets, liabilities, and owner's equity in an enterprise at a specified date is known as a **balance sheet**. The title of the statement had its origin in the equality of the elements; that is, in the balance between the sum of the assets and the sum of the liabilities and owner's equity. Sometimes the balance sheet is called a **statement of financial condition** or a **statement of financial position**.

Importance of the Balance Sheet. The balance sheet of a business is of considerable interest to various parties for several reasons. The owner or owners of a business are interested in the kinds and amounts of assets and liabilities and the amount of the owner's equity or capital element.

Persons considering buying an ownership interest in a business are greatly interested in the character and amount of the assets and

The Periodic Summary

liabilities, though this interest is probably secondary to their concern about the future earnings possibilities.

Various regulatory bodies also are interested in the financial condition of the businesses that are under their jurisdiction. Examples of regulated businesses include banks, insurance companies, public utilities, railroads, and airlines.

Form of the Balance Sheet. Traditionally, balance sheets have been presented either in **account form** or in **report form**. When the account form is followed, the assets are listed on the left side of the page (or in the left of two facing pages) and the liabilities and owner's equity on the right. This form is similar to the debit-side and credit-side arrangement of the standard ledger account. When the report form of the balance sheet is followed, the assets, liabilities, and owner's equity elements are listed underneath each other. This arrangement is usually preferable when the statement is typed on letter-size paper (8½" × 11").

The balance sheet of Karl F. Andersen, Attorney at Law, as of December 31, 1983, in account form is reproduced below and on

KARL F. ANDERSEN,
Balance
December

Assets

Current assets:			
Cash		$27,179.21	
Petty cash fund		75.00	
Clients' trust account		4,000.00	
Advances on behalf of clients		495.00	
Total current assets			$31,749.21
Long-term assets:			
Automobile	$9,650.28		
Less accumulated depreciation — automobile	6,031.43	$ 3,618.85	
Office equipment	$5,822.27		
Less accumulated depreciation — office equipment	1,993.08	3,829.19	
Total long-term assets			7,448.04
Total assets			$39,197.25

Karl F. Andersen, Attorney at Law — Balance Sheet *(Left Side)*

page 203. The data for the preparation of the statement were secured from the work sheet shown on page 195.

Whichever form is used, it is essential that the statement have the proper heading. This means that three things must be shown: **(1)** the name of the business (or name of the individual if the business or professional practice is carried on in the name of an individual); followed on the next line by **(2)** the name of the statement — usually just "Balance Sheet"; and **(3)** the date (month, day, and year) on the third line. Sometimes the expression "As of Close of Business December 31, 1983" (or whatever date is involved) is included. It must be remembered that a balance sheet relates to a particular moment of time. This is in contrast to the income statement which always refers to a certain period of time.

Classification of Data in the Balance Sheet. The purpose of the balance sheet and of all other financial statements and reports is to convey as much information as possible. This aim is furthered by some classification of the data being reported. It has become almost

ATTORNEY AT LAW
Sheet
31, 1983

Liabilities

Current liabilities:
Liability for trust funds	$ 4,000.00	
Employees income tax payable	336.80	
FICA tax payable	316.12	
FUTA tax payable	112.90	
State unemployment tax payable	81.65	
Total current liabilities		$ 4,847.47

Owner's Equity

Karl F. Andersen, capital:
Capital, January 1		$18,542.39	
Net income	$75,190.47		
Less withdrawals	59,383.08	15,807.39	
Capital, December 31			34,349.78
Total liabilities and owner's equity			$39,197.25

Karl F. Andersen, Attorney at Law — Balance Sheet *(Right Side)*

universal practice to classify both assets and liabilities in the balance sheet as either (1) current or (2) noncurrent or long-term.

Current Assets. **Current assets** include cash and all other assets that may be reasonably expected to be realized in cash or sold or consumed during the normal operating cycle of the business. In a professional practice, the current assets may include cash and receivables, such as advances on behalf of clients.

Long-Term Assets. Property that is used in the operation of a professional practice may include such assets as land, buildings, office equipment, professional equipment, and automobiles. Such assets are called **long-term assets** because they have a useful life that is comparatively long. Of these assets, only land is really permanent.

Reference to the balance sheet of Karl F. Andersen will show that the long-term assets consist of office equipment and an automobile. In each case, the amount of the accumulated depreciation is shown as a deduction from the cost of the depreciable asset. The difference between the cost of the asset and the accumulated depreciation is the **book value** of the asset. The book value represents the undepreciated amount of the asset. In future periods, the book value of a specific asset will decrease as depreciation expense is realized and the amount of accumulated depreciation increases.

Current Liabilities. **Current liabilities** include those obligations that will be due in a short time and paid with monies provided by the current assets. As of December 31, Andersen's current liabilities consisted of liability for trust funds, employees income tax payable, FICA tax payable, FUTA tax payable, and state unemployment tax payable.

Long-Term Liabilities. **Long-term liabilities**, sometimes called **fixed liabilities**, include those obligations that will not be due for a relatively long time. The most common of the long-term liabilities is Mortgages Payable.

A **mortgage payable** is a debt or an obligation that is secured by a **mortgage**, which provides for the conveyance of certain property upon failure to pay the debt at maturity. When the debt is paid, the mortgage becomes void. A mortgage payable differs little from an account payable or a note payable except that the creditor holds the mortgage as security for the payment of the debt. Usually debts secured by mortgages run for a longer period of time than ordinary notes payable or accounts payable. A mortgage payable should be classified as a long-term liability if the maturity date extends beyond the normal operating cycle of the business (usually a year). Andersen has no long-term liabilities.

Owner's Equity. As previously explained, accounts relating to the owner's equity element may be either permanent or temporary owner's equity accounts. The permanent owner's equity accounts used in recording the operations of a particular enterprise depend upon the type of organization; that is, whether the enterprise is organized as a sole proprietorship, as a partnership, or as a corporation.

In the case of a sole proprietorship, one or more accounts representing the owner's interest or equity in the assets may be kept. Reference to the chart of accounts shown on page 128 will show that the following accounts are classified as owner's equity accounts:

> Karl F. Andersen, Capital, Account No. 511
> Karl F. Andersen, Drawing, Account No. 512
> Expense and Revenue Summary, Account No. 521

Account No. 511 reflects the amount of Andersen's equity. It may be increased by additional investments or by the practice of not withdrawing cash or other assets in an amount as large as the net income of the enterprise. It may be decreased by withdrawals in excess of the amount of the net income or by sustaining a net loss during one or more accounting periods. Usually there will be no changes in the balance of this account during the accounting period, in which case the balance represents the owner's investment in the business as of the beginning of the accounting period and until the books are closed at the end of the accounting period.

Account No. 512 is Andersen's drawing account. This account is debited for any withdrawals of cash or other property for personal use. It is a temporary account in which is kept a record of the owner's personal drawings during the accounting period. Ordinarily such drawings are made in anticipation of earnings rather than as withdrawals of capital. The balance of the account, as shown by the trial balance at the close of an accounting period, represents the total amount of the owner's drawings during the period.

Reference to the work sheet shown on page 195 will reveal that the balance of Andersen's drawing account is listed in the Balance Sheet Debit column. This is because there is no provision on a work sheet for making deductions from owner's equity except by listing them in the Debit column. Since the balance of the owner's capital account is listed in the Balance Sheet Credit column, the listing of the balance of the owner's drawing account in the Debit column is equivalent to deducting the amount from the balance of the owner's capital account.

Account No. 521 is used only at the close of the accounting period for the purpose of summarizing the temporary owner's equity accounts. Sometimes this account is referred to as a **clearing account**. No entries should appear in the account before the books are closed at the end of the accounting period.

The owner's equity section of Andersen's balance sheet is arranged to show the major changes that took place during the year in the owner's equity element of the law practice. Andersen's interest in the practice amounted to $18,542.39 at the beginning of the year. The interest was increased $75,190.47 as the result of profitable operations and decreased $59,383.08 as the result of withdrawals during the year. Thus, the owner's equity increased by $15,807.39 because withdrawals were less than the income for the period. Andersen's anticipation of income was less than the amount actually earned. The owner's equity element on December 31 amounted to $34,349.78.

BUILDING YOUR ACCOUNTING KNOWLEDGE

1. Why is an income statement important?
2. Explain the two forms of the balance sheet.
3. What items are usually included in current assets?
4. Why would a mortgage payable usually not be included among the current liabilities?

Report No. 7-2

> Complete Report No. 7-2 in the study assignments and submit your working papers to the instructor for approval. After completing the report, you may continue with the textbook discussion in Chapter 8 until the next report is required.

EXPANDING YOUR BUSINESS VOCABULARY

What is the meaning of each of the following terms:

account form (p. 202)
adjusted trial balance (p. 196)
balance sheet (p. 201)
book value (p. 204)
clearing account (p. 206)
current assets (p. 204)
current liabilities (p. 204)
end-of-period adjustments (p. 193)
fixed liabilities (p. 204)
income and expense statement (p. 199)
income statement (p. 199)
long-term assets (p. 204)
long-term liabilities (p. 204)
mortgage (p. 204)
mortgage payable (p. 204)
operating statement (p. 199)
periodic summary (p. 193)
profit and loss statement (p. 199)
report form (p. 202)
report of earnings (p. 199)
revenue and expense statement (p. 199)
statement of financial condition (p. 201)
statement of financial position (p. 201)
work sheet (p. 193)

8

ADJUSTING AND CLOSING ACCOUNTS AT END OF ACCOUNTING PERIOD

CHAPTER OBJECTIVES

> The objectives of this chapter are to enable you:
> ▶ To explain and perform the steps in the accounting cycle that are needed to:
> (1) Journalize and post the adjusting entries and update the ledger account balances.
> (2) Journalize and post the closing entries and update the ledger account balances.
> (3) Take a post-closing trial balance.

As explained in the preceding chapter, the adjustment of certain accounts at the end of the accounting period is required because of changes that have occurred during the period that are not reflected in the accounts. Since the purpose of the temporary owner's equity accounts is to assemble information relating to a specified period of time, at the end of the period the balances of these accounts must be removed to allow the accounts to be ready to perform their function in the following period. Accounts of this type must be "closed."

ADJUSTING ENTRIES

In preparing the work sheet for Karl F. Andersen, Attorney at Law (reproduced on page 195), **adjustments** were made to accomplish the following purposes:

(1) To record the estimated amount of depreciation of the automobile for the year.
(2) To record the estimated amount of depreciation of the office equipment for the year.

Note that each of the **adjusting entries** affects both the balance sheet and the income statement. If an adjusting entry increases an expense, as when depreciation expense is recorded in entries **(a)**, and **(b)**, then the balance sheet accounts Accumulated Depreciation — Automobile and Accumulated Depreciation — Office Equipment are also increased. It should also be noted that adjusting entries for accumulated depreciation do not affect cash because the long-term asset has already been paid for. Depreciation, as explained in Chapter 5, is simply a way of allocating the original cost of the asset to the periods in which it is used up.

The effect of these adjustments was reflected in the financial statements reproduced on pages 201, and 202–203. To bring the ledger into agreement with the financial statements, the adjustments should be recorded in the proper accounts. It is customary, therefore, at the end of each accounting period to journalize the adjustments and to post them to the accounts.

Journalizing the Adjusting Entries

Adjusting entries may be recorded in either a general journal or a combination journal. If the entries are made in a combination journal, the only amount columns used are the General Debit and Credit columns. A portion of a page of a combination journal showing Andersen's adjusting entries is reproduced on page 210. Note that when the adjusting entries are recorded in the combination journal, they are entered in exactly the same manner as they would be entered in a general journal. Since the heading "Adjusting Entries" explains the nature of the entries, a separate explanation of each adjusting entry is unnecessary. The information needed in journalizing the adjustments was obtained from the Adjustments columns of the work sheet shown on page 195. The account numbers were not entered in the Posting Reference column at the time of journalizing; they were entered as the posting was completed.

DAY	DESCRIPTION	POST. REF.	GENERAL DEBIT	GENERAL CREDIT
	AMOUNTS FORWARDED			
30	Adjusting Entries			
	Depreciation Expense	705	241257	
	Accumulated Depr.—Automobile	212		241257
	Depreciation Expense	705	49827	
	Accumulated Depr.—Office Equip.	222		49827
			291084	291084

COMBINATION JOURNAL FOR MONTH OF December 19 83 PAGE 44

Karl F. Andersen, Attorney at Law — Adjusting Entries

Posting the Adjusting Entries

The adjusting entries should be posted individually to the proper general ledger accounts. The accounts of Andersen that were affected by the adjusting entries are reproduced on page 211. The entries in the accounts for December transactions that were posted prior to posting the adjusting entries are the same as appeared in the accounts reproduced on pages 146–151. The number of the combination journal page on which the adjusting entries were recorded was entered in the Posting Reference column of the general ledger accounts affected, and the account numbers were entered in the Posting Reference column of the combination journal as the posting was completed. This provided a cross-reference in both books.

Account: Accumulated Depreciation – Automobile   Account No. 212

DATE	ITEM	POST. REF.	DEBIT	CREDIT	BALANCE DEBIT	BALANCE CREDIT
1933 Dec. 1	Balance	✓				361886
30		CJ44		241257		603143

Account: Accumulated Depreciation – Office Equipment   Account No. 222

DATE	ITEM	POST. REF.	DEBIT	CREDIT	BALANCE DEBIT	BALANCE CREDIT
1933 Dec. 1	Balance	✓				149481
30		CJ44		49827		199308

Account: Depreciation Expense   Account No. 705

DATE	ITEM	POST. REF.	DEBIT	CREDIT	BALANCE DEBIT	BALANCE CREDIT
1933 Dec. 30		CJ44	241257			
30		CJ44	49827		291084	

Karl F. Andersen, Attorney at Law —
General Ledger Accounts After Posting Adjusting Entries

BUILDING YOUR ACCOUNTING KNOWLEDGE

1. What is the purpose of each of the adjusting entries made by Karl F. Andersen?
2. Why do adjusting entries for accumulated depreciation not affect cash?
3. Where is the information obtained that is needed in journalizing the adjustments?
4. In the posting process, how is a cross-reference provided both to the combination journal and to the general ledger?

Report No. 8-1

> *Complete Report No. 8-1 in the study assignments and submit your working papers to the instructor for approval. Continue with the following textbook discussion until Report No. 8-2 is required.*

CLOSING PROCEDURE

After the adjusting entries have been posted, all of the temporary owner's equity accounts should be closed. This means that the accountant must remove ("close out") **(1)** the balance of every account that enters into the calculation of the net income (or net loss) for the accounting period and **(2)** the balance of the owner's drawing account. The purpose of the closing procedure is to transfer the balances of the temporary owner's equity accounts to the permanent owner's equity account. This could be accomplished simply by debiting or crediting each account involved, with an offsetting credit or debit to the permanent owner's equity account. However, it is considered better practice to transfer the balances of all accounts that enter into the net income or net loss determination to a summarizing account called **Expense and Revenue Summary** (sometimes called **In-**

come Summary, **Profit and Loss Summary**, or just **Profit and Loss**. Then the resulting balance of the expense and revenue summary account (which will be the amount of the net income or net loss for the period) is transferred to the permanent owner's equity account.

The final step in the closing procedure is to transfer the balance of the owner's drawing account to the permanent owner's equity account. After this is done, only the asset accounts, the liability accounts, and the permanent owner's equity account have balances. If there has been no error, the sum of the balances of the asset accounts (less balances of any contra accounts) will be equal to the sum of the balances of the liability accounts plus the balance of the permanent owner's equity account. The accounts will agree exactly with what is shown by the balance sheet as of the close of the period. Reference to the balance sheet of Karl F. Andersen reproduced on pages 202 and 203 will show that the assets, liabilities, and owner's equity as of December 31 may be expressed in equation form as follows:

ASSETS	=	LIABILITIES	+	OWNER'S EQUITY
$39,197.25		$4,847.47		$34,349.78

Journalizing the Closing Entries

Closing entries, like adjusting entries, may be recorded in either a general journal or a combination journal. If the entries are made in a combination journal, only the General Debit and Credit columns are used. A portion of a page of a combination journal showing the closing entries for Andersen is reproduced on page 214. Since the heading "Closing Entries" explains the nature of the entries, a separate explanation of each closing entry is not necessary. The information required in preparing the closing entries was obtained from the work sheet illustrated on page 195.

The first closing entry was made to close the revenue accounts, Legal Fees Revenue and Collection Fees Revenue. Since these accounts have credit balances, each account must be debited for the amount of its balance in order to close it. The debits to these two accounts are offset by a credit of $131,881.04 to Expense and Revenue Summary.

The second closing entry was made to close the expense accounts. Since these accounts have debit balances, each account must be credited for the amount of its balance in order to close it. The credits to these accounts are offset by a debit of $56,690.57 to Expense and Revenue Summary.

DAY	DESCRIPTION	POST. REF.	GENERAL DEBIT	GENERAL CREDIT	
	COMBINATION JOURNAL FOR MONTH OF December 1983 — PAGE 45				
	AMOUNTS FORWARDED				1
30	Closing Entries				2
	Legal Fees Revenue	611	12687300		3
	Collection Fees Revenue	621	500804		4
	Expense and Revenue Summary	521		13188104	5
	Expense and Revenue Summary	521	5669057		6
	Automobile Expense	701		371313	7
	Charitable Contributions Exp.	703		99400	8
	Depreciation Expense	705		291084	9
	Law Library Expense	708		410428	10
	Miscellaneous Expense	709		66448	11
	Office Supplies Expense	710		296359	12
	Payroll Taxes Expense	712		245852	13
	Rent Expense	715		1080000	14
	Salary Expense	718		2728800	15
	Telephone Expense	720		79373	16
	Expense and Revenue Summary	521	7519047		17
	Karl F. Andersen, Capital	511		7519047	18
	Karl F. Andersen, Capital	511	5938308		19
	Karl F. Andersen, Drawing	512		5938308	20
			32314516	32314516	21

Karl F. Andersen, Attorney at Law — Closing Entries

The posting of the first two closing entries causes the expense and revenue summary account to have a credit balance of $75,190.47, the net income for the year. The account has now served its purpose and must be closed. The third closing entry closes the expense and revenue summary account by debiting that account and crediting Karl F. Andersen, Capital, for $75,190.47.

The final closing entry was made to close the Karl F. Andersen drawing account. Since this account has a debit balance, it must be credited to close it. The offsetting entry is a debit of $59,383.08 to Karl F. Andersen, Capital.

The account numbers shown in the Posting Reference column were not entered at the time the closing entries were made — they were entered as the posting was completed.

Posting the Closing Entries

Closing entries should be posted in the usual manner. Proper cross-references are provided by using the Posting Reference columns of the combination journal and the ledger accounts. After all the closing entries have been posted, the accounts affected appear as shown below and on pages 216 to 218. The income statement accounts are now in balance.

ACCOUNT **Karl F. Andersen, Capital**   ACCOUNT NO. **511**

DATE	ITEM	POST. REF.	DEBIT	CREDIT	BALANCE DEBIT	BALANCE CREDIT
1983 Dec. 1	Balance	✓				18542 39
30		CJ45		7519 047		
30		CJ45	59383 08			34349 78

ACCOUNT **Karl F. Andersen, Drawing**   ACCOUNT NO. **512**

DATE	ITEM	POST. REF.	DEBIT	CREDIT	BALANCE DEBIT	BALANCE CREDIT
1983 Dec. 1	Balance	✓			5476 068	
16		CJ42	2000 00			
27		CJ42	110 83			
29		CJ43	2500 00			
30		CJ43	11 57			
30		CJ45		59383 08	—0—	—0—

ACCOUNT **Expense and Revenue Summary**   ACCOUNT NO. **521**

DATE	ITEM	POST. REF.	DEBIT	CREDIT	BALANCE DEBIT	BALANCE CREDIT
1983 Dec. 30		CJ45		13188 04		
30		CJ45	5669 057			
30		CJ45	7519 047		—0—	—0—

Karl F. Andersen, Attorney at Law — Partial General Ledger (continued)

ACCOUNT: Legal Fees Revenue — ACCOUNT NO. 611

DATE	ITEM	POST. REF.	DEBIT	CREDIT	BALANCE DEBIT	BALANCE CREDIT
1953 Dec. 1	Balance	✓				10990800
30		CJ43		1696500		12687300
30		CJ45	12687300		—0—	—0—

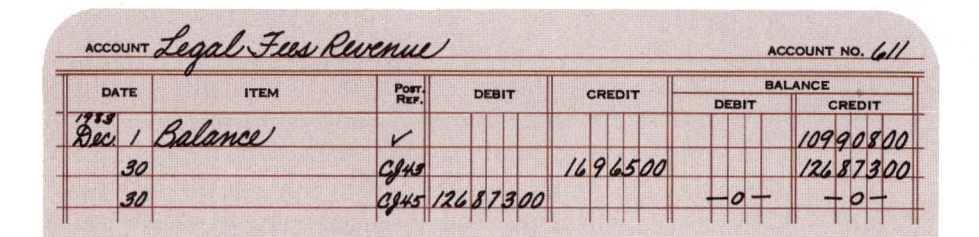

ACCOUNT: Collection Fees Revenue — ACCOUNT NO. 621

DATE	ITEM	POST. REF.	DEBIT	CREDIT	BALANCE DEBIT	BALANCE CREDIT
1953 Dec. 1	Balance	✓				473199
30		CJ43		27605		500804
30		CJ45	500804		—0—	—0—

ACCOUNT: Automobile Expense — ACCOUNT NO. 701

DATE	ITEM	POST. REF.	DEBIT	CREDIT	BALANCE DEBIT	BALANCE CREDIT
1953 Dec. 1	Balance	✓			353437	
6		CJ42	15882			
30		CJ43	1994		371313	
30		CJ45		371313	—0—	—0—

ACCOUNT: Charitable Contributions Expense — ACCOUNT NO. 703

DATE	ITEM	POST. REF.	DEBIT	CREDIT	BALANCE DEBIT	BALANCE CREDIT
1953 Dec. 1	Balance	✓			93400	
13		CJ42	5000			
30		CJ43	1000		99400	
30		CJ45		99400	—0—	—0—

ACCOUNT: Depreciation Expense — ACCOUNT NO. 705

DATE	ITEM	POST. REF.	DEBIT	CREDIT	BALANCE DEBIT	BALANCE CREDIT
1953 Dec. 30		CJ44	241257			
30		CJ44	49827		291084	
30		CJ45		291084	—0—	—0—

Karl F. Andersen, Attorney at Law — Partial General Ledger (continued)

Chapter 8 — Adjusting and Closing Accounts at End of Accounting Period

ACCOUNT Law Library Expense   **ACCOUNT NO.** 708

DATE	ITEM	POST. REF.	DEBIT	CREDIT	BALANCE DEBIT	BALANCE CREDIT
1983 Dec. 1	Balance	✓			3375 00	
12		CJ42	729 28		4104 28	
30		CJ45		4104 28	—0—	—0—

ACCOUNT Miscellaneous Expense   **ACCOUNT NO.** 709

DATE	ITEM	POST. REF.	DEBIT	CREDIT	BALANCE DEBIT	BALANCE CREDIT
1983 Dec. 1	Balance	✓			502 38	
2		CJ42	55 25			
14		CJ42	100 00			
30		CJ43	6 85		664 48	
30		CJ45		664 48	—0—	—0—

ACCOUNT Office Supplies Expense   **ACCOUNT NO.** 710

DATE	ITEM	POST. REF.	DEBIT	CREDIT	BALANCE DEBIT	BALANCE CREDIT
1983 Dec. 1	Balance	✓			2859 42	
19		CJ42	98 22			
30		CJ43	5 95		2963 59	
30		CJ45		2963 59	—0—	—0—

ACCOUNT Payroll Taxes Expense   **ACCOUNT NO.** 712

DATE	ITEM	POST. REF.	DEBIT	CREDIT	BALANCE DEBIT	BALANCE CREDIT
1983 Dec. 1	Balance	✓			2266 18	
30		CJ43	158 06			
30		CJ43	34 28		2458 52	
30		CJ45		2458 52	—0—	—0—

Karl F. Andersen, Attorney at Law — Partial General Ledger *(continued)*

Account: Rent Expense — Account No. 715

DATE	ITEM	POST. REF.	DEBIT	CREDIT	BALANCE DEBIT	BALANCE CREDIT
1983 Dec. 1	Balance	✓			990000	
1		CJ42	90000		1080000	
30		CJ45		1080000	—0—	—0—

Account: Salary Expense — Account No. 718

DATE	ITEM	POST. REF.	DEBIT	CREDIT	BALANCE DEBIT	BALANCE CREDIT
1983 Dec. 1	Balance	✓			2503000	
15		CJ42	52800			
15		CJ42	62500			
30		CJ43	48000			
30		CJ43	62500		2728800	
30		CJ45		2728800	—0—	—0—

Account: Telephone Expense — Account No. 720

DATE	ITEM	POST. REF.	DEBIT	CREDIT	BALANCE DEBIT	BALANCE CREDIT
1983 Dec. 1	Balance	✓			72984	
5		CJ42	6389		79373	
30		CJ45		79373	—0—	—0—

Karl F. Andersen, Attorney at Law — Partial General Ledger *(concluded)*

After the income statement accounts have been closed, the accounts still open are the balance sheet accounts; that is, the asset, liability, and permanent owner's equity accounts. If a new general ledger is to be opened in which to record the transactions of the new year, the balances of the open accounts which have debit balances should be entered in the Debit Balance columns. The balances of the open accounts which have credit balances should be entered in the Credit Balance columns. The date will be January 1, even though the new ledger may be opened a few days after January 1.

If the old general ledger is to be used for the new year, the December 31 balances of the open accounts automatically become the balances on January 1. The number of the new year should be entered when the first entry is made in the new year.

Trial Balance After Closing

A trial balance of the general ledger accounts that remain open after the temporary owner's equity accounts have been closed is usually referred to as a **post-closing trial balance**. The purpose of the post-closing trial balance is to prove that the general ledger is in balance at the beginning of a new accounting period. It is advisable to know that such is the case before any transactions for the new accounting period are recorded.

The post-closing trial balance should contain the same accounts and amounts as appear in the Balance Sheet columns of the work sheet, except that **(1)** the owner's drawing account is omitted because it has been closed and **(2)** the owner's capital account has been adjusted for the amount of the net income (or net loss) and the amount of the owner's drawings.

A post-closing trial balance of Andersen's general ledger is shown below. Some accountants advocate that the post-closing trial balance should be dated as of the close of the old accounting period, while others advocate that it should be dated as of the beginning of the new accounting period. In this illustration the trial balance is dated December 31, the end of the period.

KARL F. ANDERSEN, ATTORNEY AT LAW
Post-Closing Trial Balance
December 31, 1983

Account	No.	Debit	Credit
Cash	111	27,179.21	
Petty Cash Fund	112	75.00	
Clients' Trust Account	121	4,000.00	
Advances on Behalf of Clients	131	495.00	
Automobile	211	9,650.28	
Accumulated Depreciation — Automobile	212		6,031.43
Office Equipment	221	5,822.27	
Accumulated Depreciation — Office Equipment	222		1,993.08
Liability for Trust Funds	321		4,000.00
Employees Income Tax Payable	331		336.80
FICA Tax Payable	341		316.12
FUTA Tax Payable	351		112.90
State Unemployment Tax Payable	361		81.65
Karl F. Andersen, Capital	511		34,349.78
		47,221.76	47,221.76

Karl F. Andersen, Attorney at Law — Post-Closing Trial Balance

The Accounting Cycle

The steps involved in handling the effect of all transactions and events completed during an accounting period, beginning with entries in the books of original entry and ending with the post-closing trial balance, are known as the **accounting cycle**. The following is a list of the steps in the accounting cycle.

   (1) Journalizing the transactions.
   (2) Posting to the ledger accounts.
   (3) Taking a trial balance.
   (4) Determining the needed adjustments.
   (5) Completing an end-of-period work sheet.
   (6) Preparing an income statement and a balance sheet.
   (7) Journalizing and posting the adjusting and closing entries.
   (8) Taking a post-closing trial balance.

In visualizing the accounting cycle, it is important to realize that steps **(3)** through **(8)** in the foregoing list are performed *as of the last day of the accounting period*. This does not mean that they necessarily are done *on* the last day. The accountant or bookkeeper may not be able to do any of these things until the first few days of the next period. Nevertheless, the work sheet, statements, and entries are prepared or recorded as of the closing date. While the journalizing of transactions in the new period proceeds in regular fashion, it is not usual to post to the general ledger any entries relating to the new period until the steps relating to the period just ended have been completed.

Income and Self-Employment Taxes

An unincorporated business or professional practice is not subject to income taxes. The owner — not the business or practice — is subject to income taxes. The amounts of business or professional revenue and expenses must be reported in the owner's personal income tax return regardless of the amount of money or other property the owner has actually withdrawn from the enterprise during the year. In the case of a sole proprietorship or a partnership, there is no legal distinction between the enterprise and the owner.

In order to bring a large class of self-employed individuals into the federal social security program, the law requires all self-employed persons (except those specifically exempted) to pay a **self-employment tax**. The rate of tax is 2.65 percent more than the prevailing FICA rate, but the base of the "self-employment income tax" is the same as the base for the FICA tax. (If it is assumed that the combined FICA tax rate is 7 percent, the self-employment income tax rate would be 9.65 percent on the assumed base of $30,000.) The actual rate and base of the tax may be changed by Congress at any time. In general, **self-employment income** means the net income of a professional practice or business conducted by an individual or a partner's distributive share of the net income of a partnership whether or not any cash is distributed. Earnings of less than $400 from self-employment are ignored for purposes of self-employment tax.

A taxable year for the purpose of the tax on self-employment income is the same as the taxpayer's taxable year for federal income tax purposes. The self-employment tax is reported along with the regular federal income tax. For calendar-year taxpayers, the tax return and full or final payment is due on April 15 following the close of the year. Like the personal income tax, the self-employment tax is treated as a personal expense of the owner. If the taxes are paid with business funds, the amount should be charged to the owners' drawing account.

BUILDING YOUR ACCOUNTING KNOWLEDGE

1. Where is the information obtained that is needed in journalizing the closing entries?
2. Explain the function of each of the four closing entries made by Karl F. Andersen.
3. What is the purpose of a post-closing trial balance?

Report No. 8-2

> Complete Report No. 8-2 in the study assignments and submit your working papers to the instructor for approval. You will then be given instructions as to the work to be done next.

EXPANDING YOUR BUSINESS VOCABULARY

What is the meaning of each of the following terms:

accounting cycle (p. 220)
adjusting entries (p. 209)
adjustments (p. 209)
closing entries (p. 213)
Expense and Revenue Summary (p. 212)
Income Summary (p. 213)
post-closing trial balance (p. 219)
Profit and Loss (p. 213)
Profit and Loss Summary (p. 213)
self-employment income (p. 221)
self-employment tax (p. 220)

CHAPTERS 5-8

SUPPLEMENTARY PRACTICAL ACCOUNTING PROBLEMS

Problem 5-A *Journalizing; posting; trial balance*

Roberta Fitzpatrick and Rosemary Stratton are partners engaged in the practice of law. They employ a secretary-bookkeeper and a secretary. The books, which are kept on the cash basis, consist of a combination journal and a general ledger. For the combination journal, use a sheet of paper like that shown in the illustration on pages 142–145. A column for collection fees will not be needed in this journal. Number the page of the journal using number 13. The trial balance taken as of April 30, 19-- appears on the next page.

FITZPATRICK AND STRATTON, ATTORNEYS AT LAW
Trial Balance
April 30, 19--

Account	No.	Debit	Credit
Cash	110	41,200.35	
Petty Cash	112	75.00	
Clients' Trust Account	115	4,500.00	
Automobile	120	10,435.27	
Accumulated Depr. — Automobile	121		5,217.64
Furniture and Equipment	130	7,015.16	
Accumulated Depr. — Furniture and Equip.	131		2,806.06
Liability for Trust Funds	210		4,500.00
Employees Income Tax Payable	215		347.00
FICA Tax Payable	220		350.00
State Unemployment Tax Payable	225		67.50
FUTA Tax Payable	230		71.22
Roberta Fitzpatrick, Capital	310		19,347.89
Roberta Fitzpatrick, Drawing	315	12,415.38	
Rosemary Stratton, Capital	320		20,819.13
Rosemary Stratton, Drawing	325	12,232.75	
Legal Fees	410		57,115.00
Insurance Expense	510	1,424.02	
Law Library Expense	515	529.74	
Payroll Taxes Expense	520	1,058.18	
Rent Expense	525	8,000.00	
Salary Expense	530	10,174.81	
Stationery and Supplies Expense	535	760.43	
Utilities Expense	540	820.35	
		110,641.44	110,641.44

NARRATIVE OF TRANSACTIONS FOR MAY

May 2 Paid rent for May, $2,000. Check No. 400.
     2 Paid the following bills:
         Telephone bill, $165.82. Check No. 401.
         Electric bill, $47.63. Check No. 402.
     3 Received $1,500 from the U.S. Government. Fitzpatrick acted as an expert witness before a government committee.
     5 Received $4,275 from Philip Correnti for balance due on Case No. 221.
     9 Paid cash for office supplies, $65.10. Check No. 403.
    10 Received $900 for work in connection with the incorporation of the Gonzalez Manufacturing Corporation.

May 13 Paid $697 for April payroll taxes:

Employees' income tax witheld	$347
FICA tax	350
	$697

Check No. 404.
13 Paid wages of employees for first half of month as follows:
$650.00, less income tax payable, $98.40, and FICA tax payable, $45.50. Check No. 405.
$600.00, less income tax payable, $75.10, and FICA tax payable, $42.00. Check No. 406.
16 Received $2,780 from Gartland and Acosta for balance due on Case No. 219.
20 Paid for additions to the law library, $227.81. Check No. 407.
23 Received $750 for work in connection with planning the estate of R. S. McKenzie.
24 On April 20, Fitzpatrick and Stratton received $4,500 from R. L. Benedict as a deposit on a building Benedict wished to buy from C. R. Levine. The $4,500 was charged to Account No. 115, Clients' Trust Account. The transaction was completed today, May 24, and Benedict directed that the $4,500 be paid to Levine. Check No. 25. (Debit Liability for Trust Funds, Account No. 210, and credit Clients' Trust Account, Account No. 115, for $4,500.)
24 Received a fee of $1,500 from Benedict for legal work in connection with the above transaction. Case No. 227.
25 Received $50.35 for overcharge on law books purchased in April. (Law Library Expense, Account No. 515, had been debited for the total amount of the invoice.)
27 Received $2,700 for work in connection with preparing a pension plan for the Star Manufacturing Co.
31 Paid wages of employees for the second half of month as follows:
$695.00, less income tax payable, $109.10, and FICA tax payable, $48.65. Check No. 408.
$600.00, less income tax payable, $75.10, and FICA tax payable, $42.00. Check No. 409.
31 Fitzpatrick withdrew $3,000 for personal use. Check No. 410.
31 Stratton withdrew $3,000 for personal use. Check No. 411.
31 Replenished the petty cash fund. Check No. 412. The following disbursements had been made:

Stationery and Supplies Expense	$32.49
Utilities Expense — (collect telegram)	2.27
Rosemary Stratton, Drawing	18.56
Total disbursements	$53.32

31 Made an entry in the combination journal for the employer's portion of the FICA tax, for the state unemployment tax, and

for the FUTA tax for the month of May by debiting Payroll Taxes Expense for $240.21 and crediting FICA Tax Payable for $178.15, State Unemployment Tax Payable for $49.28, and FUTA Tax Payable for $12.78.

Required: (1) Record each transaction in the combination journal. (2) Prove the combination journal by footing the amount columns; total and rule the journal. (3) Open the necessary general ledger accounts using account forms like those illustrated on pages 146–150. Record the May 1 balances as shown in the April 30 trial balance and complete the individual posting from the combination journal. Determine the balances of the accounts. (4) Take a trial balance of the accounts which have balances as of May 31, using a sheet of two-column journal paper.

Problem 5-B Journalizing payroll taxes

The law firm of Murphy and Silverstein has 17 employees. The employees are paid by check on the 15th and last business day of each month. The entry to record each payroll includes the liabilities for the amounts withheld. The employer's payroll taxes are recorded on each payday. The social security and withheld income taxes exceed $3,000 on each payday, and it is therefore necessary for Murphy and Silverstein to deposit the taxes within three banking days of each payday. Thus the taxes for salaries paid on January 15 and January 31 must be paid within three banking days following January 15 and January 31.

Following is a narrative of the transactions completed during the month of February of the current year that relate to payrolls and payroll taxes.

Feb. 2   Paid $4,111.39 for January 31 payroll taxes:

Employees' income tax withheld	$2,077.50
FICA tax	2,033.89

15   Payroll for the first half of month:

Total salaries		$14,683.27
Less amounts withheld:		
Employees' income tax	$2,117.50	
FICA tax	1,027.83	3,145.33
Net amount paid		$11,537.94

15   Social security taxes imposed on employer:

FICA tax, 7.0%
State Unemployment tax, 2.5%
FUTA tax, 0.7%

Feb. 28 Payroll for the second half of month:

Total salaries...		$14,527.80
Less amounts withheld:		
Employees' income tax	$2,077.50	
FICA tax	1,016.95	3,094.45
Net amount paid		$11,433.35

    28 Social security taxes imposed on employer:
          All salaries taxable; rates same as on February 15.

Required: **(1)** Journalize the foregoing transactions, using two-column general journal paper. **(2)** Foot the debit and credit amount columns as a means of proof.

Challenge Problem 5

On March 5, 1982, Paula Walters and Joseph Rebholz received a certificate of incorporation for their individual law practices. The new firm will be known as Walters and Rebholz, P.S.C. Frances Goetz and Betty Underwood have been hired as a secretary-bookkeeper and a secretary respectively. The accounting records will consist of a combination journal and a general ledger which will be kept on the cash basis.

The corporation has been authorized to issue 1,500 shares of capital stock with a value of $50 per share. The incorporators hold the following number of shares:

Paula Walters	500 shares @ $50 =	$25,000
Joseph Rebholz..	500 shares @ $50 =	25,000
Total..	1,000	$50,000

The following selected transactions were completed during the month of April 1983:

April 1 Issued Check No. 145 for $2,000 to Douglas Phelps for rent of office for the month of April.
        2 Issued Check No. 28 for $1,207.50 to the Dietrich Construction Co. to remit a collection from the Wray Machinery Co. in the amount of $1,725 less a 30% collection fee. Collection No. 22.
        4 Purchased office supplies for cash, $128.17. Check No. 146.
        4 Declared a dividend of $10 a share to be paid to the stockholders on this date. Issued Check No. 147 for $5,000 ($10 × 500 shares) to Paula Walters.
           Issued Check No. 148 for $5,000 ($10 × 500 shares) to Joseph Rebholz.

Debit Retained Earnings, Account No. 313, for $5,000 and credit Cash, Account No. 111, for $5,000 for each check. Since the dividends are being paid on the date of declaration, it is not necessary to credit Dividends Payable when Retained Earnings is debited.

April 6 Received a check for $17,500 from the Mueller Distributing Co. in full payment of the balance due for legal fees. Case No. 37.

7 Issued Check No. 149 for $875 in payment of an invoice received from the Central Publishing Co. for law books.

8 The firm has been engaged to represent the Hilltop Plumbing Co. against Arthur Wilder. Received retainer, $300. Case No. 48.

11 Received a check for $250 for drafting a partnership agreement for Gardner and Isaacs, certified public accountants.

12 Issued Check No. 150 for $85.37 to the Central Power & Light Co. for electricity consumed during the month of March.

14 Issued Check No. 151 in the amount of $1,836.90 to the Prescott Valley National Bank in payment of the following payroll taxes on wages paid during the month of March:

Employees' income tax withheld from wages..		$ 982.90
FICA tax:		
Withheld from employees' wages..................	$427.00	
Imposed on employer	427.00	854.00
Amount of check...		$1,836.90

18 Margaret O'Hara, an attorney, invested $10,000 in the firm of Walters and Rebholz by purchasing 200 of the unissued shares of common stock at $50 a share. O'Hara will begin work with the firm on May 2. (It would be possible to change the name of the firm to include O'Hara's name, but it is not necessary to do so.)

*20 Work has been completed on the settlement of the state of Howard Jurgensen, deceased, and a check for $8,000 in payment for services rendered has been received. Case No. 32.

22 Paid the State Bar Association for annual dues for the members of the firm, $300. Check No. 152.

26 Received a check for $1,800 from Gladys Reinhardt in payment of the amount due on Collection No. 20.

    The collection docket shows that the firm had agreed to handle this collection on a 33⅓% commission basis.

28 Issued Check No. 153 in the amount of $128.10 to the Prescott Valley National Bank in payment of the FUTA tax for the quarter ended March 31, 1983.

28 Issued Check No. 154 in the amount of $494.10 to the State in payment of the state unemployment tax for the quarter ended March 31, 1983.

29 Issued the following salary checks for the month of April:
    No. 155 for $982.40 to Frances Goetz in payment of salary, $1,200.00, less $133.60 withheld for income tax and $84.00 withheld for FICA tax.

Chapters 5–8   Supplementary Practical Accounting Problems   **229**

               No. 156 for $854.20 to Betty Underwood in payment of salary, $1,100.00, less $168.80 withheld for income tax and $77.00 withheld for FICA tax.

               No. 157 for $1,558.70 to Paula Walters in payment of salary, $2,000.00, less $301.30 withheld for income tax and $140.00 withheld for FICA tax.

               No. 158 for $1,294.80 to Joseph Rebholz in payment of salary, $1,800.00, less $379.20 withheld for income tax and $126.00 withheld for FICA tax.

April 29   Made an entry in the combination journal for the employer's portion of the FICA tax for the month of April by debiting Payroll Taxes Expense and crediting FICA Tax Payable for $427.

      29   Made an entry in the combination journal by debiting Payroll Taxes Expense for $98.60 and crediting FUTA Tax Payable for $20.30 and crediting State Unemployment Tax Payable for $78.30.

              The FUTA tax is figured at 0.7% of salaries earned up to $6,000 in a year. Walters' salary reached $6,000 at the end of March. In April, all of Goetz' and Underwood's salaries are taxable, and $600 of Rebholz' salary is taxable making the total taxable wages $2,900.

              The state unemployment tax is figured at 2.7% of the first $6,000 of wages earned during the year, or $78.30 for April.

Required: (1) Open the accounts and enter the balances shown in the following April 1 trial balance. (2) Record the transactions in a com-

WALTERS & REBHOLZ, P.S.C.
Trial Balance
April 1, 1983

Cash	111	45,921.21	
Clients' Trust Account	112	1,207.50	
Government Notes	115	60,000.00	
Office Furniture and Equipment	120	26,743.22	
Accum. Depr. — Office Furniture and Equip.	121		1,395.27
Employees Income Tax Payable	201		982.90
FICA Tax Payable	211		854.00
FUTA Tax Payable	221		128.10
State Unemployment Tax Payable	231		494.10
Liability for Trust Funds	241		1,207.50
Common Stock	311		50,000.00
Retained Earnings	313		25,429.38
Legal Fees Revenue	411		83,387.00
Collection Fees Revenue	421		1,924.50
Law Library Expense	511	5,427.91	
Miscellaneous Expense	515	109.84	
Office Supplies Expense	516	189.87	
Payroll Taxes Expense	518	1,903.20	
Rent Expense	520	6,000.00	
Salary Expense	523	18,300.00	
		165,802.75	165,802.75

bination journal using the accounts listed in the trial balance on page 229. For the combination journal, use a sheet of paper like that shown in the illustration on pages 142–145 in the textbook. Foot, enter the totals, and rule the combination journal. **(3)** Post the summary columns and the General columns from the journal to the ledger accounts. In posting from the combination journal, the page number preceded by the initials "CJ" should be inserted in the Posting Reference column of the ledger. Use page number 14. The account numbers should also be entered in the Posting Reference column and immediately below the totals of the summary columns in the combination journal. **(4)** Determine and record the account balances where necessary. **(5)** Take a trial balance as of April 30, 1983.

Problem 6-A Journalizing; posting; trial balance

Dr. Michael Horwitz is a dentist. The only book of original entry is a combination journal. The accounts are kept in a general ledger. Horwitz has two employees; Joseph Berman, a dental hygienist, and Margaret Donelson, a secretary-bookkeeper. There is an auxiliary record for the patients seen by Horwitz and for the patients seen by Berman, but these records are not involved in this problem. The books are kept on the cash basis. Horwitz requests that patients pay cash for the services of the hygienist, and most do. The trial balance as of June 30 is shown on page 231.

NARRATIVE OF TRANSACTIONS FOR JULY

July 1 Paid rent for July, $2,000.
     5 Paid telephone bill for June, $65.85.
     5 Paid the Acme Dental Laboratory for laboratory work done in June, $4,019.
     8 The amount columns in the daily service records kept by Horwitz and Berman for the week ended July 8 contained the following totals:

Kind of service:	
Dentistry — Horwitz	$2,785
Oral hygiene — Berman	660
Total	$3,445

The total cash received from patients during the week ended July 8 was:

Dentistry	$2,825
Oral hygiene	630
Total	$3,455

DR. MICHAEL HORWITZ, DENTIST
Trial Balance
June 30, 19--

Account	No.	Debit	Credit
Cash	111	19,501.57	
Professional Equipment	121	28,195.20	
Accumulated Depr. — Professional Equip.	122		10,573.20
Office Equipment	131	3,462.95	
Accumulated Depr. — Office Equip.	132		1,035.90
Employees Income Tax Payable	211		368.80
FICA Tax Payable	221		357.00
State Unemployment Tax Payable	231		117.45
FUTA Tax Payable	241		84.00
Michael Horwitz, Capital	311		33,413.26
Michael Horwitz, Drawing	312	15,342.18	
Professional Fees — Dentistry	411		60,850.00
Professional Fees — Oral Hygiene	421		14,700.00
Laboratory Expense	500	24,630.00	
Laundry Expense	503	147.80	
Miscellaneous Expense	505	31.27	
Payroll Taxes Expense	508	1,479.00	
Professional Supplies Expense	510	415.75	
Rent Expense	512	12,000.00	
Salary Expense	515	15,300.00	
Stationery and Supplies Expense	518	145.10	
Telephone Expense	520	390.59	
Utilities Expense	522	458.20	
		121,499.61	121,499.61

July 10   Paid laundry bill for June, $25.27.

     11   Paid the following bills:
          Electricity bill, $30.18
          Water bill, $24.92

     15   The amount columns in the daily service records contained the following totals:

Kind of service:	
Dentistry — Horwitz	$2,510
Oral hygiene — Berman	685
Total	$3,195

The total cash received from patients during the week ended July 15 was:

Dentistry	$2,645
Oral hygiene	650
Total	$3,295

     15   Paid salary to Joseph Berman for first half of month: $650, less income tax payable, $74.80, and FICA tax payable, $45.50; and to Margaret Donelson, $625.00, less income tax payable, $109.60, and FICA tax payable $43.75.

     15   Paid $725.80 for June payroll taxes:

Employees' income tax withheld		$368.80
FICA tax		357.00
Total		$725.80

July 18 Paid for professional supplies, $82.77.

20 Paid $100 for dues to the state dental society. (Debit Miscellaneous Expense.)

22 The amount columns in the daily service records contained the following totals:

Kind of service:	
Dentistry — Horwitz	$2,837
Oral hygiene — Berman	675
Total	$3,512

The total cash received from patients during the week ended July 22 was:

Dentistry	$3,127
Oral hygiene	620
Total	$3,747

25 Paid for office supplies, $21.63.

26 Paid for subscriptions to magazines for the waiting room, $30. (Debit Miscellaneous Expense.)

29 Paid state unemployment tax for the second quarter, $117.45.

29 The amount columns in the daily service records contained the following totals:

Kind of service:	
Dentistry — Horwitz	$2,982
Oral hygiene — Berman	505
Total	$3,487

The total cash received from patients for the period July 25–29 was:

Dentistry	$2,720
Oral hygiene	590
Total	$3,310

29 Paid salary to Joseph Berman for second half of month, $650.00, less income tax payable $74.80, and FICA tax payable, $45.50; and to Margaret Donelson, $625.00, less income tax payable, $109.60, and FICA tax payable, $43.75.

29 Horwitz withdrew $2,500 for personal use.

29 Made an entry in the combination journal for the employer's portion of the FICA tax for the month of July by debiting Payroll Taxes Expense and crediting FICA Tax Payable for $178.50. The salaries of both employees have exceeded $6,000 prior to the month of July, so no entry is needed for state unemployment tax or FUTA tax.

Chapters 5–8   Supplementary Practical Accounting Problems   233

Required: **(1)** Record each transaction in the combination journal using a sheet of paper like that illustrated on pages 180–183. Number the page of the journal using number 48. **(2)** Prove the combination journal by footing the amount columns; total and rule the journal. **(3)** Open the necssary general ledger accounts using account forms like those illustrated on pages 180–189. Record the July 1 balances as shown in the June 30 trial balance and complete the posting from the combination journal. Determine the balances of the accounts. **(4)** Take a trial balance as of July 31, using a sheet of two-column journal paper.

Problem 6-B   Corrected trial balance

Dr. Gloria Contos, a physician and surgeon keeps her books on the cash basis. A trial balance taken as of September 30, 19--, does not balance. A check of the records reveals the following information:

(1) The correct total of the Cash Dr. column in the combination journal is $9,582. This amount was posted in the cash account as $9,528.
(2) The combination journal was out of balance by $213 because a payment for professional supplies was debited to the proper account but was not entered in the Cash Cr. column..
(3) The balance in the office equipment account was entered in the trial balance as $420 instead of $4,200.

DR. GLORIA CONTOS
Trial Balance
September 30, 19--

Cash	20,107.00	
Professional Equipment	48,215.50	
Accumulated Depr. — Professional Equip.		17,357.40
Office Equipment	420.00	
Accumulated Depr. — Office Equip.		1,260.00
Employees Income Tax Payable		116.90
FICA Tax Payable		168.00
FUTA Tax Payable		75.60
Gloria Contos, Capital		24,524.23
Gloria Contos, Drawing	22,637.80	
Professional Fees		84,215.00
Payroll Taxes Expense		960.00
Professional Supplies Expense		1,530.15
Rent Expense	18,000.00	
Salary Expense	10,800.00	
Utilities Expense	1,275.00	
	121,455.30	130,207.28

(4) The miscellaneous expense account in the amount of $150.68 was omitted from the trial balance.
(5) All accounts have normal balances.

Required: Prepare a corrected trial balance.

Challenge Problem 6

Elizabeth Kirkwood, Sandra Waldeck, and Clarence McClure, physicians and surgeons, are the stockholders of the Jackson Springs Medical Clinic, Inc. The corporation was formed several years ago and operates a medical practice which includes minor surgery performed in the clinic. Major surgery is performed in a nearby hospital. The clinic employs Hilda Rasmussen, R.N., Andrew Kelly, secretary-bookkeeper, and Luther Whitney, a laboratory and X-ray technologist.

The accounting records consist of a combination journal and a general ledger and are kept on the cash basis. There is also a daily service record and a patients ledger. Records of employees' earnings are maintained, but are not involved in this problem.

The corporation has been authorized to issue 5,000 shares of common stock with a value of $100 per share. The stockholders hold the following number of shares:

Elizabeth Kirkwood	1,500 shares @ $100 =	$150,000
Sandra Waldeck	1,000 shares @ $100 =	100,000
Clarence McClure	1,000 shares @ $100 =	100,000
Total	3,500	$350,000

The following selected transactions were completed during the month of March 1983. It was decided to begin a new series of check numbers and journal page numbers beginning with No. 1 on January 2, 1983:

Mar. 1 Issued Check No. 61 for $388.90 to the Midvale Gas and Electric Co. for electricity consumed during February.
2 Issued Check No. 62 for $118.30 to the Bell Telephone Co. for February service.
2 Issued Check No. 63 for $197.80 to the Medford Garage for repairs to one of the automobiles. (Debit Automobile Expense, Account No. 500.)
3 Issued Check No. 64 for $88.36 to the Superior Laundry for laundry service for the month of February.
3 Issued Check No. 65 to the Midvale National Bank in payment of the following payroll taxes based on wages paid during the month of February.

Chapters 5–8 Supplementary Practical Accounting Problems **235**

Employees' income tax withheld from wages..		$2,127.20
FICA tax:		
Withheld from employees' wages..................	$804.53	
Imposed on employer	804.53	1,609.06
Amount of check...		$3,736.26

Note: Since the undeposited taxes for the month of February are more than $3,000, they must be deposited within three banking days after February 28.

Mar. 4 Issued Check No. 66 for $56.10 to the Bennett Stationery Company for office supplies purchased in February.

     7 Declared a dividend of $5 a share on the common stock to be paid on March 30 to the stockholders of record on March 15.

        Debit Retained Earnings, Account No. 305, for $17,500 (3,500 shares × $5) and credit Dividends Payable, Account No. 251 for $17,500. No entry is needed on March 15.

     7 Issued Check No. 67 for $260.83 for the purchase of surgical instruments.

     8 Issued Check No. 68 for $79.16 to the Medical Equipment Co. for an equipment repair.

     9 Issued Check No. 69 for $2,700 to the American Medical Association for annual dues for Kirkwood, Waldeck, and McClure.

     9 Issued Check No. 70 for $100 payable to the American Red Cross.

    11 Footed the amount columns in the daily service record and obtained the following totals:

Kind of service:	
Office calls	$ 4,640
Surgery...	16,590
Total	$21,230
Patients' accounts — charges	$17,620
Cash services...	3,610
Total	$21,230

The total cash received from patients for the period March 1–11 was:

Payments	$18,870
Cash services...	3,610
Total	$22,480

    11 Issued Check No. 71 for $60.39 to the Physicians' Publishing Co. for medical books.

    14 Issued Check No. 72 for $25 to the Midvale National Bank for rental of a safe deposit box for use by the clinic. (Debit Miscellaneous Expense.)

    15 Issued Check No. 73 for $4,970 to the Collins Insurance Agency for renewal of Waldeck's professional liability insurance.

Mar. 17 Issued Check No. 74 for $789.50 to Kirkwood to reimburse her for the expense of attending a medical conference.
18 Issued Check No. 75 for $165.70 for X-ray film.
18 Footed the amount columns in the daily service record and obtained the following totals:

Kind of service:	
Office calls	$ 2,350
Surgery	10,400
Total	$12,750
Patients' accounts — charges	$10,450
Cash services	2,300
Total	$12,750

The total cash received from patients for the week was:

Payments	$ 9,920
Cash services	2,300
Total	$12,220

21 Issued Check No. 76 for $329.80 to the Physicians' Supply Co. for medical supplies.
21 Received $80,000 from Dr. Anthony Chen for the purchase of 800 shares of the unissued common stock of the clinic.

Note that Chen is not entitled to the dividend to be paid on March 30 because he was not a stockholder on March 15. Chen will begin work at the clinic on April 1.

22 Issued Check No. 77 for $115,679.37 to the Hospital Equipment Company for new X-ray equipment.
24 Issued Check No. 78 for $298.42 to the O'Malley Surgical Supply Company for surgical supplies.
25 Issued Check No. 79 for $110.16 to the Midvale Water Co. for water used during February.
25 Footed the amount columns in the daily service record and obtained the following totals:

Kind of service:	
Office calls	$ 3,325
Surgery	9,100
Total	$12,425
Patients' accounts — charges	$10,150
Cash services	2,275
Total	$12,425

The total cash received from patients for the week was:

Payments	$10,660
Cash services	2,275
Total	$12,935

Mar. 28 Issued Check No. 80 for $175.50 to the Medford Garage for gasoline and oil for the cars owned by the clinic.
29 Issued Check No. 81 for $1,015 to the Davidson Construction Co. for repairs to the building.
30 Issued Check No. 82 for $450 to the Building Maintenance Co. for cleaning services.
30 Issued the following checks in payment of the dividends payable today:
   No. 83 for $7,500 to Elizabeth Kirkwood.
   No. 84 for $5,000 to Sandra Waldeck.
   No. 85 for $5,000 to Clarence McClure.
31 Issued the following checks in payment of salaries for the month of March:
   No. 86 for $1,981.20 to Elizabeth Kirkwood in payment of salary in the amount of $3,000.00, less $808.80 withheld for federal income tax and $210.00 withheld for FICA tax.
   No. 87 for $1,833.10 to Sandra Waldeck in payment of salary in the amount of $2,500.00, less $491.90 withheld for federal income tax and $175.00 withheld for FICA tax.
   No. 88 for $1,667.00 to Clarence McClure in payment of salary in the amount of $2,200.00, less $379.00 withheld for federal income tax and $154.00 withheld for FICA tax.
   No. 89 for $975.30 to Hilda Rasmussen in payment of salary in the amount of $1,250.00, less $187.20 wihheld for federal income tax and $87.50 withheld for FICA tax.
   No. 90 for $1,046.31 to Andrew Kelly in payment of salary in the amount of $1,241.52, less $108.30 withheld for federal income tax and $86.91 withheld for FICA tax.
   No. 91 for $1,059.40 to Luther Whitney in payment of salary in the amount of $1,300.00, less $149.60 withheld for federal income tax and $91.00 withheld for FICA tax.
31 Footed the amount columns in the daily service record and obtained the following totals for the period March 28–31.

Kind of service:	
Office calls	$ 2,310
Surgery	7,830
Total	$10,140

Patients' accounts — charges	$ 7,850
Cash services	2,290
Total	$10,140

The total cash received from patients for the period March 28–31 was:

Payments	$7,600
Cash services	2,290
Total	$9,890

31 Made an entry in the combination journal for the employer's portion of the FICA tax for the month of March by debiting

Payroll Taxes Expense and crediting FICA Taxes Payable for $804.41.

Mar. 31 Made an entry in the combination journal by debiting Payroll Taxes Expense for $288.71 and crediting FUTA Tax Payable for $59.44 and crediting State Unemployment Tax Payable for $229.27.

The FUTA tax is figured at 0.7% of salaries earned up to $6,000 in a calendar year. Kirkwood's salary reached $6,000 at the end of February. In March, all other salaries are taxable for FUTA tax and state unemployment tax.

The state unemployment tax is figured at 2.7% of the first $6,000 of salaries earned in a calendar year.

Required: **(1)** Open the accounts and enter the balances shown in the March 1 trial balance on page 239. **(2)** Record the transactions in the combination journal using the account titles listed in the trial balance on page 239. For the combination journal, use a sheet of paper like that shown in the illustration on pages 180–183 in the textbook. Foot, enter the totals, and rule the combination journal. **(3)** Post the summary columns and the General columns from the journal to the ledger accounts. In posting from the combination journal, the page number preceded by the initials "CJ" should be inserted in the Posting Reference column of the ledger. Use page number 6. The account numbers should also be entered in the Posting Reference column and immediately below the totals of the summary columns in the combination journal. **(4)** Determine and record the account balances where necessary. **(5)** Take a trial balance as of March 31, 1983.

JACKSON SPRINGS MEDICAL CLINIC, INC.
Trial Balance
March 1, 1983

Account	No.	Debit	Credit
Cash	100	55,081.17	
Government Notes	105	25,000.00	
Automobiles	115	20,453.80	
Accumulated Depr. — Automobiles	116		12,783.63
Building	120	305,515.30	
Accumulated Depr. — Building	121		38,189.41
Land*	125	50,000.00	
Laboratory and X-ray Equipment	130	55,920.18	
Accumulated Depr. — Laboratory and X-ray Equip.	131		27,960.00
Medical Equipment	135	24,038.82	
Accumulated Depr. — Medical Equip.	136		10,817.47
Office Equipment	140	18,672.35	
Accumulated Depr. — Office Equip.	141		9,336.18
Prepaid Insurance	150	21,904.60	
Employees Income Tax Payable	211		2,127.20
FICA Tax Payable	221		1,609.06
FUTA Tax Payable	231		160.60
State Unemployment Tax Payable	241		619.47
Dividends Payable	251		
Common Stock	300		350,000.00
Retained Earnings	305		48,750.16
Professional Fees	400		105,480.00
Automobile Expense	500	475.26	
Charitable Contributions Expense	503	375.00	
Dues and Subscriptions Expense	508	625.00	
Electricity, Gas, and Water Expense	510	813.38	
Laboratory & X-ray Expense	515	419.72	
Laundry Expense	518	178.47	
Medical Library Expense	520	72.88	
Medical Supplies Expense	522	836.19	
Miscellaneous Expense	525	132.93	
Office Supplies & Postage Expense	528	175.07	
Payroll Taxes Expense	530	2,386.10	
Repairs & Maintenance Expense	533	299.08	
Salary Expense	535	22,943.28	
Surgical Instruments Expense	538	377.52	
Surgical Supplies Expense	540	151.62	
Telephone Expense	542	225.17	
Traveling & Meetings Expense	545	760.29	
		607,833.18	607,833.18

*Note that there is no accumulated depreciation account for land. Land does not depreciate.

Problem 7-A Adjusting entries in a work sheet

Charles Phillips and Robert Olsen have formed a partnership for the practice of civil engineering. They employ ten engineers and drafters, a secretary, and a secretary-bookkeeper. The partners share profits and losses equally. The Trial Balance columns of the work sheet for the current year ended December 31 are shown below.

PHILLIPS AND OLSEN, CIVIL ENGINEERS
Work Sheet
For the Year Ended December 31, 19—

Account	Acct. No.	Trial Balance Debit	Trial Balance Credit
Cash	100	52,897.49	
Petty Cash	105	75.00	
Office Equipment	120	35,427.98	
Accumulated Depr. — Office Equip.	121		14,171.20
Professional Equipment	130	47,819.37	
Accumulated Depr. — Professional Equip.	131		23,909.68
Automotive Equipment	140	60,248.42	
Accumulated Depr. — Automotive Equip.	141		30,124.21
Employees Income Tax Payable	210		2,425.20
FICA Tax Payable	220		2,606.92
FUTA Tax Payable	230		
State Unemployment Tax Payable	240		
Charles Phillips, Capital	310		18,500.47
Charles Phillips, Drawing	315	31,529.80	
Robert Olsen, Capital	320		16,400.10
Robert Olsen, Drawing	325	30,118.73	
Expense and Revenue Summary	330		
Professional Fees	400		453,200.00
Automotive Expense	500	8,462.30	
Charitable Contributions Expense	503	2,140.00	
Depreciation Expense	505		
Insurance Expense	508	5,750.00	
Miscellaneous Expense	510	530.13	
Payroll Taxes Expense	512	18,089.50	
Rent Expense	515	36,000.00	
Salary Expense	518	223,450.00	
Stationery, Supplies, and Blueprint Expense	520	7,270.36	
Telephone Expense	522	1,528.70	
		561,337.78	561,337.78

Required: Prepare a ten-column work sheet making the necessary entries in the Adjustments columns to record the following:

Depreciation:
Office equipment, 10% a year, $3,542.80
Professional equipment, 12½% a year, $5,977.42
Automotive equipment, 25% a year, $15,062.11

Note: Problems 7-B and 8-A are based on the work sheet for Phillips and Olsen. If these problems are to be solved, the work sheet should be retained for reference until they are solved, at which time the solutions of all three problems may be submitted to the instructor.

Chapters 5–8   Supplementary Practical Accounting Problems   **241**

Problem 7-B Financial statements

Refer to the work sheet for Phillips and Olsen (based on Problem 7-A) and from it prepare the following financial statements:

(1) An income statement for the year ended December 31.
(2) A balance sheet in account form as of December 31.

Challenge Problem 7

Michael Johansen and Marcia Schulte are attorneys who started a law practice on January 3, 1983. They share profits and losses equally. They employ a secretary-bookkeeper and a secretary. The trial balance taken on December 31, 1983, is given below:

JOHANSEN AND SCHULTE, ATTORNEYS AT LAW
Trial Balance
December 31, 1983

Account	No.	Debit	Credit
Cash	110	9,987.78	
Clients' Trust Account	115	770.00	
Advances on Behalf of Clients	120	345.00	
Office Supplies	125	1,214.87	
Prepaid Insurance	130	5,295.15	
Automobile	150	11,428.72	
Accumulated Depr. — Automobile	151		
Building	160	52,038.47	
Accumulated Depr. — Building	161		
Land	170	10,000.00	
Office Equipment	180	3,750.38	
Accumulated Depr. — Office Equipment	181		
Liability for Trust Funds	210		770.00
Employees Income Tax Payable	220		264.60
FICA Tax Payable	230		294.00
Mortgage Payable	250		46,528.85
Michael Johansen, Capital	300		40,740.16
Michael Johansen, Drawing	305	20,400.00	
Marcia Schulte, Capital	310		39,643.13
Marcia Schulte, Drawing	315	19,338.26	
Legal Fees Revenue	400		39,850.00
Collection Fees Revenue	410		1,370.25
Automobile Expense	500	1,680.47	
Depreciation Expense	505		
Insurance Expense	510		
Law Library Expense	515	3,840.12	
Miscellaneous Expense	520	102.42	
Office Supplies Expense	525		
Payroll Taxes Expense	530	2,172.00	
Salary Expense	535	25,200.00	
Telephone Expense	540	1,897.35	
		169,460.99	169,460.99

Required: (1) Copy the trial balance in the first two columns of a ten-column work sheet. Complete the work sheet for the year ended December 31, 1983, making the required adjustments from the information given below:

> Depreciation: (Be sure to allow three lines for Depreciation Expense.)
> Automobile, 25% a year.
> Building, 2½% a year.
> Office Equipment, 10% a year.

The amount of office supplies on hand on December 31 was $330.29. (Make the adjusting entry for the difference between the balance in Account No. 125, Office Supplies, and the amount on hand on December 31.)

One-third of the prepaid insurance has expired and is now an expense. (2) Prepare an income statement for the year ended December 31, 1983. (3) Prepare a balance sheet in report form as of December 31, 1983.

Note: Challenge Problem 8 is based on the work sheet for Johansen and Schulte. If Challenge Problem 8 is to be solved, the work sheet should be retained for reference until it is solved, at which time the solutions for both problems may be submitted to the instructor.

Problem 8-A Adjusting and closing entries

Refer to the work sheet for Phillips and Olsen (based on Problem 7-A) and draft the general journal entries required: (1) To adjust the general ledger accounts so they will be in agreement with the financial statements. (2) To close the temporary owners' equity accounts on December 31.

Problem 8-B Complete accounting cycle

Louise Matthews and Maria Michalski for several years have been partners engaged in the practice of architecture. They share profits and losses equally. The accounting records consist of a combination journal and a general ledger. The column headings in the combination journal are as follows:

Cash Dr.
Cash Cr.
Check Number
Day
Description
Post. Ref.
General Dr.

General Cr.
Professional Fees Cr.
Stationery, Office, and Blueprint Supplies Expense Dr.
Salary Expense Dr.
Employees Income Tax Payable Cr.
FICA Tax Payable Cr.

The account forms in the general ledger are like those illustrated on pages 180–189.

The trial balance as of November 30 is shown below. The trial balance includes all the accounts in the general ledger, some of which do not have balances as of November 30.

MATTHEWS AND MICHALSKI, ARCHITECTS
Trial Balance
November 30, 19--

Account	No.	Debit	Credit
Cash	100	110,065.35	
Petty Cash	110	100.00	
Office and Professional Equipment	120	65,314.28	
Accumulated Depr. — Office and Professional Equip.	121		20,410.71
Automobiles	130	21,892.35	
Accumulated Depreciation — Automobiles	131		10,946.18
Employees Income Tax Payable	200		1,813.60
FICA Tax Payable	210		1,603.00
FUTA Tax Payable	220		
State Unemployment Tax Payable	230		
Louise Matthews, Capital	300		35,778.95
Louise Matthews, Drawing	310	55,437.50	
Maria Michalski, Capital	320		38,037.88
Maria Michalski, Drawing	330	30,018.20	
Expense and Revenue Summary	340		
Professional Fees	400		409,026.00
Automobile Expense	500	5,666.33	
Charitable Contributions Expense	505	6,225.00	
Depreciation Expense	510		
Electricity Expense	515	3,650.09	
Insurance Expense	520	1,273.00	
Miscellaneous Expense	525	579.15	
Payroll Taxes Expense	530	10,274.98	
Rent Expense	535	55,000.00	
Repairs and Maintenance Expense	540	6,778.47	
Salary Expense	545	126,385.38	
Stationery, Office, and Blueprint Supplies Exp.	550	7,117.02	
Telephone Expense	555	3,998.57	
Travel and Entertainment Expense	560	7,840.65	
		517,616.32	517,616.32

The firm employs seven persons, two architects, two drafters, two secretaries, and a secretary-bookkeeper.

NARRATIVE OF TRANSACTIONS FOR DECEMBER

Dec. 1 Paid the Doyle Realty Co. $5,000 for rent of the office for the month of December. Check No. 926.
1 Received $7,875 from R. W. Pavone Co. for work completed.
2 Paid the Bell Telephone Co. bill, $360.51. Check No. 927.
5 Paid the following payroll taxes based on salaries paid during the month of November by sending Check No. 928 in the amount of $3,416.60 to the Hastings National Bank. Since the amount is in excess of $3,000, it must be deposited within three business days following the end of the month.

Employees' income tax withheld from salaries..		$1,813.60
FICA tax:		
Withheld from employees' salaries.............	$801.50	
Imposed on employer..................................	801.50	1,603.00
Total..		$3,416.60

A Federal Tax Deposit, Form 501, was filled out and sent with the check.
6 Paid the Hastings Gas and Electric Co. for electricity used during the month of November, $325.64. Check No. 929.
6 Paid for gasoline and oil used in the company cars during November, $258.33. Check No. 930.
7 Received $3,775 from the Goldschmidt Co. for work completed.
8 Paid the Professional Supply Co. for blueprint supplies, $260.88. Check No. 931.
9 Reimbursed Michalski for expenses incurred in attending a professional meeting, $540.82. Check No. 932.
12 Paid the Scardina Insurance Agency $5,875 for a one-year professional liability insurance policy. Check No. 933.
14 Paid the Summit Country Club $60.75 for entertainment of a client. Check No. 934.
15 Paid salaries for the first half of the month, $5,725 less employees' withholding tax, $906.80, and FICA tax payable, $400.75. Checks No. 935–941 inclusive were issued for the net amounts payable to the employees.
15 Paid the Quality Cleaning Co. $625 for office cleaning services rendered during November. Check No. 942.
16 Received $10,700 from James Schroeder for work completed.
16 Paid the Square Deal Garage $185.75 for repairs to one of the company cars. Check No. 943.
19 Paid the Heffner Stationery Co. $175.38 for stationery and supplies. Check No. 944.
19 Received $6,900 from Lucas County in payment for work completed.
20 Contributed $50 to the Community Christmas Fund. Check No. 945.
21 Paid the Fine Line Furniture Co. $2,975 for office furniture. Check No. 946.

Dec. 22 Paid the Simmons Stationery Co. $227.35 for office supplies. Check No. 947.
22 Paid the balance due on the pledge to the United Fund, $500. Check No. 948.
23 Paid $15 for a subscription to a professional journal. Check No. 949. Debit Miscellaneous Expense, Account No. 525.
27 Received $10,000 from the Lucas County Airport for work completed.
28 Paid the Hastings National Bank $25 for annual rental of a safe deposit box for use of the partnership. Check No. 950. Debit Miscellaneous Expense, Account No. 525.
29 Paid the Faulkner Office Equipment Co. $47.80 for typewriter repairs. Check No. 951.
30 Matthews withdrew $4,500 for personal use. Check No. 952.
30 Michalski withdrew $3,000 for personal use. Check No. 953.
30 Paid salaries for the second half of the month $ $5,801.15, less employees' withholding tax, $919.80, and FICA tax payable, $406.08. Checks No. 954-960 inclusive were issued for the net amounts payable to the employees.
30 Issued Check No. 961 to replenish the petty cash fund. A statement of petty cash disbursements for December follows:

Louise Matthews, Drawing	$15.00
Automobile Expense	17.50
Charitable Contributions Expense	5.00
Miscellaneous Expense	8.50
Stationery, Office, and Blueprint Supplies Expense	4.80
Travel and Entertainment Expense	47.28
Total disbursements	$98.08

30 Made an entry in the combination journal for the employer's portion of the FICA tax for the month of December, $806.83.

Required: **(1)** Journalize the December transactions. **(2)** Open the necessary general ledger accounts and record the December 1 balances, using the November 30 trial balance as the source of the needed information. Complete the individual and summary posting from the combination journal. **(3)** Take a trial balance of the general ledger accounts and enter the figures in the first two columns of a ten-column work sheet. **(4)** Complete the ten-column work sheet making the required adjustments from the information given below.

Depreciation:
Office and professional equipment, 12½% a year, $8,164.29, based on the balance at the beginning of the year. No depreciation is taken this year on the purchase of December 21.
Automobiles, 25% a year, $5,473.09.

(5) Prepare an income statement for the year ending December 31 and a balance sheet in report form as of December 31. **(6)** Record the adjusting entries in the combination journal and post. **(7)** Record the closing entries in the combination journal and post. The page numbers of the combination journal begin with No. 23. **(8)** Take a post-closing trial balance.

Challenge Problem 8

Refer to the work sheet for Johansen and Schulte (based on Challenge Problem 7) and draft the general journal entries required: **(1)** To adjust the general ledger accounts so they will be in agreement with the financial statements. **(2)** To close the temporary owners' equity accounts on December 31. (The expense and revenue summary account is No. 320.)

INDEX

A

ABA numbers, 66
Access to stockholder and employee fringe benefits, 156
Account, 13; books of, 130, 165; capital, 29; cash, 54; checking, 63; clearing, 206; clients' trust, 129; common stock, 157; corporation income tax payable, 157; dividends payable, 157; expense and revenue summary, 129; income tax expense, 158; patient's 168; payable, 5; receivable, 4; retained earnings, 158; savings, 79; standard form, 13; T, 14, *illustrated*, 14
Accountant, 4
Accountants, certified management, 3; certified public, 2; public, 2; registered, 2
Account form, 202, *illustrated*, Karl F. Andersen, 202–203, Robert Half, 50–51
Accounting, 4; business, 3; cash basis of, 126, 164; elements, 4; for cash, 53; for employee earnings and deductions, 99; for employer payroll taxes, 104; for personal service, 125, 163; nature of business, 1; payroll, 82; process, 3
Accounting cycle, 220
Accounting equation, 6; effect of transactions on, 8
Accounting procedure, 25, 135, 172
Accounting process, 3
Accounting systems, computer-based, 172
Accounts, chart of, 29, 127, 164; contra, 127; receivable system, 172; temporary owner's equity, 19; use of asset, 15; use of expense, 19; use of liability, 15; use of owner's equity, 15; use of revenue, 19
Accounts receivable system, 172
Accumulated depreciation, 127

Additional withholding allowances, 87
Adjusted trial balance columns, 196
Adjusting accounts at end of accounting period, 208
Adjusting entries, 209; journalizing, 209, *illustrated*, 210; posting, 210, *illustrated*, 211
Adjustments, 209; columns, 194; end-of-period, 193
Advances on behalf of clients, 128
Allowance, withholding, 87
Amount, invested, 49; withdrawn, 49
Analyzing, 3
Application for Social Security Number (Form SS-5), *illustrated*, 86
Assets, 4; current, 204; long-term, 204
Assignment, 168
Auditing, 2
Automated systems, 90
Automatic teller machines, 67
Auxiliary records, 131, 166

B

Balance, 21
Balance-column account form, 131
Balance sheet, 11, 49, 201; body of, 49; classification of data, 203; columns, 197; form of, 202; heading of, 49; *illustrated*, Karl F. Andersen, 202–203, Edward Foote, 11, Robert Half, 50–51; importance of, 201
Banking procedures, 63
Banking transactions, recording, 72
Bank statement, 73, *illustrated*, 74; reconciling, 75
Blank indorsement, 64
Body of, balance sheet, 49; income statement, 47
Bookkeeper, 4
Bookkeeping, 4; double-entry, 12
Book of original entry, 27
Books of account, 130, 165
Book value, 127, 204
Blue Cross, 168
Blue Shield, 168
Business accounting, 3; nature of, 1
Business enterprises, 125
Business entity, 4

C

Capital, 5; account, 29
Cash, 54; account, 54; accounting for, 53; disbursements, 54, 56; proving, 56; receipts, 54; register, 55; short and over, 56
Cash basis of accounting, attorneys, 126; for a personal service enterprise, 126, 164; physicians and dentists, 164
Certified, management accountants, 3; public accountants, 2
Characteristics of the corporate form of organization, 155
Charge, 14
Chart of accounts, 29, 127, 164, *illustrated*, Karl F. Andersen, 128, Robert Half, 30, Kennedy & Weiss, 165
Check 63; dishonored, 67; indorsing the, 64; negotiable, 64; payroll, 94; stub, 70; writing a, 70
Checkbook, 70
Checking account, 63; opening a, 65
Checks, and stubs, *illustrated*, 71; electronic processing of, 72; NSF, 68; outstanding, 75; postdated, 69
Checkwriter, 71
Classification of data in the balance sheet, 203
Classifying, 4
Clearing account, 206
Clients' trust account, 129
Closing accounts at end of accounting period, 208
Closing entries, 213; journalizing, 213, *illustrated*, 214; posting, 215, *illustrated*, 215–218
Closing procedure, 212
Collection docket, 132
Collection fees revenue, 129
Column, credit amount, 28; date, 27; debit amount, 28; description, 27; posting reference, 28
Columns, adjusted trial balance, 196; adjustments, 194; balance sheet, 197; income statement, 196; trial balance, 194
Combination journal, 130, 166, *illustrated*, Karl F. Andersen, 142–145, partial, 158–161; Kennedy & Weiss, 180–183
Commercial insurance companies, 168
Common stock account, 157
Company health insurance plans, 168
Compensation, types of, 84
Completing the work sheet, 197
Compound entry, 62
Computer-based accounting system, 172
Computer, programs, 172; service bureaus, 172
Constructively received, 127
Contra accounts, 127

Index

Control, internal, 53
Corporate earnings, taxation of, 156
Corporate form of organization, characteristics of, 155
Corporation, income tax payable account, 157; professional, 152
Credit, 14; advice, *illustrated*, 73; amount column, 28; balances, 21
Current assets, 204; liabilities, 204

D

Daily service record, 163, 166, *illustrated*, 167
Date column, 27
Debit, 14; amount column, 28; balances, 21
Debit advice, 67, *illustrated*, 68
Decrease in an asset, offset by a decrease in a liability, 17; offset by a decrease in owner's equity resulting from expense, 10, 20
Deductions from total earnings, 85
Defendant, 126
Deposits, by mail, 69; in transit, 75; making, 65; night, 69
Deposit ticket, 65, *illustrated*, 66
Depreciate, 127
Depreciation, accumulated, 127; expense, 127
Description column, 27
Determination of total earnings, 84
Direct deposit, 94
Disbursements, cash, 54, 56
Dishonored check, 67
Dividends payable account, 157
Docket, collection, 132; office, 132
Double-entry, bookkeeping, 12; framework, 12
Drawee, 64
Drawer, 63
Drawing account, lack of, 156

E

Earnings, deductions from total, 85; determination of total, 84; report of, 199
Effect of transactions on the accounting equation, 8
Electronic processing of checks, 72
Employee earnings and deductions, 83; accounting for, 99
Employee's earnings record, 94, 135, *illustrated*, 96–97

Employees, 83; FICA tax withheld, 85; income tax payable, 100; income tax withheld, 86
Employer payroll taxes, accounting for, 104; imposed on, 102; journalizing, 106
Employer's, FICA tax, 102; FUTA tax, 102; identification number, 98; quarterly federal tax return and quarterly report (Form 941), *illustrated*, 110; state unemployment tax, 103
End-of-period, adjustments, 193; work sheet, 193
Enterprise, business, 125; manufacturing, 125; mercantile, 125; personal service, 125; professional, 125
Entries, adjusting, 209; closing 213
Equity, owner's, 5, 205
Expense, 17, 18; depreciation, 127; payroll, 99; payroll taxes, 104
Expense and revenue summary, 212; account, 129

F

Federal tax deposit form (Form 501), *illustrated*, 109
Fee, 83
FICA tax, employees, 85; employer, 102; payable, 100, 105; withheld, 85
Filing returns and making payroll tax payments, 107
Final processing, 4
Financial condition, statement of, 11, 201
Financial position, statement of, 11, 201
Financial statements, 10, 46, 199
Fiscal year, 18
Fixed liabilities, 204
Foot, 44
Footing, 21; accounts, *illustrated*, 44; *illustrated*, 21
Form, 501, *illustrated*, 109; 941, *illustrated*, 110; SS-5, *illustrated*, 86; W-2, *illustrated*, 99; W-4, *illustrated*, 88
Form of, the balance sheet, 202; the income statement, 200
Fund, petty cash, 57
FUTA tax, 102; employer's, 102; payable, 105

G

General ledger, 38, 131, 166
General ledger accounts, *illustrated*, Karl F. Andersen, 146–151, Robert Half, 41–

43, partial, 160–162, Kennedy & Weiss, 180–189
Government regulation, 156
Gross pay, 85

H

Heading, of a balance sheet, 49; of an income statement, 47

I

Importance of, the balance sheet, 201; the income statement, 199
Imprest method, 58
In balance, 21
Income, and expense statement, 199; net, 18, 49; self-employment, 221; summary, 213
Income statement, 10, 47, 199; body of, 47; columns, 196; form of, 200; heading, 47; *illustrated*, Karl F. Andersen, 201, Edward Foote, 11, Robert Half, 48; importance of, 199
Income tax expense account, 158
Income tax payable, employees, 100
Income tax withheld, employees, 86
Income taxes, 220
Increase in an asset, offset by an increase in a liability, 8, 16; offset by an increase in owner's equity, 8, 15; offset by an increase in owner's equity resulting from revenue, 9, 20
Increase in one asset, offset by a decrease in another asset, 9, 16
Independent contractors, 83
Indorsing the check, 64
Information processor, 4
Insurance, prepaid, 164
Internal control, 53
Interpreting, 4

J

Journal, 26; combination, 130, 166; proving, 35, *illustrated*, 36–37
Journalizing, 26, 28, 53; employer's payroll taxes, 106; *illustrated*, 29; payroll transactions, 100; the adjusting entries, 209, *illustrated*, 210; the closing entries, 213, *illustrated*, 214; transactions, 26

K

Keeping a ledger account for each bank, 78

L

Lack of the drawing account, 156
Lawyer's, collection docket, 132, *illustrated*, 134; office docket, 132, *illustrated*, 133
Ledger, 26; general, 38, 131, 166; patients', 168; posting to, 38
Legal fees revenue, 129
Liabilities, 5; current, 204; fixed, 204; long-term 204
Liability for trust funds, 129
Limited liability of owners, 155
Local taxes, 86
Long-term, assets, 204; liabilities, 204

M

Machines, automatic teller, 67
Making, deposits, 65; deposits by mail, 69; payroll tax payments, 107; withdrawals, 70
Management accountants, certified, 3
Manual system, 90
Manufacturing enterprise, 125
Matching, concept, 47; principle, 126
Mechanical system, 90
Medicaid, 168
Medicare, 168
Mercantile enterprise, 125
Merit-rating system, 104
MICR numbers, 66
Minicomputers, 172
Monthly statement, *illustrated*, 55
Mortgage, 204; payable, 204

N

Nature of business accounting, 1
Negotiable check, 64
Net, income, 18, 49; loss, 18; pay, 85; worth, 5
Night deposits, 69
Notes payable, 5
NSF checks, 68

Index

O

Office docket, 132; lawyers, 132
Opening a checking account, 65
Operating, a petty cash fund, 57; statement, 10, 199
Organizing a professional corporation, 152
Outstanding checks, 75
Overdraft, 68
Owner's, equity, 5, 205; limited liability of, 155

P

Passbook, 79
Patient's account, 168, *illustrated*, 169; ledger, 168
Pay, gross, 85; net, 85
Payable, account, 5; corporation income tax, 157; dividends, 157; employees income tax, 100; FICA tax, 100, 105; FUTA tax, 105; mortgage, 204; notes, 5; state unemployment tax, 105
Paycheck and deduction stub, *illustrated*, 95
Payee, 64
Payment for services, 168
Payroll, accounting, 82; check, 94; expense, 99; records, 90; register, 92, *illustrated*, 92-93
Payroll taxes, expense, 104; imposed on employer, 102
Payroll transactions, journalizing, 100
Periodic summary, 192
Personal service, accounting for attorneys, 125; accounting for physicians and dentists, 163; enterprise, 125
Petty cash disbursements record, 58, 132, 166, *illustrated*, 60-61; proving, 61
Petty cash fund, 57; operating, 57
Petty cash voucher, *illustrated*, 58
Plaintiff, 126
Post-closing trial balance, 219, *illustrated*, 219
Postdated checks, 69
Posting, 39, 53, *illustrated*, 41-43; reference column, 28; the adjusting entries, 210, *illustrated*, 211; the closing entries, 215, *illustrated*, 215-218; to the ledger, 38
Prepaid insurance, 164
Preparing the trial balance, 45
Processing of checks, electronic, 72
Professional corporation, 152; organizing a, 152
Professional enterprise, 125
Profit and loss, 213; statement, 10, 199; summary, 213
Proprietorship, 5
Proving, cash, 56; the journal, 35; the petty cash disbursements record, 61; the work sheet, 198
Public accountants, 2

Q

Quarterly federal tax return and quarterly report, employer's (Form 501), *illustrated*, 110

R

Receipts, cash, 54
Reconciling the bank statement, 75
Record, daily service, 163, 166; employee's earnings, 94, 135; petty cash disbursements, 58, 132, 166
Recording, 3; banking transactions, 72
Records, auxiliary, 131, 166; payroll 90; time, 126
Register, cash, 55; payroll, 92
Registered accountants, 2
Regulation, government, 156
Report form, 202
Reporting, 4
Report of earnings, 199
Request for medicare payment, *illustrated*, 171
Restrictive indorsement, 64; for deposit, *illustrated*, 64
Retained earnings account, 158
Revenue, 17; and expense statement, 199; collection fees, 129; legal fees, 129

S

Salary, 84
Savings account, 79
Self-employment, income, 221; taxes, 220
Service bureaus, 91; computer, 172
Services, payment for, 168
Signature card, 65
Source documents, 26

Index

Standard, form of account, 13, *illustrated*, 13; two-column journal, 27, *illustrated*, 27
Statement, bank, 73; income, 10, 47, 199; income and expense, 199; monthly, 55; of financial condition, 11, 201; of financial position, 11, 201; of petty cash disbursements, *illustrated*, 62; operating, 10, 199; profit and loss, 10, 199; revenue and expense, 199; wage and tax, 98
Statements, financial, 10, 46, 199
State taxes, 86
State unemployment tax, employer's, 103; payable, 105
Stockholder and employee fringe benefits, access to, 156
Suitability for large scale operations, 155
Summarizing, 4
Summary, expense and revenue, 212; income, 213, periodic, 192; profit and loss, 213
System, accounts receivable, 172; automated, 90; manual, 90; mechanical, 90; merit rating, 104

T

T account, 14; *illustrated*, 14
Taxation of corporate earnings, 156
Taxes, FICA, 85, 102; FUTA, 102; income, 220; local, 86; self-employment, 220; state, 86
Temporary owner's equity accounts, 19
Time, records, 126; sharing 91
Total earnings, deductions from, 85; determination of, 84
Transactions, 7; journalizing, 26
Transferable ownership units, 155
Transposition error, 77
Trial balance, 21, 38, 43; after closing, 219; columns, 194; *illustrated*, 22, 45, 150, 190; postclosing, 219, *illustrated*, 219; preparing, 45
Trust funds, liability for, 129
Two-column journal, 27
Types of compensation, 84

U

Unlimited life, 155
Use of, asset accounts, 15; expense accounts, 19; liability accounts, 15; owner's equity accounts, 15; revenue accounts, 19

V

Value, book, 127, 204

W

Wage and tax statement, 98; Form W-2, *illustrated*, 99
Wage bracket method, 88
Wages, 84
Weekly federal income tax wage bracket withholding table for married persons, *illustrated*, 89
Withdrawals, making, 70
Withholding allowance, 87; certificate (Form W-4), *illustrated*, 88
Withholding allowances, additional, 87
Work sheet, 193; completing, 197; end-of-period, 193; for an attorney, 193; *illustrated*, Karl F. Andersen, 195; proving, 198
Write it once principle, 91
Writing a check, 70

Z

Zero bracket amounts, 87